Praise for 2

"Demonstrating an impressive c... ... ...y of each neighbourhood of the old city of Bangkok at the grassroots level, Kenneth Barrett has written the first book in the English language that really introduces the districts of this culturally and architecturally diverse city. Written in lively prose, *22 Walks in Bangkok* is both local history to be read at home, and heritage guide to be clutched in hand while exploring the back lanes of the city on foot."

—James Stent, chairman, Siamese Heritage Trust of the Siam Society under Royal Patronage

"The metamorphosis of Bangkok from a water town to an overland city in less than three generations left behind a trail of the unexpected and undecided in the urban fabric. Strolling in and out of the alleys of Bangkok with Kenneth Barrett will reveal the unlikely and the co-existence of the opposite in the built forms and lifestyle of the inhabitants."

—Sumet Jumsai, architect

"The best way to truly get to know this city is on foot, and *22 Walks in Bangkok* is a book that opens historical windows to the past ... as well as telling how the city has become what it is today. For tourists as well as residents, this publication adds to the store of knowledge about Bangkok and offers a hands-on, foot-down way of getting to know the City of Angels."—Naphalai Areesorn, editor-in-chief, *Thailand Tatler*

"I thought I knew Bangkok but Kenneth Barrett proved me wrong. He's shown me a whole different side to the city that I never knew existed. It's as if you're walking through the city with a friend who has lived there his whole life."

—Stephen Leather, author, *Private Dancer*

"My journalism thesis at university was an attempt to define New York as a multitude of neighbourhoods in search of a city. Kenneth Barrett has topped me in doing the same thing for messy Bangkok, a vast sprawl of unfocused energy I had always, until now, considered unwalkable. It takes a photographer's eye to see all that he's found and a writer's skill to share it so engagingly."

—Jerry Hopkins, author, *Romancing the East*

KENNETH BARRETT

22 WALKS
IN BANGKOK

EXPLORING THE CITY'S HISTORIC
BACK LANES AND BYWAYS

TUTTLE Publishing

Tokyo | Rutland, Vermont | Singapore

Published by Tuttle Publishing, an imprint of Periplus Editions (HK) Ltd

www.tuttlepublishing.com

Copyright © 2013 Kenneth Barrett

ISBN: 978-0-8048-4343-0

Distributed by

North America, Latin America & Europe
Tuttle Publishing
364 Innovation Drive
North Clarendon, VT 05759-9436 U.S.A.
Tel: 1 (802) 773-8930
Fax: 1 (802) 773-6993
info@tuttlepublishing.com
www.tuttlepublishing.com

Japan
Tuttle Publishing
Yaekari Building, 3rd Floor
5-4-12 Osaki
Shinagawa-ku
Tokyo 141-0032
Tel: (81) 3 5437-0171
Fax: (81) 3 5437-0755
sales@tuttle.co.jp
www.tuttle.co.jp

Asia Pacific
Berkeley Books Pte. Ltd.
61 Tai Seng Avenue, #02-12
Singapore 534167
Tel: (65) 6280-1330
Fax: (65) 6280-6290
inquiries@periplus.com.sg
www.periplus.com

16 15 14 13   5 4 3 2 1

Printed in Singapore   1311MP

CONTENTS

Preface

Bangkok is not an easy city to understand. Visitors are perplexed by what appears to be an endless sprawl, and information is not easily available. Tour groups will be taken to the main sights, where they will be dazzled by the splendour but have little context in which to understand what they are looking at. Independent travellers will seek out sights and find the friendly little brown notice boards installed by the Bangkok Metropolitan Administration to be a big help, but again there is little available to guide them there in the first place, and to provide the background information that those with a serious interest in exploring this fascinating city will need.

22 *Walks in Bangkok* is designed as both a history of the city and as an exploration guide. The idea grew out of a series of columns I wrote for a local magazine some years ago, in which I took a number of localities and attempted to explain what they were and how they got there. When I first set out on the series, I wondered why it hadn't been tried before. I soon found out. The information is widely scattered, and there was little in the way of informative guidebooks for a

journalist with limited time and a looming deadline. The series was successful and ran for three years, but I was never entirely happy with the content, feeling it could have been much better.

I had been intending for a long time to return to the concept and create a full-length book, but the scale of the task was formidable. Simply rewriting the columns was not possible, as the book needed to be packed full of detail, and to have a narration that actually walked the reader into, and around, the historic districts. For a long time I kept the idea in my mind, where it sat as a continually nagging presence. Eventually, with the encouragement (and immense patience) of publisher Eric Oey, I started, and finished. The book has involved an enormous amount of research, a lot of help from a lot of kind people, and an extraordinary amount of shoe leather. For me, it has been worth every minute. Before I started, I thought I knew Bangkok well. I now know it a whole lot better.

My hope is that anyone with an interest in getting below the surface of Bangkok, and in discovering its old districts, temples and palaces, and its various nooks and corners, will use this book as a guide and find the same satisfaction in exploring the city that I have.

INTRODUCTION

Bangkok Begins

Brown as the earth it flows upon, warm and languid and sensual, the Chao Phraya River winds and loops southwards across the central plain of Thailand towards the South China Sea, a distance of 370 kilometres (230 miles), the alluvial terrain at its lowest point only 1.8 metres (6 ft) higher than the surface of the ocean. Across this fertile plain has moved a changing cast of people who have left scattered remains behind them, the earliest recognisable civilisations having been those of the Mon, the Khmer, and the Malay.

Around the seventh century A.D., the Tai people living in the mountainous regions of southern China began to move further southwards, away from the spreading influence of the Han Chinese, establishing settlements in the northern highlands of what are now Thailand, Laos and Vietnam. One group of migrants founded a town named Chiang Saen on the southern bank of the Mekong River, which rose to be a small but powerful kingdom. Over the centuries the migrants spread westwards and southwards, settling into the river valleys of the mountainous regions, founding villages and towns and kingdoms. By 1100 A.D. the Tai were firmly established at Nakhon Sawan, on the fringe of the central plain, where the Ping and the Nan rivers come together to form the Chao Phraya.

The migration of the Tai people into the Upper Chao Phraya Valley brought them into contact with the outer reaches of the Khmer empire. Centred at Angkor, the empire had spread westward across the central plain of Thailand, absorbing Mon kingdoms that had earlier spread into the region from Burma. One of these was Sukhothai, a trading settlement on the banks of the Yom River, the main tributary of the Nan. Sukhothai seems to have been loosely controlled by both the Khmer and the Mon at various periods, and possibly this is why the Tai were able to seize the city in 1238.

The Sukhothai era is considered to be the beginning of modern Thai identity, because for the two centuries it lasted this period saw an extraordinary flowering of power, wealth and culture. Within twenty years the kingdom covered the entire Upper Chao Phraya Valley. Under its third king, Ramkhamhaeng, the city-state adopted Theravada, the oldest form of Buddhism, as its official religion. Ramkhamhaeng also established the modern Thai script, basing it on the written language of the Khmer, which was itself derived from the very old Tamil script known as *vattezhuttu*, meaning "rounded writing", which in turn was derived from the ancient Brahmi. The Buddhist and Hindu cultural influences that had originated in India and Sri Lanka and been propagated by the Khmer empire began to coalesce into a distinctively Thai form in religious art and temple architecture.

Sukhothai developed into an important trading centre, trading with China, India and the Khmer empire. As the city-state grew in wealth and influence, its reach expanded out of the Upper Chao Phraya Valley until it encompassed Lampang in the north, Martaban in Burma, Vientiane and Luang Prabang in Laos, and parts of the Malay peninsula in the south. This same period saw the rise of the Lanna kingdom in the far north of Thailand, as the Tai settlements in that region evolved. Based initially at Chiang Rai and then at Chiang Mai, Lanna was another great flowering of Thai culture.

Relationships between Sukhothai and Lanna were largely peaceful. Lanna had more cause to fear Burma, a continual menacing presence, and the rise of the Mongol empire in China.

Against this background the founding of Ayutthaya, much further to the south, appears at first to have been of little consequence. There had been earlier kingdoms at this part of the lower Chao Phraya floodplain, and in the middle of the fourteenth century a man who was either a Tai nobleman or a rich Chinese merchant, and who is known to history as King Uthong, established himself on an island formed by the gathering of three rivers: the Chao Phraya, the Pasak and the Lopburi. Ayutthaya had two natural advantages: as an island it was well protected from aggressors, and it had easy access to the sea, just a hundred kilometres further down the Chao Phraya. Overseas trading had started to become significant, and the rise of Ayutthaya was therefore a natural development. It also happened fast. Ayutthaya was founded in 1351, and less than thirty years later had subsumed Sukhothai, which had begun to decline after the death of Ramkhamhaeng.

Ayutthaya became one of the richest and most beautiful cities in Asia and the most powerful kingdom on the Southeast Asian mainland. It also became one of the most cosmopolitan. The greatest volume of trade was with China, and such was the importance of the relationship that Ayutthaya entered willingly into a tributary relationship with the Chinese emperors. Chinese merchants and workers settled in Ayutthaya and many of them rose to positions of power and wealth. Muslim merchants came from India, and Japanese and Persians followed. The Portuguese were the first Europeans to arrive, in 1511, at the time of their ventures in Malacca, and a year after they had conquered Goa. They received permission to settle in Ayutthaya in return for supplying guns and ammunition to the king. The Spanish arrived towards the end of the same century, followed by the Dutch and the British in the early seventeenth century. The French arrived in 1662, during the reign of King Narai, and their influence grew immensely when Narai and Louis XIV exchanged lavishly-funded delegations.

Despite the short distance to the sea, the meandering course of the Chao Phraya doubled the distance and meant that sailing to and from Ayutthaya took several days. During the first half of the sixteenth century canal works were undertaken at various points to improve navigation, and 1542 saw the most ambitious, a two-kilometre (1.24-mile) cut across a 14-kilometre (8.7-mile) loop that saved a complete day of sailing time. Rather than remaining a canal, however, the action of the river water widened the cutting so that it became the main course.

There had already been for many years a customs post and storage depot on the land within the loop: records from a century before the canal was cut referring to the official in charge as Nai Phra Khanon Thonburi, the earliest documented appearance of the name "Thonburi", which can be translated loosely as "Money Town". Now an island, the town gained in importance as a customs port, entrepot and garrison. Ships wishing to sail upriver were required to pay a tax there, and to deposit their cannon, which they would collect on the way down. A grand name was required for the now fortified port, and in 1557 it became Thonburi Sri Maha Samut, "City of Treasures Gracing the Ocean".

The area through which the canal had been dug had, however, always been known colloquially as Bang Kok, or Bang Makok. No one seems to know which, or why. There are no Thai records, and the early European accounts give several versions of the spelling. *Bang* is the Thai word for a settlement near to water. *Kok* or *makok* is a variety of plum, so it is possible that orchards covered the area. There is some significance in the fact that Wat Arun, meaning "Temple of the Dawn", was originally a small temple named Wat Makok. Another possibility is that the name was actually Bang Koh, which means "Village on an Island" and certainly, when the word *koh* is spoken, it is short and sharp, bearing little relation to the way it is written in English. There is even a possibility that the Malay word *bengkok*, which means "bend", could have been borrowed to describe the meandering river. Quite possibly the name derives from all these sources. Whatever the origin, when the canal was cut across the land, the name Bangkok continued to be used for both banks and was entrenched by the Portuguese and all the European nations who followed them.

The origins of the word Siam evolved in a similar haphazard way. It is not of native origin. There is a Sanskrit word, *syama*, which describes a shade of dark brown, and a Hindi word, *shyam*, used for dark-skinned people. A twelfth-century A.D. inscription at Angkor Wat is the first written evidence of this word being used to refer to the Tai, and it has carried over to the Shan in Burma, who are of Tai origin. Early sources say that the people of Ayutthaya continued to call themselves Tai, and their kingdom Krung Tai, or "the City of the Tais". The name Syam, Siem or Siam was propagated by the Portuguese, who possibly encountered it at Goa. Incidentally, the word "Tai" is not the linguistic root for the name of modern Thailand. The latter is a confection that dates from the 1930s, when the absolute monarchy had been overthrown and the new government was striving for an international identity that would also please the local population. "Thai", it was decided, is generally held to mean "free", while "land", of course, is not even a Thai word. With more than forty ethnic groupings in the country, the new name was not universally popular, and there is even today a small but vociferous group of scholars who are lobbying for the name to revert to Siam.

The rise of Thonburi

With the main force of the river water coursing through the route of the canal, the original loop silted up and the waterway eventually became four canals: Bangkok Noi, Bang Ramat, Taling Chan and Bangkok Yai. From these, other small canals and streams connected and became the basis of transporting produce from the farms and orchards of the outlying districts. With the growth of residential areas came the building of temples. The garrison was strengthened in 1665 when King Narai the Great ordered the construction of Wichaiprasit Fort at the mouth of the Bangkok Yai canal to protect Ayutthaya from invasion by sea. Narai had greatly expanded relations with the European powers, which had unleashed an unprecedented foreign influence at the Ayutthaya court. Advised that a stronger French presence would provide a counterweight to the Portuguese and the Dutch, who were causing the most concern, in 1688 Narai allowed the French to increase their military presence at Bangkok, occupying the Thonburi fort and building another on the opposite bank of the river. A chain was laid between the two, which could be raised in the event of uninvited shipping attempting to travel upriver.

For the Ayutthaya courtiers, increasingly hostile to the foreign communities and to Narai's chief minister, a Greek adventurer named Constantine Phaulkon, this was the final insult. The French were intent not only on trade and influence; they were flooding the city-state with missionaries in an attempt to convert the royal family and the people to Roman Catholicism. In what became known as the Siamese Revolution of 1688, the commander of the royal elephant corps, Phra Phetracha, staged a coup d'état and the king was arrested. Narai, who was already gravely ill, died a few weeks later. Phetracha became king. Phaulkon was beheaded. The Siamese then set to dislodge the French, who left the Thonburi fort and grouped at their new fortification on the open, swampy ground of the eastern bank. Cannon balls were hurled across the river at the French, and their fortress was besieged for four months. Eventually the French were ejected from the country, and aside from the ever-present Portuguese, who had largely intermingled with the local population, and a small number of Dutch traders, who had supplied material help, other European nations were no longer as welcome as they once had been.

The fall of Ayutthaya

King Narai's era is regarded as the time when Ayutthaya was at its peak. After the dynastic convulsions that followed him had subsided there was a brief period of stability in the first half of the eighteenth century, but Ayutthaya's influence was waning. The city-state had always controlled its provinces and vassal states with a relatively loose hand, and as a consequence many had become powerful in their own right and less inclined to be subservient to the king. Although the Khmer empire had been eclipsed by Ayutthaya, and the Europeans no longer presented a threat, the Burmese had risen in power in the middle of the sixteenth century and had overrun Chiang Mai and the Lanna kingdom in the north, where they stayed for two centuries. During the second half of the sixteenth century the Burmese had laid siege to Ayutthaya and captured the city for a brief period before they were driven out.

In the middle of the eighteenth century there were more struggles over the royal succession in Ayutthaya, amounting almost to civil war and culminating in the crowning of King Ekkathat. He was to be the last monarch. Ayutthaya had formed an alliance with the Mons who were fighting the Burmese, and in 1760 the Burmese attempted to invade Ayutthaya. Ekkathat, his kingdom weakened by internal turmoil, managed to repel them, but in 1765 they returned with enormous armies converging on Ayutthaya from both the west and the north, capturing peripheral cities to remove any chance of support for the capital. The Burmese laid siege for two years and when they broke through in 1767 they utterly destroyed the city, looting and burning its palaces, temples, libraries and houses. Ekkathat fled, and was discovered by monks in woodland several days later, dead from starvation.

During the siege, about a year before Ayutthaya fell, a Siamese general named Taksin managed to break out of the city with five hundred troops and he headed for the east coast, to Rayong, far away from Burmese influence. He was too late to save Ayutthaya, but at Chantaburi and along the eastern coast he built up an army of 5,000. With a land assault impractical, Taksin assembled a fleet of ships and sailed up the Chao Phraya to Thonburi, where the Burmese had installed a puppet governor. The Thonburi forces were overpowered and the governor executed. Taksin and his men sailed on up the river and drove the invaders out of Ayutthaya and back across the border into their own country. Ayutthaya was no longer habitable, and so Taksin as the new ruler had to make a very fast choice of location for a new capital. He selected Thonburi. There was already a thriving community, a port and fortifications, and the river and canals formed a moat.

Taksin's kingdom

Taksin is one of the most remarkable figures in Thai history. He was part Chinese, his tax-collector father having been Teochew Chinese and his mother Siamese. The boy was given the name of Sin, and showing great promise he had joined the service of King Ekkathat. Eventually he rose to become the governor of Tak, a province in the north of Thailand that borders Burma. This brought him the title of Phraya Tak, or Lord Tak, and from there he became popularly known as Phraya Tak Sin. He was crowned king at Wang Derm Palace in Thonburi on 28th December 1768, at the age of 34.

Much of the new king's reign was devoted to warfare. Several of the provinces in the east, north and south had broken away and were declaring themselves independent. Taksin waged campaigns against the rebels, he drove the Burmese out of Lanna, and he extended his power into Laos, Cambodia, and part of the Malay peninsula. Despite an almost continual state of warfare—and Taksin was a king and a general who led from the front—he still paid a great deal of attention to the transformation of Thonburi from garrison town to capital, renovating temples and building new ones, ordering canals to be dug, promoting trade with other countries including China, Britain and the Netherlands, and encouraging education and the arts. He brought in prisoners of war from his battles and used them as labour.

Craftsmen who had survived the destruction of Ayutthaya settled in Thonburi and formed their own communities. With China supplying money and manpower, Chinese traders thrived. The Portuguese, who supplied Taksin with arms and ammunition, were given a plot of land on the riverside. Indian and Malay Muslim traders established themselves along the canal banks.

Although much was accomplished in a short time, Siam was still in chaos. The breakdown of institutions and society proved a harder battle than retaking the provinces. Internally, the country was almost ungovernable. There were other contenders for the throne, and even the priesthood was in rebellion. Perhaps the strain was too much, for Taksin began to exhibit symptoms of mental derangement. He attempted to tame the priesthood by declaring himself an incarnation of the Buddha, punishing monks who would not worship him. He imprisoned, tortured and executed court officials who he believed were plotting against him, and certainly, with no royal bloodline to connect him to the old nobility of Ayutthaya, there were many who regarded him as a usurper. Morale in Thonburi sank to the point where, with the country largely held together by a mix of force and patronage, it was felt that the kingdom was yet again in danger of disintegration.

A court rebellion in early 1782 signalled the end for Taksin. Siam's highest ranking noble, Thong Duang, more usually known by his title, Chao Phraya Maha Chakri, was away fighting in Cambodia, but he returned to Thonburi and rounded up the leaders. Chakri decided that the king had to be removed permanently. The generally accepted version of history is that Taksin was taken to Wat Arun, where he was placed inside a velvet sack and beaten to death with a scented sandalwood club, the traditional method of execution for anyone of royal bloodline, the belief being that no drop of royal blood should be spilled upon the ground. Another account says he was beheaded in front of Wichaiprasit Fort. A conspiracy theory of the time says that he faked his madness, as the country had become ungovernable and he was deeply in debt to the Chinese who had supplied much of the funding for his wars and nation building, and that he was secretly removed to a remote temple in the mountains of Nakhon Si Thammarat, where he lived to a ripe old age, dying in 1825. Whatever actually happened, the reign of King Taksin ended on 6th April 1782.

The Bangkok era

Chao Phraya Maha Chakri immediately proclaimed himself king, initially as Phra Buddha Yodfa Chulaloke, later becoming known as Rama I when the method of naming monarchs in this fashion was introduced by Rama VI. He was the founder of the Chakri dynasty that rules Thailand to this day.

Thonburi was capital of Thailand for only fifteen years, from 1767 until 1782, and Taksin was its only king. When Rama I came to the throne he was very much aware that the canal moat would not provide an effective barrier against a determined invasion by the Burmese. The area contained within the waterways was also too small for what was now a growing city. The king turned his thoughts to the land on the eastern bank of the river. There were numerous settlements and temples but they were scattered amongst the farmlands, orchards and marshy countryside. Directly opposite Thonburi the riverbank was occupied mainly by Chinese merchants and their godowns and the land was reasonably clear and dry, for the French fortifications had been extensive, and Taksin had already dug canals behind the merchant community for drainage and transportation. Enlarging these canals would form a protective moat and create an island. Predatory Burmese in the west would be kept at bay by the river, while to the east lay a broad expanse of impassable delta land known as the Sea of Mud. Heavy fortifications could be built along the river to discourage a sea-born invasion. Rama I could see that a city of similar grandeur to Ayutthaya would be able to rise from such a secure setting. The Chinese merchants were offered an area of land not far from their original settlement, and do not appear to have offered any resistance to the move. With a new capital city to be constructed on their doorstep they were probably delighted.

At the auspicious time and date of 6:45 a.m. on the 21st April 1782, the stakes were driven into the soil of Bangkok for the City Pillar, marking the official founding of the new city. Rama I gave his new capital a grand ceremonial name: Krung Thep Maha Nakhon Amon Rattanakosin Mahinthara Yuthaya Mahadilok Phop

Noppharat Ratchathani Burirom Udomratchaniwet Mahasathan Amon Phiman Awatan Sathit Sakkathattiya Witsanukam Prasit. The longest place-name in the world, it translates as: "The City of Angels, the Great City, the Eternal Jewel City, the Impregnable City of God Indra, the Grand Capital of the World Endowed with Nine Precious Gems, the Happy City, Abounding in an Enormous Royal Palace that Resembles the Heavenly Abode where Reigns the Reincarnated God, a City given by Indra and Built by Vishnukarma".

Foreigners, perhaps unsurprisingly, continued to use the name they had always known and which appeared on all their maps. Eventually Bangkok was registered as the official English language name. Thais call their capital Krung Thep Maha Nakhon, or more usually just Krung Thep, which translates loosely as "City of the Angels".

PART I

THONBURI

These three walks will take us through Thonburi, which was briefly the capital before Bangkok was founded. We explore the southern bank of the Bangkok Yai canal, walking alongside the old coastal railway line to the former betel nut market and visiting landmarks known to Thonburi's only monarch, King Taksin. Our second walk takes us through the old harbour district to neighbourhoods settled by the Portuguese, Hokkien Chinese and Cham Muslims, ending at a Lao community of bamboo flute makers. The third of the walks leads us through what was the fortified part of the city, taking in famous landmarks such as the Temple of the Dawn and Wat Rakhang, before visiting a small community founded by bronzesmiths who had fled the destruction of Ayutthaya, with our journey ending at a macabre museum.

A Buddha image in the grounds of a canal-side temple in Bangkok Yai.

In Search of King Taksin

Starting from Wong Wian Yai Skytrain station, the walk takes us alongside the Bangkok Yai canal to the temple that is the final resting place of King Taksin.
Duration: 2 hours

Once Bangkok had been founded as the new capital of Siam, Thonburi became something of a rural backwater. A place of market gardens and canals and old temples, it snoozed all the way through the nineteenth century as the Chakri dynasty built Bangkok into a powerful city. Only in the early part of the twentieth century did the world intrude again upon Thonburi, and even then it was to use the former kingdom as a transit point. The turn of the century saw the beginning of the railway era in Siam, and to service the south a line was opened to Petchaburi in 1903, later continuing down to Butterworth, across the Malay border. As there was no bridge across the Chao Phraya, a station was built in Thonburi, next to the Bangkok Noi canal, and passengers made their way across the river by boat.

For several years the northern and southern railway systems operated independently of each other, divided by the river. As rail traffic grew, however, the decision was made to build a bridge across the river and link all the lines at a new station on the east bank next to Chinatown. The Rama VI Bridge, opening in 1927 at Bang Sue, on the northern side of the city, was Bangkok's first river bridge. Thonburi railway station continued to operate, serving local passengers and also the new railway line that was built to Kanchanaburi, in the west, but the southern railway line now bypassed Thonburi, looping around its northern edge. Five years later, in 1932, the second bridge opened. The Memorial Bridge carries the roadway across the river and has its Thonburi landing near to the mouth of the Bangkok Yai canal. Here, two traffic circles were laid out to link eleven new road projects in Thonburi that in turn connect to highways leading west, south and east.

With a suburban railway service and the laying out of the roads came commercial and residential development, and in recent years the BTS Skytrain has vaulted the river and planted commuter stations, but Thonburi has obstinately refused to follow the same style of growth as Bangkok. No central business district has evolved here, the only international hotels are a smattering along the riverbank, and the shops are for the locals. Thonburi remained officially an independent city and province until it was merged into Bangkok in 1971. Today, although Bangkok residents refer to the west bank in general as Thonburi, the name is officially affixed to only one small district, or *khet*, of which Bangkok has fifty.

Taksin and his brief kingdom could easily have been forgotten were it not for a revival of nationalism immediately following World War II, and the change of name from Siam to Thailand. Wong Wian Yai, the larger of the two traffic circles, had been a blank traffic island for twenty years. There is in existence a black-and-white aerial photograph taken in 1950, and the only features on the island are the pathways that cross it and what appears to be a tall lamppost in the centre. But the island stands at a point near the old harbour, and outside what had been the fortified walls of Thonburi, and Taksin would have mustered his troops on this ground. Part of the nationalist campaign during this time of great turbulence in Thailand, with a military government newly installed, a changed constitution and a great deal of popular unrest, was to rehabilitate the reputation of King Taksin. The government decided to erect a statue and place it in Wong Wian Yai. The statue was unveiled in 1954, and a ceremony

of homage takes place every year on 28th December, the anniversary of Taksin's coronation.

The first thing to be learned when taking the Skytrain across the river today is that Wong Wian Yai station is not quite at Wong Wian Yai: it is two-thirds of a kilometre away, being located on Krung Thonburi Road. The station steps lead down next to Bang Sai Gai canal, a small waterway that threads its way through this district. On the bank, and visible from the main road, are the red roof and white walls of the Chao Mae Aniew Shrine, a small and ancient Chinese shrine with a small stage in its courtyard for community meetings and performances. Hemmed in by timber houses with open verandas, this quiet setting is the first intimation of the pleasant rural area this must have been within living memory. The canal path leads to a dead end, the water disappearing under a low bridge, so a return to the main road is necessary, followed by a right turn into Somdet Phra Chao Taksin Road. Wong Wian Yai is directly ahead. Of course, long

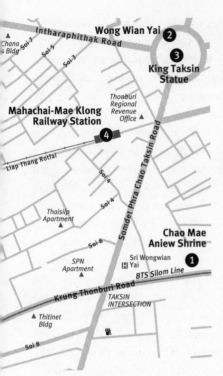

gone is the tranquillity of that old 1950 photograph, the king rising high above a sea of traffic, and pedestrians and advertising signs. Corrado Feroci, the Italian sculptor who spent almost forty years in Bangkok and is regarded as the founder of modern art in Thailand, has cast him in metal and placed him on a reinforced concrete pedestal some nine metres above street level. The king, brandishing his sabre in the direction of Ayutthaya, is mounted on his horse, or to be more correct a Thai pony, an indigenous breed that stands naturally at about twelve hands and which has the toughness and stamina for both military and pack animal use. The circle is a brilliant splash of colour, its gardens planted with red, green and yellow blooms, and the place is frequently lively with gatherings, for it is a focal point for local rallies and community activities. Around the circle is a large selection of shops, prominent amongst them the haunted shell of the Merry King department store, closed for many years now, the darkened entrance to its basement carpark the stuff of B-grade werewolf movies.

Just off the circle is Thailand's strangest railway line. The Mahachai-Mae Klong line was built by the Tha Cheen Railway Company under a private concession and opened in early 1905, its purpose being to bring fish and farm produce from the coast. The trains run down to the Tha Cheen River, near to where it empties into the sea at Samut Sakhon, a fishing port also known by its older name of Mahachai. There is no bridge there so everyone disembarks, catches a ferry, and boards a train on the other side, which then goes further along the coast to Samut Songkhram, or Mae Klong. Both stretches are the same length, almost thirty kilometres. The line is completely independent of the national railway system and is a single track. Although Wong Wian Yai is the terminus, it is the most modest terminus that can be imagined, for passengers simply walk through a gap between two blocks of nondescript commercial buildings on Somdet Phra Chao Taksin Road, and the platform and ticket office is there, sitting next to the pavement. Railway anoraks love this line, as indeed does anyone who travels on it, because it is rather like a grown-up train set that winds its way out of the city and through the rice fields, orchards and plantations. They coo over its whimsical rolling stock and wayside stations, marvel at the occasionally wiggly rail lines, and hold their breaths during the rainy season as the little trains plough manfully through the lakes that appear at certain stretches, the line disappearing under the muddy water and no one being quite sure whether or not the rail bed has dissolved. The grand soul-sucking moment for everyone comes when the train eases into the centre of the market at Samut Songkhram, where railway and market are not easily distinguishable, the stallholders politely removing their produce from the sleepers and folding their umbrella shades to allow it through. The Thais have a wry sense of humour, and the market is known locally as Talad Lom Hoop, or "Closing Umbrella Market". Despite its Toytown quality, the Mahachai-Mae Klong line is a hard-working one with a frequent service, crowds of commuters along with pickups stacked high with boxes of fish, fruit and vegetables regularly emerging between the two grimy buildings at Wong Wian Yai and adding to the general traffic chaos.

There is a narrow road that runs alongside the railway track. Liap Thang Rot Fai is almost rural, with old timber houses and modest brick buildings along the route, the clamour and traffic of Wong Wian Yai left behind within minutes. A lone foreigner trudging down this odd little country lane is assumed to be lost, and along with the smiles and waves there will be offers of help and even of food and drink from residents sitting in their gardens. A landmark on the right-hand side, not far from the station, is the Suan Phlu Mosque, marking one of about twenty Muslim communities in Thonburi, descended mainly from the communities that had existed in Ayutthaya or from prisoners of war brought back by Taksin from his campaigns in the east and the south. Off to the left is a maze of little lanes, with a few old and rather splendid houses behind high gates, a huddle of more modest dwellings, and a couple of neighbourhood temples. One of these, Wat Kantathararam, was privately endowed. There is a plaque on the wall outside that says the one-and-a-half acres of land were donated by a couple named Mr Kan and Mrs Chan in 1891, and that they and their children also contributed to the construction of the ordination hall. The family were successful farmers and traders, and when Talat Phlu station comes into view a few minutes later, the name indicates at once what this area was: a betel market. It was in fact the main betel market for Bangkok.

Talat Phlu is on the bank of the Bangkok Yai canal and can be traced back to the time of Taksin, when Teochew people who had migrated from southern China settled in the area. Farmers and traders, they cultivated plantations of piper betel, or *phlu*, which stretched along the bank of the Bang Sai Gai canal, the Bang Waek canal, and other areas next to waterways. Chewing betel was popular at that time, people using it during social occasions, as a breath freshener, and to blacken their teeth, the height of fashion. The ingredients were kept in little ceremonial boxes, and consisted of dried pieces of betel palm nut and betel leaf folded into a cone shape and daubed with *poon daeng*, a paste of slaked lime, turmeric and water. Some users added shredded tobacco leaves. Farmers paddled boats loaded with betel leaves along the canals to the wholesale market at Talat Phlu, which grew as Bangkok grew, and eventually occupied a long stretch of the canal bank.

The betel-chewing habit continued long after Taksin's time. It only ended during World War II, when the government of Field Marshal Plaek Phibunsongkhram banned the growing and trading of betel to put a stop to the random spitting by chewers that soiled the city's streets, lanes and buildings with red stains. Talat Phlu ceased trading betel, but the canny Chinese traders transformed it into a successful wet market. This has also become one of Thonburi's most popular eating areas, famous for its traditional Teochew food that can be found in countless little family-owned restaurants and food stalls

The King Taksin statue in the compound of Wat Intharam, where his ashes are interred.

around the market and station. This reputation actually began many years ago, having gained considerable ground in the latter part of the nineteenth century when King Rama v visited Jeen Ree restaurant to sample its *mee krob*, a dish of crispy rice noodles stir-fried with pork, shrimp and egg. Located in a graceful old building next to the Talat Phlu Pier, and with a soothing interior of greys and blues, Jeen Ree is still there, serving the same dish. Presumably because of its royal fame this is one of the most expensive items on the menu, but at only 150 baht (less than five dollars) no one is going to complain, and it makes a satisfying lunch: mix the crispy noodles with pickled garlic, chives, bean sprouts and kaffir lime, and wash it down with Chinese tea. Elsewhere in this area, look for Teochew specialities such as chive dumplings, fish-ball soup and (my own favourite) duck noodles.

Heading back towards Wong Wian Yai there is the choice of Thoet Thai Road, which runs parallel to the railway line, or the back-ways and alleys next to the canal. The latter are more picturesque, with only the occasional possibility of ending up in someone's back-yard. Go past the Baptist Church, past the fire station, past some old timber shophouses, over a small canal and past the pumping station, and then through Wat Klang Market, where the rooftops of

Wat Mon can be seen glittering red, white and gold above the huddled roofs.

Wat Mon was built around the end of the Ayutthaya era by a community of Mons led by a soldier whose name is no longer known, but who may have been in charge of a small garrison here. Temple legend says that woodland on this bank provided cover for troops and that shallow water on the far bank drove boats close to the wooded shore, where if they were enemy boats they would be attacked. The settlement was known as Bung Ying Rua, which means, "to hide and shoot at boats". The name was later corrupted to Bang Yi Rua, which means "Boat Village", and as rural temples usually took their name from the locality, this was the early name of the temple.

During the Thonburi period, one of Taksin's closest allies was a general named Phraya Pichai, who was also the governor of Uttaradit province, in the north of the country. Within this province is a village named Namphi, and nearby is mined an ore that goes into the making of a very tough steel traditionally used to forge swords for Siamese nobility. During one of the battles to drive the Burmese out of the country, Pichai confronted the enemy with a sword made from Namphi steel in his left hand and an ordinary sword in his right. The right-hand sword snapped during the fighting, but Pichai fought on two-handed with the Namphi sword and the broken blade. He won his battle, and entered into Thai history as Dap Hak, or "Broken Sword", a heroic figure who is also revered as one of the great masters of Thai boxing. Pichai renovated and enlarged Wat Mon as a way of making merit for the men who had died during the battle.

Although Rama I made subsequent additions, Dap Hak's chapel still remains, and carries his name. The artificial mountain near the temple wall dates from his time and is clad in seashells and rocks taken from the beach; there is a Buddha footprint on the top. Next to the temple gate is a small chapel containing an image of the Buddha lying flat on its back, symbolising the time immediately before cremation, the pose being known as Tawai Phra Ploeng. The image is about two-and-a-half metres long, almost filling the

Longtail boats ply between communities alongside the Thonburi canals.

room, and is wrapped in a gold sheet, with an angel at the foot of the bier. Installed by Dap Hak, the image is the only one of its kind in Thailand. Pichai, 41 at his death, was cremated and his ashes interred here at Wat Mon, in the stupa. Devotees leave offerings at a small altar in front of a portrait, and next to the stupa is a topiary of Pichai in a fighting stance.

There were three temples at Bang Yi Rua that were so close they all bore the same name, being differentiated by the suffix *Nai* (inner), *Klang* (centre), and *Nok* (outer). While Phraya Pichai was renovating Wat Bang Yi Rua Nai, King Taksin found peace at Wat Bang Yi Rua Nok, where he would rest and meditate. He became fond of the temple and decided to adopt it as his own, carrying out extensive renovations and naming it as a royal temple. The temple became the most splendid of those along the canal bank, and an important place of worship for the noblemen and courtiers who were building homes alongside Klong Bangkok Yai. As befits Taksin's Chinese ancestry, the architecture is a mix of Chinese and Thai. Inside the chapel, or *wiharn*, carved from a single piece of wood and flanked by four pillars and flower curtains, is the seat upon which the king would sit cross-legged in meditation. In front of the *wiharn* are two stupas, shaped like lotuses, and here is the final resting place of this great king. After Taksin's death, his body was cremated and his ashes brought here and interred in the stupa on the right, the ashes of his queen being buried in the stupa on the left. Rama III bestowed the temple's present name, Wat Intharam, when the temple was enlarged. The statue of the king upon his horse, sabre held high in his right hand, horse and king alike freckled with gold leaf, is a recent one, and a far more modest monument than the one at Wong Wian Yai. Sculpted life-size, it was commissioned soon after the end of World War II, when several miniature models were made by prospective sculptors and it was left to the public to decide which they liked best. Wat Intharam is today a place of pilgrimage for the Thais, especially those of Chinese descent, who in addition to coming here on the anniversary of Taksin's coronation also pay homage at Chinese New Year. The third of the Bang Yi Rua temples, incidentally, still exists and is known as Wat Chantharam.

Wat Intharam's compound backs directly onto the canal bank, where a frequent longtail boat service whisks visitors along Bangkok Yai and out to the Chao Phraya River. Next to the pier is a fine old two-storey wooden house whose front entrance uses a traditional Teochew method for securing the building against intruders. Erected inside the doorway are three or four wooden pillars. To get in or out, a person inside the house needs to remove a pillar. The pillars cannot be lifted from outside. As long as there is someone waiting at home, and as long as you don't severely upset that person, it's a pretty good system, as there is no key to be lost.

The Old Harbour

This quiet stretch of riverbank contains remnants of Thonburi's original communities along with temples, shrines, mosques and churches, and even a pagoda that affords a magnificent view.
Duration: 3 hours

The reason why the Wong Wian Yai terminus of the Mahachai-Mae Klong railway is such a modest little affair is that it was never actually built as a terminus. It was originally the penultimate station, with the line tootling on towards the river and terminating at Klong San ferry pier. From here, the produce was loaded onto boats and floated straight over to the piers that served the commercial heart of the city, which in those days was Charoen Krung Road and Chinatown. The railway had been built and operated under a forty-year concession by the Tha Cheen Railway Company, headed by Celestino Xavier, one of the most influential members of the Portuguese community in Bangkok, who served at the Siamese ministry of foreign affairs and was awarded the title Phraya Phiphat Kosa. When the concession expired in the early 1940s, the line was bought by the government and eventually became part of the State Railway of Thailand. In 1961, the traffic around the Klong San-Wong Wian Yai area having become congested, military dictator Field Marshal Sarit Thanarat decided to axe the section of line that ran through the increasingly busy streets.

He had wanted to cut the line a few stops down, at Wat Singh, but the residents and traders persuaded him that Wong Wian Yai would be more appropriate.

Today, crossing over Somdet Phra Chao Taksin Road from the Wong Wian Yai terminus, it can immediately be seen where the railway line used to run, for concrete slabs have simply been laid over the course of the track. On the corner of Charoen Rat Road, along which the line had passed, is one of Bangkok's leading leather markets. Further along this road there are some attractive old houses, one of them being home to the Thonburi Full Gospel Church, a conspicuous pink landmark with a huge red cross on its frontage. Keep walking, following the ghost of the line, and Klong San Market comes into view. At first sight this looks like any other small urban market in Bangkok, but look a little closer and it becomes apparent the market has been laid out exactly on the site of the old Klong San station, and consequently has a long, linear footprint. Although there is a wet market off to the left, the main attraction is the garment market, which occupies the site of the line and the platforms, and is one of the best-known markets for young Thais to shop for inexpensive fashion. Klong San is, for compulsive non-shoppers (I think you know who I mean), a rather tedious market to negotiate, because much of the thoroughfare is a single alley: you go up and you come down the same way. At the end of the market, next to the steps that lead up to the river pier, there is a long, single-storey timber building that housed the ticket office.

Klong San is today an almost forgotten corner of Bangkok, important only to those who live here or the ferry passengers passing through. But in the days of Ayutthaya and subsequently the Thonburi kingdom, the entire bank of the river, starting from here, was the port where the ships moored to offload their produce onto smaller vessels or into warehouses, and for the captains to pay their taxes and tea money. This continued into the Rattanakosin era, with the old harbour busy with the produce of the rice mills and timber yards located along the Thonburi bank, and remnants can be found today. Turn northwards at Klong San Market, and an enormous marine mast can be seen towering above the rooftops.

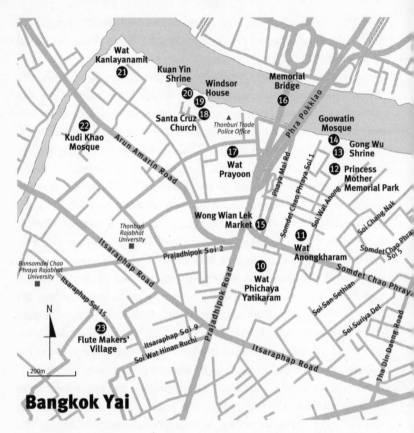

Bangkok Yai

When Rama IV built the third and final moat around Bangkok, he ordered the construction of five forts along the canal and also the building of a fort on the Thonburi bank, thereby forming a strong line of defence against any sea-borne invasion. Pong Patchamit Fort was built at the inlet of the San canal, the waterway from which the district derives its name, and it was directly opposite to the fort on the opposite bank that guarded the entrance to the new moat. Three years later, in 1855, the Bowring Treaty was signed and Siam opened to foreign trade. Steam ships began replacing Chinese junks and foreign shipping began to crowd into the harbour. In the reign of Rama V, the Harbour Department installed a signal flagpole at Pong Patchamit Fort where flags were hoisted to indicate the owners of the trading vessels that were arriving or departing. During

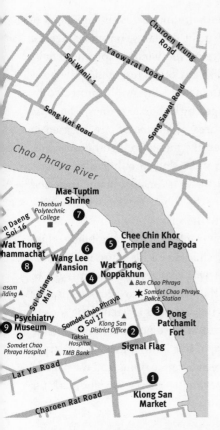

Rama VI's reign the signal flag was moved downriver to Klong Toei, and the flagpole at the fort was changed to indicate weather conditions that were provided by the Meteorological Department. Later, when the weather forecasting system was modernised, the signal flag method ceased. The mast however remains, as does part of the fort. The Fine Arts Department rescued what was left in 1949. Unless the visitor knows it is there, he or she will never find it, because the fort is hidden away behind the Klong San District Office. Enter Soi Lat Ya 21, the lane beside the mast, and walk through the District Office compound. There is a flight of steps leading up to the ramparts, and a small garden with stone seats.

On the other side of the mast is the Taksin Hospital, and the lane alongside here, Soi Lat Ya 17, leads between old timbered houses to a tiny canal. On its bank is Wat Thong Noppakhun, a temple of unknown age, in whose forecourt is a stone *yannawa*, an ocean-going Chinese ship. About seven metres long, painted cream and red, and with a bodhi tree for a mast, the vessel carries an inscription in Thai that commemorates the arrival of Buddhist monks from China and Japan. The vessel is a shrine, with offerings made at the base of the tree, and directly behind the rudder is a single Chinese grave, encased in plaster, where offerings are also made. The temple is believed to pre-date the Bangkok era but to have been restored during the reign of Rama II, the Chinese porcelain on the gable ends of the *wiharn* having become popular then, signifying the scale of trade with China. Inside the *wiharn* are murals, with depictions of Siamese cats perched above the main doorway, on guard against mice, cockroaches and other vermin. The windows on the temple *ubosot*, or ordination hall, are unlike any other, resembling the port-holes of a ship, set deep within the thick white walls, protected by gold and lacquer shutters and ringed by elaborate frames. The *sema* stones, used to mark the sacred area of an *ubosot*, are encased in cylindrical columns looking rather like miniature lighthouses, with the stones visible only through a small slot on either side. Several *chedis* surround the temple, and there are many small *chedis* and grave markers outside the house of the abbot, beyond which can be seen a Chinese pagoda rearing into the sky.

Follow the lane around past the front of Wat Thong Noppakhun and some of the most exuberant Chinese architecture in Bangkok will be revealed. Chee Chin Khor was a society formed in 1952 to undertake charitable works for the poor and to provide disaster relief supplies. During the first forty years of its existence the society headquarters had a rather peripatetic existence, but this riverside site became home in 1993. A temple was built, a four-storey struc-ture with multiple roofs clad in green ceramic tiling, and the pagoda was added as recently as 2001, becoming an instant landmark for

The towering stupas and prang of Wat Phichaya, built with materials from China.

river travellers. Saturday morning is a good time to visit Chee Chin Khor Temple, as there is a service at that time and a sizeable crowd gathers at the open-air restaurant at the side of the compound. There are four altars within the temple, with fat Chinese Buddhas and gongs and incense, and the crowd surges into the building to disperse amongst the various floors and altars. A climb up the circular interior staircase of the pagoda is irresistible, and from the top there are beautiful views of the river and the city.

From here, too, is a view of Wang Lee Mansion, one of the few remaining walled Chinese courtyard houses that were once a feature of Thonburi and Bangkok. Wang Lee Mansion is not open to the public, and in fact is still a residence and a company compound. There is no alley through from Chee Chin Khor to the imposing gate of the mansion, so a return to Somdet Chao Phraya Road is necessary before entering the neighbouring Chiang Mai Road. The road is short and runs directly down to what was a harbour known as Huay Chun Long, which means "Steam Boat Pier". There is a shrine here to the goddess Mae Tuptim, where Chinese sailors would pray for a safe passage across the ocean. Chinese operas are still performed from time to time in front of the shrine. On both sides of the road are godowns and shophouses belonging to Chinese merchants, and the entrance to the Wang Lee compound is busy with trucks and pickups. Tan Chu Huang, the founder of the Wang Lee business, was an immigrant from Shantou who arrived in Bangkok in 1871. He established a business in rice trading and milling, which eventually was to become one of the largest of its kind, with a rice mill here next to the pier and another four further downstream. Following his marriage to a Siamese lady of Chinese descent, he built Wang Lee Mansion beside the harbour in 1881. Designed in a U-shape around a central courtyard paved with flagstones brought from China as ballast, the house is still in the hands of the same family, and has recently been carefully restored.

Opposite to the Wang Lee Mansion is a lane leading to Wat Thong Thammachat, an Ayutthaya-era temple in a woodland glade that seems far removed from the booming traffic, despite being only five minutes away from the main road. The *ubosot*, with its neat red window frames and its neat red fence, sits in a well-tended courtyard with a red meeting hall behind. The lane will take the visitors round behind the temple, through a small area of old houses, and back out to Somdet Chao Phraya Road. Little can have changed in this locality over the past century.

A long, straight canal, Klong Somdet Chao Phraya, runs alongside this road. Appearing on late nineteenth century maps as Regent Canal, it led directly to a small island on which were three palaces, one of them belonging to Dit Bunnag, who had acted as regent for Rama IV and who was elevated to Somdet Chao Phraya, the highest title a commoner could attain, equal to royalty. Only the king and the king's brother, who was appointed "second king", a position invented by Rama IV but later discontinued, were higher. Alongside this canal too were mansions and even a zoological garden. One of the canal-side mansions belonged to another member of the Bunnag family, who were descended from a Persian merchant who had settled in Ayutthaya around the year 1600. Built in the last years of Rama IV's reign, the two-storey mansion is a romantic blend of English Tudor and Moorish. When the Somdet Chao Phraya Hospital was built nearby, an annex for the psychiatric unit was built next to the mansion, and the old house taken over as the residence for the hospital director. Today, beautifully conserved, it acts as the hospital reception, while on the second floor is the Institute of Psychiatry Museum. Alas, Regent Island is no more the home of palaces: the surrounding canal was filled in to become Arun Amarin Road, and although there are a couple of gracious old houses behind high walls, the island is now fringed with standard mid-twentieth-century housing.

Not far from Regent Island and on the bank of the Somdet Chao Phraya canal is a glorious riot of white stupas. This is Wat Phichaya Yatikaram, an Ayutthaya-era temple that was greatly enlarged during the years 1829–1832, in the time of Rama III, by Tat Bunnag, the brother of Dit. The two brothers were so powerful in the court of Siam that they were known as the Sun and the Moon, and Tat also took the title of Somdet Chao Phraya. The temple architecture is heavily influenced by Chinese style, very much a characteristic of Rama III's reign, when almost all of Siam's trade was with China. The Bunnags owned junks, and most of the materials used in the construction of the temple were brought in from China, including the boundary stones that were carved by Chinese stoneworkers. Instead of the overlapping roof leaves and the finials of the traditional Siamese temple, the roof of the *ubosot* resembles the hood of a Chinese carriage, and the eaves are decorated with stucco flowers and dragons. At the main entrance of the *ubosot* is a painting of a Chinese warrior with a lion at his feet, a theme that is repeated on another door, where a dagger-wielding angel is subduing a lion. Two enormous white *prangs* tower over the compound, the largest of them housing four Buddha images looking out towards each of the cardinal directions. A bronze statue of Tat Bunnag is seated at the temple entrance, looking across the canal towards the river, the face modelled after a photograph taken of him in middle age.

A few years later, in 1850, Tat Bunnag completed Wat Anongkharam, on the opposite side of the road. The architectural style here is very different, the *wiharn* being built in the classic early Bangkok style that originated in the time of Rama I. The principal Buddha image, Phra Chunlanak, is from Sukhothai although it was installed as recently as 1949, a century after the temple was built. The image is in the "Subduing Mara" position, conquering evil, the right hand over the knee, the fingers touching the ground, the left hand remaining palm up in the lap. There are other Buddha images in the crowded temple compound, which also includes a school.

Wander down the quiet little lane that runs beside Wat Anongkharam, heading towards the river, and in this neglected corner of Klong San once lived the most famous of the temple school's former pupils. The late Princess Srinagarindra, the Princess Mother, who was born in 1900 and passed away in 1995, was the mother of two kings: Rama XIII, who became king in 1935 at the age of nine, and died in mysterious circumstances in 1946, and King Bhumibol Adulyadej, Rama IX. Yet she was born a commoner, the child of a Chinese father and a Siamese mother, and she grew up on this very street, attending what was then the all-girls school at Wat Anongkharam, founded by an enlightened abbot who believed in the need for girls to have an education, not a generally accepted practice at that time. Her father was a goldsmith and the family lived in a modest rented house. In those days when Siamese were not required to have family names, the young girl was simply known as Sangwan. She went on to study nursing at Siriraj Hospital, further along the riverbank, and after graduating she was one of only two girls in that year to win a scholarship to study nursing in America. It was in the United States that she met Prince Mahidol, the sixty-ninth son of Rama V, who was studying medicine at the Massachusetts Institute of Technology. The couple later returned to Siam, where the prince worked to form a public health system, but he died young, passing away at Sra Pathum Palace in 1929. In 1993, shortly before his mother's death, King Bhumibol made known his wish to renovate the area around the Princess Mother's childhood home to provide a public park. Her family home no longer existed but there were some similar buildings nearby, which the owners gladly donated. The Princess Mother Memorial Park is a lovely, leafy area of some one-and-a-half acres, sheltered by tall trees and with fragments of walls and crumbling arches embedded amongst the greenery. There are two house-sized exhibition halls, which display photographs and mementos from the Princess Mother's life, and there is a reconstruction of her childhood home. This plot of land had once held the mansion home of another member of the Bunnag family, Pae Bunnag, who had been director general of the Royal Cargo Department during the reign of Rama V. Part of his kitchens still exist, now forming the Pae Bunnag Art Centre at the back of the park. To one side of the park, seated on a bench, is a life-size bronze statue of the Princess Mother, gazing across the greenery.

Leave the park by the rear gate and there is a small patch of wasteland and, behind that, sitting directly on the riverbank, one of Bangkok's most florid Chinese shrines. Gong Wu Shrine has a long history, predating Bangkok and even predating the Taksin era. There are three statues here of Gong Wu. The smallest was brought to Siam by Hokkien traders around the year 1736, during the period of the Qing Dynasty Emperor Chen Long. Later, in 1802, the second Gong Wu statue arrived, and in 1822 a wealthy Chinese named Kung Seng renovated the shrine, installed a bell tower, and brought in a third statue. The Gong Wu Shrine has its own jetty, and from the end of this can be seen a small green onion-shaped dome at a neighbouring jetty.

There is a small public garden between the two jetties, so the only way to find out what the dome belongs to is to walk around the garden and into a rather dusty little corner, where through an almost hidden gate is the courtyard of the Goowatin Mosque. This is, however, a very unusual mosque. The dome is mounted over the jetty, and the only indication that this tiny building is a place of worship is the traditional row of taps outside for the washing of hands and feet. Originally the building had belonged to (yes, you have guessed correctly), Tat Bunnag. It had been used as a warehouse, and next door, boarded up and crumbling away, is a splendid colonnaded building that must have been the offices. The Persian ancestor of the Bunnags, Sheikh Ahmad, had been a Muslim, and many of his descendants had held high office for Islamic affairs in Siam. The Bunnag line had become Buddhist, but clearly there were strong family connections because when a group of Muslims arrived from the Indian city of Surat in the time of Rama IV, Tat Bunnag had handed over this property for them to use as a mosque. The Indians were traders but some became skilled translators in the Bunnag business. One of them was named Ali Bai Nana. Everyone knew him as Clerk Ali, but he had ambitions beyond translating, and he rose to become one of the wealthiest members of the Indian community, the founder of the powerful Nana family. His descendant Lek Nana owned part of the land on which the Princess Mother Memorial Park was laid out, and the family today own huge plots of land on Sukhumvit Road, where the name is given to the district that is served by the BTS Skytrain Nana station.

Crossing a bridge over the small canal that runs through here to connect with Klong Somdet Chao Phraya takes us under the concrete span of Pokklao Bridge to, just a few metres further on, the green girders of the far more aesthetically pleasing Memorial Bridge. Opened in April 1932, the name commemorates the 150th anniversary of the Chakri dynasty, although in Thai it is simply named after Rama I, King Buddha Yodfa, and is known as Saphan Phra Phutta Yodfa, or colloquially, Saphan Phut. The designers and builders were a British company, Dorman Long, who also built Sydney Harbour Bridge and who remain in business to this day. Work began on 3rd December 1929. A riveted steel truss structure, using 1,100 tons of structural steel, the bridge has three spans. The two outer spans, each of 74.9 metres (246 ft), are fixed. The centre span, measuring 61.8 metres (202 ft 11 ins) and 7.3 metres (24 ft) above the water at its highest point, is a bascule span, composed of two separate parts, each of which could originally be tilted upwards to allow tall vessels or ceremonial river processions to pass underneath. The bascule arms turned on fixed trunnions and were balanced by 450-ton cast-iron weights hanging inside concrete piers on both sides of the river. An electric motor operating the gearing could raise the two bascule leaves in less than five minutes, and a petrol engine was on standby in case the power supply failed. The operator sat in a cabin on the east pier, with an electrical cable on the riverbed connecting the gearing in each pier. Another cabin was located on the opposite bank for the sake of design symmetry, but the only mechanism controlled from there was the safety locking gear. Sadly, this ingenious mechanism, designed by a British engineer named Frederick Thompson and manufactured by Thomas Broadbent and Sons of Huddersfield, is no longer in use. When the Pokklao Bridge was being built in 1983, ending the possibility of tall ships sailing any further upriver, the two bascule sections were permanently connected and hold-down tendons and bearings installed to dampen any movement. As the entire lifting gear is contained inside the piers and is not visible from the shore or the river, the curious-minded, strolling along the pedestrian walkway to try and see how the mechanism worked, will find little to enlighten him.

At the foot of the bridge is Wong Wian Lek, the smaller of the two Thonburi traffic circles. Or at least, this is where it used to be. With the opening of the Pokklao Bridge and its access roads, the circle was cut in two and its landmark clock tower moved east towards Somdet Chao Phraya Road, where there is still the Wong Wian Lek Market. From here operated a bus service over the bridge to business areas such as Chinatown and the Indian district of Pahurat. The terraced houses alongside the road connecting to the bridge were of two storeys, with a tin roof, and many of them survive today. In the vicinity of the circle there were shops and parking areas for horse-drawn carriages and cycle rickshaws waiting to take people over to

Miniature mansions for the departed, set into the candle-wax mountain at Wat Prayoon.

the Bangkok side. The food shops along the footpath meant that the area was a busy and colourful one, especially at night. In the years between the opening of the bridge and the start of World War II, bands played here on Saturday and Sunday evenings and the circle, with its buses bringing in passengers and moving them out, must have been very pleasant, especially compared to the impersonal roar of today's traffic over the bridge. Wong Wian Lek Market, however, still retains its garden atmosphere and is a noted place to buy Buddha amulets, while on the other side of the bridge approach road there is a small and pretty garden ringed all the way round by a handsome wrought-iron fence painted in fire-engine red.

Take a closer look at this fence, and it is seen to be fashioned in the shape of lances and arrows and that its arched sections bristle with axes and swords. The fence was ordered from Britain in the time of Rama III, the payment being in sugar cane equal to the weight of the fence, and it was originally for part of the Grand Palace. The king, however, decided he didn't want it. That left the minister of the treasury, Dit Bunnag, with an awful lot of fence. He was, however, building a temple on land he had previously used as a coffee plantation, and when Wat Prayoon was completed a home was found for the fencing. There was so much of the stuff that it was used to enclose the entire compound, and the locals were quick to dub the temple Wat Rua Lek, or Iron Fence Temple. When the Memorial Bridge was built a slip road was cut through the compound and this distinctly un-Buddhist design was partly replaced with a less militant fence for the temple entrance, although there is a remnant leading from the gateway to the pagoda, an enormous white structure that towers 61 metres (200 ft) and forms a clearly visible landmark from the opposite side of the river. Designed in the shape of a bell, Wat Prayoon's pagoda was the first in Bangkok to be built in Sri Lankan style. The interior fencing divides the temple grounds into two distinct halves. The buildings on the south side are all in traditional Thai style. In the ordination hall can be found a 5.79 metre (19 ft) tall Buddha image named Phra Buddha Nak, which was brought to Wat Prayoon from a temple in Sukhothai in 1831, and which is one of a pair, the other being in Wat Suthat Thepwararam on the other side of the river. The buildings on the north side of the iron fence are mostly in Western architectural styles, including a single-storey structure with beautiful stained-glass windows that was built in 1885 as a gathering place for members of the Bunnag family. Monks and novices also used the building for studying the Dharma, but in 1916 the Thammakan Ministry, the forerunner of the Ministry of Education, changed it into a public reading room, and it thereby became the first public library in Thailand.

In the temple grounds is a monument depicting three up-ended cannons, built to commemorate a huge gunpowder explosion during the fireworks display staged to mark the temple's official opening on 13th January 1837. Dr Dan Beach Bradley, one of the first Protestant missionaries allowed to work in Bangkok, recorded that thousands of people had turned out to watch and that many injuries were caused when a cannon exploded. Bradley, who was a medical doctor, was summoned to treat a monk's injured arm, amputating it at the shoulder in what was the first case of a Western surgical procedure used during this era. Possibly it was the fireworks accident that led to the twenty-six large octagonal water basins, bearing various designs such as dragons, trees, bamboo and flowers, that were imported from China and installed around the pagoda. Similar basins can be found at the ancient royal palace of Gu Gong in Beijing, where they were intended for extinguishing fires, rather than sacred purposes. The lion figures were also brought from China. If you see children trying to pull the crystal ball out of the male lion's mouth, it is because they have been told that if they can do so, the ball will turn to pure gold. For all its other distinguished qualities, Wat Prayoon is best known for a whimsical structure tucked into the corner of the grounds nearest the river, where it can be found by passing under an arch bearing the name Khao Mor, or Mor Mountain. Inside this enclosure is a pond with fish and turtles, and rising out of the water is an artificial mountain that was designed by Dit Bunnag to resemble the wax of a melting candle. The mountain is a shrine, with caves and niches occupied by Buddha images and miniature buildings, along with monuments to the departed. A set of steps leads to the top of the mountain where a bronze pagoda is situated. Locals call this place Turtle Mountain, and bring their families to feed banana and papaya to the turtles.

The Portuguese had been the first Europeans to settle in Siam, arriving in Ayutthaya shortly after they captured Malacca in 1511, shrewdly dispatching an envoy to the king beforehand to reassure him that they had no territorial ambitions. In 1516, Portugal signed a treaty with Siam to supply firearms and munitions, and with the treaty came the rights to reside, trade and practice their religion in the country. This brought the first Portuguese friars in 1567, and they established the Catholic Church in Ayutthaya. After the fall of Ayutthaya, the Portuguese continued with their military support of Taksin in his efforts to drive the Burmese out of Siam, and the supply of cannon and muskets contributed significantly to the strength of Taksin's army. With Thonburi as the new capital, the king, in recognition of their services, presented the Portuguese with an area of land on the riverbank and granted them permission to build a church. He visited this community himself on 14th September 1769. A wooden church was completed the following year, and as 14th September marks the Feast of the Triumph of the Cross, the church was named Santa Cruz, or Holy Cross. Taksin was also encouraging Chinese immigrants to settle in the adjacent area of land, which was quickly becoming heavily populated, and when in 1835 a new church was built to replace the wooden structure it was designed in a Chinese style. The church became known to residents as Kudi Cheen, or Chinese Church, the term *kudi* meaning "an abode for priests or monks", and the name became attached to the entire neighbourhood, and even to the foreign residents, who were known as "*farang* Kudi Cheen". The Chinese Church lasted for less than a century, and in 1916 the third and present version of Santa Cruz was built. This time the design was by two Italian architects, Annibale Rigotti and Mario Tamagno, and with its characteristic octagonal dome and classical proportions is resolutely Italianate in style. The name Kudi Cheen, however, remains firmly in usage, for both the church and for the neighbourhood.

Santa Cruz is only a few minutes' walk from the Memorial Bridge via the attractive walkway that has been built along the riverbank in recent years. An equally picturesque entry can be made by ferry from Pak Klong Talat, the flower market on the other side of the river, for the church has its own pier. The neighbourhood is quiet and neat, and the church precincts are almost silent. Unless your visit is at a time of worship the only other visitors are likely to be local residents passing through on their way to and from the river. During school hours the voices of children can be heard from the Santa Cruz Suksa School and Santa Cruz Convent, and nuns can sometimes be seen flitting through the precinct, but otherwise the visitor is alone. A number of statues stand in the grounds, including one of Mary set in a garden grotto near the river, and there is a large crucifix next to the pier. Santa Cruz Church is painted in delicate pastels of cream and red ochre, with stained glass fanlights above the windows. The roof is a barrel vault structure, and there is a classic pediment and Italian frescoes over the altar. A handsome two-storey presbytery stands on one side of the precinct, and to the rear of the church, away from the river, there is a tiny cemetery with the graves of former pastors.

Thonburi, of course, was short-lived. In 1786, four years after Bangkok was established as the capital, King Rama I granted the Portuguese land on the riverbank at Chinatown, and here they built Holy Rosary Church. Their influence was nonetheless dwindling, especially in religious work where French missionaries largely eclipsed them during the nineteenth century. Santa Cruz Convent, for example, was founded by the Sisters of Saint Paul of Chartres, a French order, in 1906.

The Portuguese have, however, left behind a very tangible legacy. The Thais had not known the art of baking until the Portuguese settled in Ayutthaya, and indeed the Thai word for bread, *pung*, comes from a word for bread used by the Portuguese at that time. The Kudi Cheen community baked their own bread and cakes, and today there are still bakeries here producing a sponge cake known as *khanom farang* Kudi Cheen, using apple and jujube and made to the same recipe used in the time of the Portuguese merchants and priests who had thrived in Ayutthaya. The largest bakery is located directly to one side of the precinct, entered via an unmarked doorway set between a statue of Jesus as the Good Shepherd and a modern three-storey house that is only one room wide. No one appears to mind if you wander inside. There are a handful of women putting the mix and fruit into star-shaped moulds, while the baking is done by a man who places the moulds in a tandoor-like oven and then puts a tray over the top, which he heaps with glowing coals. The baking done, the cakes are packed into cellophane bags and every so often a bicycle-powered cart will depart from the premises and deliver them to shops in the locality.

The Kudi Cheen houses in the vicinity of Santa Cruz are smart and have a prosperous air about them, and as there are no roads here, only footpaths, there is an agreeably sleepy atmosphere. This is still very much a Catholic community, even though the blood of those Portuguese settlers has long since mingled with Thai and Chinese blood, and Christian images can be seen on the houses and fences. Each of the tiny lanes is neatly numbered, although many are cul de sacs, and charting a way through the maze is not easy. Soon, though, the path emerges onto the riverside walkway. There is an intriguing old house here that looks as if it has been abandoned for many years, but in fact is still occupied, after a fashion. Standing on church land, the house is constructed of golden teak and is founded upon a solid stone platform, which has protected it from the waterlogged ground. Faded and blackened with age, its shutters firmly closed, its front door occasionally open to allow the river breezes to blow through,

The riverside shrine to Kuan Yin is in a classic Chinese design.

this is Windsor House, or Baan Windsor, a classic example of the gingerbread style that is known as Ruen Manila. Louis Windsor, a wealthy British merchant who had settled in Bangkok during the reign of King Rama IV and who married a Thai woman, Somboon, built the house. Their home was passed down the generations to the modern-day Jutayothin family, who leased it to expatriates during World War II and have ever since lived in a nearby residence, leaving caretakers in place. There has been a recent move to register Windsor House with the Fine Arts Department and turn it into a museum for the Kudi Cheen area.

A few metres along the walkway the Catholic community ends at a small waterway and the Chinese district begins. Taksin had encouraged the Hokkien Chinese to settle here. Residents had originally built two shrines on this site, but during the reign of Rama III the shrines were pulled down and replaced with a single temple to the goddess of mercy, Kuan Yin. Over the course of a number of years the temple fell into a state of dilapidation until the reign of Rama V, when one of Siam's best-known historians, Prince Damrong Rachanuphap, passed through the community on his way to neighbouring Wat Kanlayanamit to take part in the casting of a large bell. He noted the decayed condition of the building, the cracking of the mural paintings, the deterioration of the carvings on the roof, and the depredations of rain and bats, and he urged the conservation of the temple that was, he said, a masterpiece created by skilled artists who even then were becoming hard to find. Today, the temple remains faded on the exterior, although a bright red archway has recently been added at the walkway, leading through to a red-tiled courtyard. Two dragons writhe on the roof. There are some beautiful bas-reliefs and murals on the exterior walls, framed in blue, but they have become weathered and much of the paint has disappeared. Inside, seen through swirling clouds of incense smoke, the wall paintings are vivid, traditional golden silk lanterns hang from the roof beams, and a one-metre-high statue of Kuan Yin sits serenely at the back of the altar, facing the river. The shrine is cared for by a local family and has a steady stream of Chinese visitors, albeit ones with a tendency to become somewhat agitated when a large foreigner hoves into view with a camera.

From the walkway of the Memorial Bridge, Wat Kanlayanamit, an enormous barn-like structure that rises above the neighbouring rooftops, dominates this part of the riverbank. Oddly, though, it is easy to walk straight past the entrance when following the riverside pathway, because it is an unassuming one next to a clutter of wooden shops and eating houses, and the temple is set further back from the river than it appears from a distance. Passing through the gate one is within another distinctive aspect of the Chinese community. A Chinese nobleman named Toh Kanlayanamit, who owned a residence on this piece of land, founded Wat Kanlayanamit in 1825 and the design is a blending of Chinese and Thai styles. At the river entrance are two Chinese pavilions, built from brick and encased in mortar to give the appearance of stone, and next to the small *wiharn* to the rear of the compound is a Chinese *chedi*. On the other side of the *wiharn* is an elegant bell tower housing the giant bell, the biggest bronze bell in Thailand, which Prince Damrong had watched being cast. Inside the *wiharn* are murals dating from the founding of the temple. The gable of the *ubosot* is Chinese in style, the distinction being the lack of finials and overhanging eaves, and a floral design covers the flat gable frontage. The *ubosot* also has murals depicting life from the time of Rama III, but parts of them are sadly deteriorated. Beneath the floor is reportedly the basement of Toh Kanlayanamit's house. Wat Kanlayanamit is a second grade royal temple, and it is the royal *wiharn*, the hall of worship, that towers over the compound. The reason for its great size soon becomes clear, for the *wiharn* was built to house a huge Buddha image, 15.2 metres (50 ft) high and 11.6 metres (38 ft) wide, which almost fills the entire structure. Fashioned after a Buddha figure in Ayutthaya, the image is named Samporkong, and attracts crowds of Chinese devotees during the Chinese New Year period.

Leaving Wat Kanlayanamit by the side gate takes us straight to the bank of Bangkok Yai canal, where one will see the lock gate used to control the water flow, and envy the gatekeeper who has a cosy little office on top of the structure. Following the pathway will take us to Arun Amarin Road. Cross over here, following the narrow waterway that runs briefly alongside Bangkok Yai, and we are in another distinctive community in this most ethnically diverse of districts, for this is Kudi Khao, one of the oldest Muslim communities in Bangkok. Three religions—Christian, Buddhist and Muslim—live peaceably together in an area that can be traversed on foot within half an hour.

The Muslims of Kudi Khao are Sunnis. They are Cham in origin, whose ancestors migrated from Borneo, some going into Vietnam and Cambodia, and others finding their way to Ayutthaya, where they became traders and farmers, living on rafts on the rivers and canals of the capital. Early settlers had also made their homes on the Bangkok Yai canal, and when Thonburi was founded more made their way down the Chao Phraya to join them. The largest community formed on the north bank, around the Tonson Mosque, but others settled here on the south bank, where in the time of Rama I they built their own mosque, officially Bang Luang Mosque, taking its name from the early name for the canal, but usually referred to as Kudi Khao: the word *khao* meaning "white". There are no roads in this tiny community, only narrow pathways built around the course of the waterway, which forms the shape of a square and which is worryingly unguarded for much of its length. Kudi Khao is in the centre of this maze of timber houses, in a small clearing of residences and shops and so tightly hemmed in that the thoroughfare is only a few metres wide. This is no conventional mosque for at first glance it could easily be mistaken for a Thai temple, the architectural form following the traditional Thai style. The structure is entirely white, except for the roof, whose tiles are of an Islamic green. Closer examination reveals the symbol of Islam on the gable, adorned with Chinese-style stucco flowers. Thirty pillars support the structure, signifying the thirty principles of the Koran, while the twelve windows and one door represent the thirteen principles of daily prayer. On the north side of the mosque is a timber *sala*, or pavilion, serving as a gathering place for community members. The only mosque in Bangkok built to this style, Kudi Khao is an architectural gem that draws Muslim visitors from throughout Asia.

It is possible for the most adventurous of us to chart a way through the back lanes from Kudi Khao into another of Thonburi's oldest communities, for Bang Sai Gai is only a few minutes away on foot, and the campus of Bansomdej Chao Phraya Rajabhat University is the main landmark. We are, however, looking for a village within this village, and it can be found along Itsaraphap 15, alongside the university, where there is a roadside shrine and, quite possibly, the sounds of someone down the tiny alley opposite tootling an experimental tune on a flute. Ban Lao is a settlement that has its origins in the time of King Taksin. One of his first campaigns was against a rebellion in Vientiane, and he had sent General Chakri there to bring back the Emerald Buddha, which had been taken by Lao invaders from its Chiang Mai temple two hundred years before. The soldiers stormed Vientiane and along with the holy image they brought back with them a considerable number of prisoners of war. Some of the Lao were skilled in the ancient craft of making flutes from bamboo. They settled in this little area near the canal junction and their ancestors remain here to this day, still making their flutes. I had last entered this little alley, or *trok*, a dozen years previously when I met the patriarch of Ban Lao, Jarin Glinbuppha. Jarin passed away a few years ago, and his daughter Nitaya is now head of the community. She produced her father's guestbook, which I had signed at the time, and which is full of the signatures of musicians, academics, television producers, writers, and dealers in musical instruments. Prominent is the signature of former prime minister Chuan Leekpai, who had made his own way to Ban Lao and to Jarin's workshop. Jarin had drawn a frame in biro around the entry.

A traditional Thai musical ensemble will often use a *khlui* flute, made from a species of bamboo known as *mai mak*. Because of the quality and reputation of the *khlui* made at Ban Lao, the flutes find a ready market. Most of them are delivered to Duriyaban, a music store on Tanao Road, on the other side of the river. The bamboo comes from Taipikul Putthabat, a village in the province of Saraburi, about a hundred kilometres northeast of Bangkok. This is limestone country, and the villagers cut the bamboo from the mountain behind Wat Phra Phutthabat, the stands growing on the mountain ledges providing exceptionally strong wood. First it is cut to length then left to dry in the sun, where it takes from fifteen to twenty days for the wood to dry completely, the villagers turning the bamboo over continuously to ensure consistent drying, the colour turning from green to a light yellow. The dried wood is cut according to the tone required, a short one producing a high tone and a long one a low tone. The surface is polished using ground brick wrapped in coconut husk, and holes drilled based on precise dimensions and spacing according to a formula passed down through the generations. Bees' wax is poured into the flute and a heated rod inserted to melt the wax, leaving a smooth coating on the uneven inner surface and ensuring a consistency of sound. The more elaborate flutes are covered in rich markings made by dribbling liquid lead, which is heated in a charcoal-fired kiln. Ban Lao makes flutes from other materials too, and foreign buyers often order to specification. Nitaya showed me some ebony instruments tipped with ivory. Others are made from hardwoods brought out of the northern forests, and from ceramics. The most popular ones now, however, are made from PVC, and retail for about 50 baht. These sell in the mass market, being especially popular in schools. Ban Lao occupies two parallel alleys, and only about half a dozen families are making the flutes now. I couldn't resist buying a bamboo flute, along with a PVC model as a comparison, but as my musicals skills do not extend beyond switching on a radio, they live upon my bookcase as souvenirs.

Money Town

This walk takes us through the earliest part of the Thonburi settlement, when it was a customs port and garrison town for the capital of Ayutthaya, further upriver.
Duration: 4 hours

The earliest maps of Thonburi, dating from the latter half of the seventeenth century, show a very modest sized township. King Narai's Wichaiprasit Fort, built in the 1660s and expanded by the French under the naval officer Chevalier de Forbin, sits formidably at the mouth of Klong Bangkok Yai, a watchful presence for ships heading upriver to Ayutthaya. With the fort at its southeast corner, a rectangle of fortifications spreads back almost as far as Klong Bangkok Noi, and outside of this rectangle the land is marked as being agricultural. On the east bank of the river, the Bangkok side, the corresponding fort built by the French is an enormous star-shape, and outside of this, again, the land is marked as farms and orchards. Clearly, Money Town had been essentially for officialdom and the military, while the community that depended upon it had lived largely outside the walls, on the river and alongside the canals, for this was the era when ordinary folk dwelled upon the water rather than on the usually marshy land. When King Taksin established Thonburi as his capital he took the original fortified area and strengthened it by having a canal dug as a moat, the southern

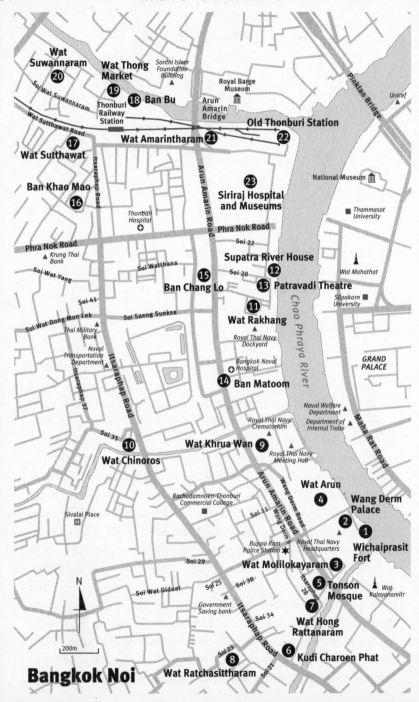

Wat Suwannaram **20**

Wat Thong Market **19**

18 Ban Bu

Sonthi Islam Foundation Building

Royal Barge Museum

Thonburi Railway Station

Arun Amarin Bridge

Pinklao Bridge

Unicef

Old Thonburi Station **22**

21 Wat Amarintharam

Wat Sutthawat Road

17

Wat Sutthawat

Ban Khao Mao **16**

Itsaraphap Road

Arun Amarin Road

23

Siriraj Hospital and Museums

National Museum

Thonburi Hospital

Phra Nok Road

Soi 22

Thammasat University

Phra Nok Road

Krung Thai Bank

Soi Wat Yang

Soi Watthana

Supatra River House **12**

Soi 20

Wat Mahathat

15

Ban Chang Lo

13 Patravadi Theatre

Silpakorn University

Soi 41

Soi Saeng Sueksa

11

Soi Wat Dong Mun Lek

Wat Rakhang

Chao Phraya River

Thai Military Bank

Royal Thai Navy Dockyard

Naval Transportation Department

Bangkok Naval Hospital

14 Ban Matoom

GRAND PALACE

Itsaraphap 37

Naval Welfare Department

Department of Internal Trade

Soi 35

Royal Thai Navy Crematorium

10

Wat Khrua Wan **9**

Wat Chinoros

Royal Thai Navy Meeting Hall

Maha Rat Road

Wat Arun

4

Rachadamnoen-Thonburi Commercial College

Soi 11

Arun Amarin Road

Wang Derm Road

Wang Derm 5

Wang Derm Palace

2

1

Sivalai Place

Buppa Ram Police Station

Royal Thai Navy Headquarters

Wichaiprasit Fort

Itsaraphap Road

Soi 29

Wat Molilokayaram **3**

5

Itsaraphap 28

Tonson Mosque

N

Soi Wat Diduat

Soi 25

Soi 38

7

Wat Kalayanamitr

Government Saving bank

Soi 34

Wat Hong Rattanaram

200m

Soi 23

8

6 Kudi Charoen Phat

Bangkok Noi

Wat Ratchasittharam

Soi 21

end connecting to Klong Bangkok Yai next to Wat Molilokkayaram, and the waterway passing behind Wat Arun, running parallel to the river until it reached Klong Bangkok Noi, at Wat Amarin. These three temples had all existed since the Ayutthaya era, with no one really knowing when they were founded, and indeed at this period they were all known by different names to those of today. Taksin made this area his royal court, building his palace directly next to Wichaiprasit Fort, with Wat Arun as his immediate neighbour on the other side. As a protection from marauders, he had the safest place in the kingdom.

Taksin's moat still exists and it is possible to follow its course all the way across the heart of Thonburi, a journey that can be accomplished on foot within an hour and which will pass some of the old city's most historic sites, skirting the naval dockyards before the canal finally runs to ground just before reaching Klong Bangkok Noi, the waterway having been filled in at this point by Rama v for the building of Thonburi Railway Station. Wichaiprasit Fort, however, is visible only from the Chao Phraya River, and the landward approach will reveal only a massive gate guarded by what must be some of the friendliest-looking sentries in the business. The fort is the home of the Royal Thai Navy, which flies the flag of its commander-in-chief here and fires off salvos from its cannon on state occasions. Taksin's palace has been absorbed into the fort compound and is similarly off-limits except to the occasional specialist tour that has to be invited in. These invitations are very, very hard to get if you are a non-Thai. (They won't even let me in, although possibly they can't be faulted on that.) Now known as Wang Derm, or Former Palace, it was occupied after Taksin's time by a succession of princes. Three sons of Rama II were born here, two of who would become king as Rama III and Rama IV, while the third would become Second King Pinklao. When the last royal resident, Prince Chakrapadibhongse died in 1900, Rama v granted ownership of the palace to the Royal Thai Navy, which manages it jointly with the Phra Racha Wang Derm Restoration Foundation. There are some architectural gems in here. Taksin had built the Throne Hall in Chinese style, and the Navy uses it as a reception hall and a conference centre. There is a large Chinese bell at the

Throne Hall, the clapper being in the form of a dragon with a crystal ball in its mouth, while the bell stand is Thai in style, the capital of its pillar carved in the shape of a lotus flower and a *naga* that twists its body around the pillar. Two Chinese-style mansions are located close to the eastern gate of the palace, the inner one having been Taksin's personal quarters and which is now used as Navy offices. A shrine to King Taksin is here, built late in the nineteenth century in a blending of Thai and Western styles, while nearby is a small modern shrine housing—curiously—whale bones that were found beneath the Taksin shrine when renovations were being undertaken.

The Navy in fact has a substantial frontage at Thonburi from the Bangkok Yai to the Bangkok Noi canals, denoting the importance that this stretch of water had for shipbuilding and military use from the Taksin era onwards. In the early years of the Ayutthaya period river barges manned by teams of rowers had been the chief element of Siamese shipping, as the capital was not a seaport and rivers and canals formed the main transportation highways. When wars erupted, the barges were fitted with cannons for battle. In 1608 the style began to change when King Ekatosarot requested assistance from the Dutch to send shipbuilders to build and equip a number of two- or three-mast brigs. By the latter half of the century the Siamese shipbuilding industry was flourishing, helped by the easy availability of timber, and both Western-style ships and Chinese junks were being built, along with oar-driven barges. Siam therefore had a good capability for building ships, and the vessels that Taksin constructed in the dockyards at Chantaburi in a very short period of time to fight the Burmese invader shows the degree of expertise there must have been. He was able, late in 1767, to move 5,000 men on a fleet of commandeered and new vessels along the Gulf coast, stopping on the way to quell unrest at Chonburi and then sailing up the Chao Phraya to Thonburi, which he took by force, executing the governor, Chao Thong-in, who had been placed in command by the Burmese. The fleet then travelled on to Ayutthaya and Taksin's army attacked the Burmese at Pho Sam Ton, driving them back across the border. Thus the naval fleet played an important role in regaining Siam's independence. In 1769, with Taksin now king and attempting to win

A sailor image marks the jetty for those visiting the Bangkok Naval Hospital.

back errant provinces, he led a fleet of 10,000 men with another 10,000 oarsmen to Nakhon Si Thammarat, in the south, where the governor had been unwilling to comply. The fleet passed through the mouth of the Samut Songkhram River, and was almost destroyed by a great storm, but the province was taken. Taksin ordered the building of another hundred warships for future battles.

During the reigns of Rama II and Rama III, with China trade fuelling Siam's growth, junks were the most widely built vessels in Siam. The reign of Rama IV saw the new era of steamships, and the beginning of Western trade. The first steamship was built in Bangkok in 1865, 22.8 metres (75 ft) long and 9.14 metres (30 ft) wide, with a 15 horsepower engine. Warships in the reign of Rama IV also started using steam propulsion, first with side paddle wheels then with rear propellers. Eventually, the hulls were also changed from wood to iron. As the nineteenth century progressed, and the volume of Western shipping increased, shipbuilding and repair was undertaken on both sides of the river. During this period the Siamese military forces were regrouped along British lines. Before, there had been no navy. The fighting forces were regarded as soldiers, whether they went by land or water. Now, under Rama V, the Royal Navy was formed. (Language clings stubbornly to the old ways: the Thai word for soldier is *taharn*, and for sailor is *taharn rua*, or "boat soldier". (A member of the Royal Thai Air Force is a *taharn agaht*, or "air soldier".) Early in 1890, Rama V officially designated the land directly to the south of Wat Rakhang as the Thonburi Naval Dockyard, and a decade later Taksin's palace was brought into the Navy complex, being designated in 1906 as the Royal Thai Navy Academy. After World War II it became apparent that Thonburi was no longer large enough to build and maintain modern fighting ships, and other Navy bases were opened at Samut Prakharn and Sattahip, near to Pattaya. This part of Thonburi, however, remains dotted with Navy buildings, including the Department of Naval Engineering, the Bangkok Naval Hospital, and the Royal Thai Navy Crematorium, which is attached to Wat Khrua Wan, a temple noted for having the most complete and best preserved set of Jataka paintings in Thailand.

When Rama I moved the capital across the river and Wang Derm ceased to be a royal palace, the two temples that had previously been encompassed in the compound by King Taksin were released to become public temples once more.

Wat Molilokkayaram stands at the mouth of Taksin's moat, tucked in beside Wichaiprasit Fort, but to casual visitors it is almost invisible and indeed takes some effort to actually find. Approaching by road over the bridge across Klong Bangkok Yai, the temple is visible fleetingly as a huddle of red roofs, and a U-turn is required to enter the tiny lane that takes its name from the temple and which will lead the visitor over the moat and into the compound, which is surprisingly large, covering five acres of land. When Taksin established his court, this temple was already here. It was known as Wat Tai Talat, which means "the temple behind the market", so there must have been a market here right against the walls of the fort. Taksin incorporated the temple into his palace boundary. Under Siamese tradition no monks are allowed to reside in a temple in a royal compound between dusk and dawn, the religious activities being reserved for the monarchy, but when Rama I moved the capital across the river he allowed monks to take up residence. The oldest building in the compound is the *wiharn*, which, oddly, Taksin used for storing salt, and the building is still known as Phra Wiharn Chag Klua. The *wiharn* is a mix of Thai and Chinese styles, with ceramic roof tiles, and gable spires and ridges decorated with stucco. Rama I built the *ubosot*, which has very fine Siamese painting on the interior walls and the ceiling, and beautifully carved and lacquered door and window frames. A library was later added, an unusual construction with masonry on the first level, a wooden structure at the second, and a *chedi* at each end. There are deep alcoves around the base housing statues in military uniforms, although they have badly deteriorated. The building is now living quarters for the monks.

The temple, which was upgraded to second tier royal status in the reign of Rama VI, has been a significant one for the Chakri dynasty. Rama II, III, IV and V all made additions and renovations, and Rama VI elevated it to the royal second tier. Most of the sons of Rama II, including the future kings Rama III and IV and Second King Pinklao, had their elementary study here. Wat Molilokkayaram has evolved over the years to become a study centre for the Pali language and in 1991 was appointed as the monastic educational institute providing Dharma education. Temples from elsewhere in Bangkok and other parts of Thailand send students here, where there are twenty teachers and up to two hundred monks and novices studying each year.

Wat Arun, of course, needs little introduction. It is one of Thailand's best-known symbols, and its Khmer-style *prang* decorates the logo of the Tourism Authority of Thailand. To most visitors it is just a dramatic spire, and those who puff their way to the upper terrace are certainly rewarded with a gorgeous view of the river and the city beyond, but the temple is a complex place with deep symbolic meanings and a beauty that continues to reveal itself, no matter how often one visits. No one knows when Wat Arun was founded, but it dates back to the Ayutthaya era, when it was known as Wat Makok, denoting that this area was used for growing the type of plum that the Thais call *makok*, and lending weight to the theory that Bangkok, or Bang Kok, or Bang Makok, gained its name from the surrounding plum orchards. The temple appears to have had little significance until General Taksin, on his way back to Ayutthaya with his fleet intent on driving out the Burmese, arrived here as dawn was breaking. When he became king and established Thonburi as the capital, he had the temple incorporated within his royal compound, renovated it, and gave the name Wat Chaeng, which means "Temple of the Dawn". In 1779 the Emerald Buddha was brought back from Vientiane by General Chakri and enshrined here for five years until being transferred by Rama I across the river to the purpose-built Wat Phra Kaeo. The mystique and holiness of the Emerald Buddha was conferred upon Wat Chaeng, which has continued throughout the Chakri dynasty. Wat Chaeng was the crown temple of Rama II, who renamed it Wat Arun, after the Hindu god of the dawn, and whose ashes are buried under a Buddha statue in the ordination hall, the face of the image believed to have been moulded in the king's likeness.

The temple appears to have had a very modest-sized *prang* during its early days, thought to be less than two metres high, and construction of its present structure began only in the time of Rama II, who passed away when it was still in the foundation stage. Rama III completed construction, and although there is some dispute as to how high the *prang* actually is, the generally accepted figure is 67 metres (219 ft), with a circumference around the base of 234 metres (767 ft). Whatever the height, it is the highest *prang* in Thailand. A *prang* symbolises Mount Meru, the mountain that stands in the middle of Hindu-Buddhist cosmology, and in the case of Wat Arun it rises from the fabulous region of Himavant, which is covered in forests and lakes and is the home of sages, imps, demons and dragons, represented here by carved and moulded figures against a background of porcelain flowers and leaves. The main *prang* is called the *phra prang*, and there are four smaller *prangs* at the base, known as *prang thit*, symbolising the four continents and housing statues of the gods within alcoves. The *phra prang* has four terraces, and four *mondops*, or pavilions bearing images, are located on the second terrace.

There are sixteen structures of importance within this large site, which covers thirteen acres, and many of them have been built or changed during successive reigns. The *wiharn* was built in the reign of Rama I, and rebuilt in the reigns of both Rama II and III. Inside the *wiharn* is the principal Buddha image, brought from Vientiane in 1858 and named Phra Arun. The *ubosot* dates from the time of Rama II and is distinctive with its yellow and green tiled roofs, with the eight metal statues of elephants near the entrance having been cast in 1846. Seated inside the peripheral gallery are 120 Buddha images, and there are 144 stone lions, 112 soldiers, and 16 noblemen, all Chinese in style. The eight boundary markers, the *sema*, are housed in marble porches and intricately carved. There are six riverside pavilions, all Chinese in style, built from green sandstone and dating from the reign of Rama III, and the *mondop* housing the Buddha footprint also dates from this period and was designed with a Chinese-style roof.

Those in search of history rather than symbolism should visit the old *ubosot*, which dates back to the earliest days of the temple and is located in front of the *prang*. The *Siam Chronicles* record that King Taksin lived in this ordination hall for a brief period before his execution, and his bedstead, a modest teak slab, can be seen there today. Near to the old ordination hall is the original chapel, dating back to the same era. Near here is a gilded statue of Nai Raung, a monk who burned himself to death in 1790 in front of the sermon hall, promising that if he achieved Nirvana, he would make a nearby lotus bloom. The lotus duly bloomed and when the monk was properly cremated his ashes turned green, white, yellow and purple. The ashes were kept in the hall for sermons. Another pavilion honours in a similar way Nai Nok, a monk who burned himself to death in 1861 in front of the old ordination hall. A small area in the garden, under a bodhi tree, has become a shrine with decapitated figures placed here in commemoration of the death of King Taksin.

There is a strong Chinese influence in the architecture of Wat Arun, vying with the Khmer influence, the mingling of Hindu and Buddhist symbolism, and Siamese tradition and identity. China had played a significant role in supporting Taksin's campaigns against the Burmese and in establishing his kingdom, and he was greatly in debt to the Chinese at the time of his death. During the reigns of Rama I, II and III, almost all of Siam's trade was with China, reaching its peak under Rama III, whose enthusiasm manifested itself in Chinese styling for many of the temples he built or restored. Chinese junks shipping out of Siam loaded with rice or timber would need to be loaded with bulk goods to act as ballast when they returned, and much of this was crockery, porcelain and rock and stone carvings. Although largely foundation and building material, a useful commodity in muddy delta country, some of it would have been good quality and delivered for a specific purpose. The *phra prang* of Wat Arun is studded with porcelain, a mixture of Chinese and Siamese, which catches the light and causes the structure to glitter, and craftsmen have fashioned porcelain flowers and leaves. The stone figures in and around the temple structures and in the garden are often beautifully carved and provide a valuable insight as to how the Chinese looked and dressed at that time, and there are also depictions of other races, such as the European sailors and soldiers that can be seen in the gardens.

The little paved lane that runs behind Wat Arun, Wang Derm Road, is one of the most pleasant thoroughfares in Bangkok, with the temple wall on one side and old houses with eating places and cafés on the other and in the small *sois* that lead through to Arun Amarin Road. Walk the few metres back to the beginning of Taksin's moat, pass under the bridge, follow the footpath along Bangkok Yai canal, and another ancient community will be revealed.

As we have seen on the other side of the canal, there has been a Muslim community on this part of Klong Bangkok Yai since before the Thonburi period. They were Cham Muslims, coming from parts of what are now Cambodia and Vietnam, and they arrived in the first half of the sixteenth century as labourers to help with the river works that eased navigation along the Chao Phraya, and as mercenaries to fight in the war against Burma that saw the first siege of Ayutthaya in 1548. Some of the Cham who helped dig the canal that led to the creation of the Bangkok Yai and Noi canals stayed on the bank of the Yai. They were certainly at Thonburi during the reign of King Songtham (1611–1628), as a surviving record written on a palm leaf notes a soldier named Jiam attempting to send a set of garments to his father on the Bangkok Yai canal. Another record notes the construction of a mosque in 1688, during King Narai's reign, by a Siamese Muslim of Persian lineage named Okya Rajavangsansenee, who was a commander in charge of the 400 French-led mercenaries hired by Narai to man Wichaiprasit Fort, largely comprising North Africans, presumably Muslims.

There had also been Cham Muslims living in Ayutthaya, where they made their homes on rafts on the waterways and worked as farmers, boat builders and traders. When Ayutthaya fell and Thonburi was founded, they sailed their rafts down the river and joined the existing community. So large did the Cham community become that they occupied both banks of the canal, with mosques on both sides. Tonson Mosque, here on the north bank, is the oldest mosque in Bangkok, while Kudi Khao on the south bank dates from the time of Rama I.

Tonson Mosque was originally a teak structure raised on a platform and roofed with terracotta tiles. In style it followed the Siamese pattern. In 1827, in the reign of Rama II, the mosque was rebuilt as a brick structure, again following the Siamese style and with elaborate mouldings on its stucco-clad gables. By the middle of the twentieth century this building had deteriorated so badly it was completely rebuilt, being finished in 1954, this time as a reinforced concrete structure with a traditional Islamic dome. The arched *mihrab*, the pavilion indicating the direction of Mecca, carries an engraved teak tablet that is believed to have come from a mosque in Ayutthaya, and which displays burn marks. A century-old copy of the Koran has been written in very fine script using either a fish bone or rice husk, and is contained in a decorated teak box with mother-of-pearl inlay. A prominent feature is a suspended lamp that has a square brass lampshade inlaid on all sides with green glass and engraved in memory of Rama V. In the mosque compound, two older buildings have survived: a structure erected to welcome visiting royalty in 1915, and an octagonal pavilion built in 1930. The graveyard is also of historical interest, containing the final resting place of many prominent members of the Muslim community, including high-ranking court officials and royal consorts.

The Cham are the remnants of the Champa kingdom, which prevailed in what is now southern and central Vietnam and parts of southern Cambodia from the seventh through to the eighteenth

centuries. They had used Sanskrit as their scholarly language and
were initially Hindu, but Arab maritime trade from the tenth century
onwards saw the spread of Islam into parts of the kingdom. The late
fifteenth century saw much of Champa wiped out, as the Vietnamese
moved south. Early in the seventeenth century, as the Ming Dynasty
collapsed, thousands of Chinese refugees poured into the Cham
region. Many Cham fled their homelands during this period, some to
Cambodia, some to Siam, some to the Malay peninsula, and some to
the Chinese island of Hainan. Although avowedly Muslim, the communities at Tonson and Kudi Khao have largely been absorbed into
the Thai identity, and are no longer aware of their Cham ancestry.
They study Arabic, in order to read the Koran, and they celebrate
Muslim festivals such as Eid, but they speak Thai and regard themselves as Thai. Their children attend Thai schools, which in this district are either Buddhist or Catholic oriented and where provision is
made for them as Muslims, but otherwise they follow the standard
Thai curriculum. Aside from eschewing pork, their food is essentially Thai, the stalls and eating-houses around the mosques serving
noodles, and beef, chicken and seafood. The casual visitor passing
through these communities would probably not notice any difference to the traditional Thai Buddhist communities in the city, except
for the sight of the occasional woman wearing a headscarf.

The Cham Muslims are Sunni, but as if to emphasise yet another
level of tolerance in this most tolerant of societies, there is another
Muslim community almost directly next door, this time formed of
Shias, and with their own mosque, Kudi Charoen Phat. This can be
found by following the footpath from Tonson Mosque past the big
old bodhi tree and heading alongside the canal where within a couple of minutes it leads to Itsaraphap Road. The mosque is on the corner, and is in yet another distinctive architectural style, a Western
panya building, a form that was a familiar sight alongside the canal
during the reign of Rama v. A single-storey structure with a green
tiled roof, it has no dome. Kudi Charoen Phat was founded by a
group of Muslims who had played an active role in court life during the Ayutthaya era, and who had resettled here when Thonburi
became the capital. A Muslim place of worship registering with the

Ministry of Interior becomes known officially as a mosque, or *masy-id* in Thai, and the fact that Kudi Charoen Phat retains the old word *kudi* in its name indicates that it is not registered as such, and is run quite independently under its own administrative council.

Around the bodhi tree that stands between the two Muslim communities are clustered the buildings of an Ayutthaya-era Buddhist temple, Wat Hong Rattanaram. Founded by a wealthy Chinese named Nai Hong, it was designated a royal monastery by King Taksin, being adjacent to the palace, and was a significant centre of religious education. Taksin had the temple area expanded greatly, and a large ordination hall was constructed in front of the old one, together with other structures, and consequently the compound today sprawls over an extensive area. More renovations took place in the time of Rama III. The grand ordination hall is built of brick and lime, and its two-tiered roof has gables decorated with the design known as *hamsa*, with two niches housing gilded stucco *hamsa* figures, facing each other, and the projected eaves supported by square columns and brackets with more *hamsa* figures. The door arch has elements of both Chinese and Western styles, and the door and window panels are finely decorated with stucco-moulded

Tonson Mosque was founded by Cham Muslims and is the oldest mosque in Bangkok.

figures. Within the ordination hall there are tempera paintings in glass frames depicting the story of the Emerald Buddha, painted during the reigns of Rama III and Rama IV. The *wiharn* houses an ancient golden Buddha image that had previously been encased in lime, the image having been discovered when its casing was broken. It dates from the Sukhothai period, and an old U-Thong script can be seen etched along the base. The scripture hall is carved with a floral motif from the early Rattanakosin period and is used as monks' living quarters, while the bell tower is pure white, built in brick and mortar, and is Chinese in style.

Occasionally, in this urban area, one stumbles across temples that could easily be in the middle of the countryside, such is their atmosphere of detachment from the outside world. Wat Ratchasittharam, on Itsaraphap Soi 23, is one. Standing by the side of a small canal, and with two *chedis* at the entrance, the temple is set amongst lovely old rain trees. During the final days of Ayutthaya, a forest monk known as the Venerable Suk Kaithuean (1733–1822) had played an important role in promulgating the meditation practices that had originated with the historical Buddha. A forest monk undertakes what the Thais call *thudong*, which is the ascetic practice of wandering the forests developing themselves spiritually by becoming one with nature. During the Thonburi era the Venerable Suk had settled at Wat Thahoi, on the outskirts of the now-ruined Ayutthaya, where his affinity towards wild creatures had them nesting in the temple grounds. Suk appears to have been a charismatic and possibly unpredictable man, the name Kaithuean being a nickname that translates as "wild chicken", but his form of ancient meditation was important and authentic during this time of turmoil, and Rama I invited him to Bangkok where he was installed at Wat Phlab in 1782 as head of meditation instruction.

At the same time Wat Ratchasittharam was built adjacent to Wat Phlab and the two temples were merged. Rama II, when he was king, studied here, and Suk was appointed Supreme Patriarch in 1819. During the reign of Rama II his system of meditation was promoted as the main medium of instruction for the entire monastic community of Siam, and Suk was meditation instructor to the young princes

Jessadabodindra and Mongkut, who became Rama III and Rama IV, respectively. His system of meditation, however, eventually fell into disuse. It did not die out completely, as he kept records in the form of *samut khoi*, the traditional Siamese folded manuscript books, and it is taught today at Wat Ratchasittharam as the Matchima meditation system, the home of this form of meditation being one of the very few places in Thailand to still teach it. Wat Ratchasittharam attracts devotees to this form of meditation, and also because of its very fine mural of the death of the Lord Buddha. The outside wall depicts the scene of the Royal Barge Procession. The temple is a second-tier royal temple. Inside the compound can be seen the teak building that was used as the residence for Rama II when he entered the monkhood.

Further along Itsaraphap Road the road lifts to pass over Klong Morn, the main canal that bisects Money Town between the Bangkok Yai and Noi canals, and as it does so an enormous temple building can be seen rising high above the bridge. This is the recently constructed dormitory building for Wat Chinoros, a temple that is built to a far more modest scale than its living accommodation and which dates back to 1836. The princely monk Krom Phra Poramanuchit Chinoros, who was one of Siam's most famous poets, and who became Supreme Patriarch in 1851, built the temple. The ceiling of the *ubosot* is painted red and decorated with *naga* fretwork covered with gold leaf, and there are unusual murals here that depict in map form the temple, the canal, the river and the Grand Palace, although the paintings are in a sad state of deterioration. There are two other unusual aspects to Wat Chinoros. One is the curved shape of the *ubosot*, which gives an odd distorting effect, while the other is the heaped cannonballs that form the *sema* stones. Venerable Chinoros, who was a son of Rama I, was also known as Prince Wasukri. He had been ordained at Wat Pho and resided there for much of his life. He passed away in 1853 and his ashes are buried there at what is now known as Wasukri Residence.

One of the first acts King Taksin performed after driving out the Burmese in 1769 and establishing Thonburi as the capital was to form a commission that would work to ensure the purity of Buddhism

The former residence of Rama I at Wat Rakhang, converted into a library.

continued, even though the temples and libraries of Ayutthaya had been burned and destroyed. A temple named Wat Bang Wa Yai that existed on the riverbank near to the king's palace was given royal status and used by the king to host a congress of senior monks, the stipulation being that they must be learned both in the Dharma and in meditation. Taksin was conducting a military campaign in the south of Siam, where Nakhon Sri Thammarat, an ancient kingdom that had always had shaky allegiance to Siam, had made a bid for independence following the fall of Ayutthaya. Thammarat, on the east coast of the Malay peninsula, had for centuries been an important trading post, and in the seventeenth century British, Portuguese and Dutch merchants had established factories there. It was also a centre for Buddhist study and pilgrimage, Wat Phra Mahathat being as old as the city itself and housing a tooth relic of the Buddha.

Taksin had the Buddhist scriptures, the Tripitaka, brought up from the south for the monks to study under the supervision of a learned monk named Phra Archan Si, who was appointed abbot of Wat Bang Wa Yai. Rama I continued the royal patronage of the temple. During the late Thonburi period he had used a set of timber buildings near to Taksin's palace as his residence, and he moved these to the temple compound for use as a library. During the renovation work a particularly melodious bell, or *rakhang*, was found in the eastern part of the compound. The king ordered the bell shipped across the river for installation in the Temple of the Emerald Buddha, and had five new bells sent back in exchange. He also decreed that the temple be renamed Wat Rakhang, the Temple of the Bell.

The most picturesque way to approach Wat Rakhang is by ferry, boarding at Tha Chang Pier and disembarking at the jetty with its two uniformed matelot statues, for the pier also services the Naval Hospital next door, which provides medical treatment for sailors and their families. Vendors line the short distance from the jetty to the temple, and weekends, especially Sundays, are a lively time to visit for there is something almost like a carnival atmosphere. Several vendors sell turtles that merit-makers buy and release into the river, and a number of urchins stand by with wide grins waiting to dive into the warm brown waters and retrieve the hapless creatures ready for the next worshipper. Being a turtle in Bangkok is not exactly a blast. There are bells everywhere. Two beautiful blue-and-gold bells hang in front of the *ubosot*, there are bell designs on the door and the window shutters, and if devotees ring each of the long row of bells hanging in the courtyard they will be blessed with good luck; which explains why the air is continually filled with the tinkling and clanging of bells. The five bells presented by Rama I hang in a bell tower to the front of the temple, four of them painted a light blue, the centre bell a dark blue.

A few steps from the bell tower is the king's former residence, now known as the Tripitaka Hall. When the buildings were moved to the temple grounds a pond was dug so that they could stand on stilts in the water, and thereby keep insects away from the paper and parchment documents. That has now been filled in, and the building stands framed in green trees, a classical piece of Siamese teak architecture. Stained in red ochre are three buildings, each with a distinctive gable. Entering the front door, one is standing inside the central room. The unit on the right side is the reading room, and that on the left the retiring room. The inside walls are covered with murals depicting the daily life of that time, painted by Acharn Nak, who was a monk in the time of Rama I. The paints used to create these murals were tempera mixed with latex, a form of colouring that yields neither shading nor the brightness that can be seen in works of art created in the Ayutthaya period, but the artist was working in a time of great turmoil for Siam and possibly paints from China or India were not easily available.

There is a pleasant little stony lane here, and if the lane is followed around to the left one comes to the former home of a remarkable lady. Khunying Supatra Singholka, who passed away in 1993 at the age of 83, was from an aristocratic family. Her father was Phya Rajamountre, a noble in the court of Rama VI, and her mother was Khunying Boonpan. Rama VI was the literary king, a monarch who produced many learned works in addition to plays. One of his papers was entitled "The Status of Women is an Indicator of a Society's Civilisation", and it was a profound and controversial work for its era and the conservative Siamese beliefs of the time. Supatra herself first became involved with women's rights when she entered Thammasat University as a law student, and she made this her mission in life, helping to produce legislation to amend laws that discriminated against women. Amongst her achievements over the years were the obtaining of equal rights for wives to handle legal matters without a husband's prior consent, in ensuring a husband's automatic approval of his wife's business dealings, and other changes in the law relating to marriage registration and divorce alimony.

In addition to being a very prominent lawyer, Supatra was a successful businesswoman, the owner of Bangkok's largest ferry and express boat business. She also owned a large area of land along the riverbank here in the vicinity of Wat Rakhang, and she left a very prominent legacy. Firstly there is Supatra's house, which has been converted into a stylish restaurant named Supatra River House. On the terrace each weekend is staged a theatrical display, the players being from the Patravadi Theatre next door. Owner Patravadi Meechuthon is the daughter of Supatra, and one of Thailand's most accomplished actresses. The theatre is very much the preserve of ancient Siamese traditions, in addition to exploring more modern forms, and there is a small shop at the entrance where khon masks are displayed. Supatra's other daughter, Supapan Pichaironnarongsongkram, has inherited her mother's business acumen, and today operates the family Chao Phraya Express riverboat service.

Opposite the Naval Hospital is a little alley named Soi Arun Amarin 23, and here, in the houses straddling Taksin's moat, is a community that is known as Ban Matoom and which for generations has been famous for selling and preserving the fruit of the bael tree (*matoom* in Thai), a tree that is native to India but which has spread through parts of Southeast Asia. The bael fruit is the size of a large grapefruit and has a woody shell that is so hard it has to be cracked open with a hammer or a machete. The pulp has a floral aroma and a bitter-sweet flavour, and can be eaten fresh, boiled with syrup, dried, or taken as a particularly refreshing drink. Today, there are only four families in Ban Matoom selling bael fruit, a contrast to the past when the entire community made a living from it. The families buy the fresh fruit from Sukhothai and Phichit provinces. The best time to visit is from July to April, when the fruit is in season, but outside this period the community sells preserved bael and bael fruit tea.

Following the Ban Matoom alley round into the lane that runs alongside Taksin's moat, across Itsaraphap 39 and into the continuation of the lane, which becomes Soi Ban Chang Lo, one passes through yet another community that has recently become almost extinct. Ban Chang Lo is where Buddha images were cast, the earliest craftsmen having come down from Ayutthaya during the Thonburi era and settled here, which at the time was just outside the palace walls. These were foundry workers, skilled at mould making and metal casting, and during Taksin's time and on into the early Rattanakosin periods they produced weapons such as swords, guns and cannon for the army. One of their masterpieces is a cannon named Phra Piroon, now on display at the National Museum. They started to focus on making Buddha statues during the reigns of Rama II and III, when both kings built and restored many temples, and this continued through to the modern era. Each family specialised in a certain skill, such as sculpting, making moulds, mixing gold, pouring hot metal, and polishing and decorating with gold lacquer and mirrors. They used clay moulds until Corrado Feroci introduced plaster moulds, which can be used half a dozen times or more. Pollution control regulation in 1992 forced the craftsmen to move elsewhere, mostly to Nakhon Pathom's Phutthamonthon area. There is some small-scale work that is still done here, and a few offices continuing to take orders for the factories, but otherwise this is now just a quiet residential lane. Substantial space was needed for some of the image-making activities and several families have capitalised on the freeing up of their land, so that in recent years new residential developments have appeared in this area.

Strolling north along Soi Ban Chang Lo, turning left into Phran Nok Road and then right into Itsaraphap Road will lead to a small alley named Soi Khao Mao 1, which runs behind Wat Sutthawat. A couple of minutes down here, just when it seems the visitor is heading into a pleasant but featureless residential area, there is a junction with a signboard that advises he is in Ban Khao Mao, another Thonburi-era community that has known days of greatness but which is now sadly diminished. In the days when this land was fruit orchards threaded by waterways, boats would arrive from rice-growing districts carrying young green rice, *khao mao*. The community, which traces its roots directly from Khao Mao village in the Uthai district in Ayutthaya, would pound the green rice and make dishes such as crispy fried noodles (*khao mao mee*), toffee (*kalamae med*), and desserts such as *khao niew daeng*. *Khao mao* was a good food supply during times of war since it can be kept for a long time and becomes soft and edible once sprinkled with water. King Taksin kept his troops supplied with *khao mao* as regular army rations. Ban Khao Mao supplied the households of royalty and nobility with traditional Siamese desserts and other delicacies during the Thonburi period and throughout the nineteenth century. A few families here still make and sell *khao mao*, and there is a small museum nearby, in the grounds of Wat Sutthawat, that tells of this and other traditional skills that once flourished in the area.

Many of the refugees who managed to get out of Ayutthaya when the Burmese destroyed the city were skilled craftsmen who travelled down the river to Thonburi, where they once again flourished, briefly under Taksin and then to a greater degree under the Chakri dynasty, as Bangkok was founded. One little band of travellers set up a community in Thonburi on the bank of the Bangkok Noi canal. They called their village Ban Bu, after the trade they had brought with them. The word *bu* doesn't translate directly, but it means to hammer gently and rhythmically, as a smithy does when he is forming something delicate like a plate or cup. These people were bronzesmiths, making the ornamental bronze bowls and goblets for the temples and palaces of Ayutthaya.

Ancient timber houses straggle along the bank of the Bangkok Noi canal beside Wat Suwannaram, and there is a century-old market hall, Wat Thong Talat, with a handsome truss-beam roof. Ban Bu main street is nothing more than a pathway a few feet wide, just broad enough to take the motorcycles that buzz down here, past the temple and over the humped bridge that crosses a small inlet from the canal. There is a pleasantly timeless feel, but time has changed the village of the bronzesmiths, for the number of manufacturers has dwindled to just one, a family-owned firm named Jiam Sangsajja. They are now the only craftsmen in Bangkok producing the traditional stonewashed bronze bowls known as *khan long hin*. There used to be a tiny shop on the main street but it burned down a few years ago, set alight when a gas canister in the neighbouring house exploded in the early hours of the morning, says Metta Salanon, matriarch of the business. A gazebo has replaced the shop, and the small timber house that stood behind it now serves as Metta's office and showroom. Metta is a tiny, compact woman with glossy hair and a cherubic smile. The fire had done the image of the business no good, and what was a dying trade now has only a few years left. The two remaining smiths are now about sixty years old. When they retire, there will be no one else to replace them, as nobody is interested in learning this craft.

The workshop is a ramshackle mix of corrugated zinc and timber, lit mainly by daylight from the open doorway. The heat hits you straight away, and the smell of burning coals and red hot metal hangs heavily in the air. There is a startling plop and hiss as someone tosses something hot into a tub of cold water. Two open furnaces protected by structures like zinc sentry boxes throw out a cherry-red glow. Here sit the two smithies, each with a helper, practicing their ancient art. A smithy places slivers of copper, tin and a gold known as *thong mah lau* into an earthen mould and heats it for about ten minutes over the charcoal. The contents melt and blend into liquid bronze, which is poured into a mould called a *din ngann*. The bronze forms a pancake shape. The smithy bakes the flat metal until it turns hard like stone, washing it in water to make it harder. He and his helper then alternately beat the metal into its finished form, the final stage being known as *karn laai*, in which a much smaller hammer is used for final shaping. A middle-aged lady carries this out, and the remainder of the tiny workforce is also female, three women carrying out the cleaning and polishing stages. In earlier days the craftsmen would polish their work with fine stones wrapped in a piece of cloth, hence the name "stone washed". Nowadays they grind the mould into powder and use that instead, a method that gives a depth and lustre unmatched by the metal polish used by modern factories. The bronze glows in the light that filters through the doorway, and if you ping a large bowl with your finger, it gives out the resonant sound of a temple bell.

Ban Bu is tucked in directly behind Wat Suwannaram, a temple whose beauty is at distinct odds with its grim history. King Taksin had used the grounds of this Ayutthaya-era temple as a place to execute a large number of Burmese prisoners of war, who were brought down from a holding camp at Bang Kaew in Phitsanulok Province to meet their fate. Quite why Taksin chose the temple for this purpose is unknown. There is, however, nothing to mark the temple's former notoriety. The original building no longer stands, having been demolished by Rama I, who then had the present structure erected. Off to the side of the temple a royal crematorium was built (it was Siam's first funeral facility built of concrete) and used until the reign of Rama V, when it was demolished. Bangkok Noi District Office occupies the site today.

Enter the temple *ubosot* and there is the most exquisitely painted interior, with frescoes on all four walls painted by Master Thongyu and Master Kongpae, two of the leading artists of Rama III's reign.

They had worked side by side here, and Suwannaram is one of the greatest surviving examples of first period Rattanakosin mural painting. This style followed the traditions of Ayutthaya, being essentially light and airy and with a two-dimensional form that pre-dated the Siamese use of perspective and which lends a zigzag appearance to the scenes and episodes depicted. There is, however, a curious perspective that gives the impression the viewer is looking down from above, into the scenes, and below the stylised representations of celestial and noble beings can be seen the antics of the common folk. Often comical, and always very human, they are a record of everyday life of that time. Here there is added interest for the visitor with scenes depicting European characters, including a man in late-seventeenth century dress peering over battlements with a telescope and another taking a pop with a rifle, possibly representing the siege of Bangkok. Another scene shows foreign troops clad in turbans, and judging by the style of dress and their facial characteristics these are believed to be Persians, there having been an influential group of Persian merchants at Ayutthaya. The golden image of the Buddha is in the Subduing Mara position. A curious tradition is attached to this image, which is believed to have the power of fulfilling wishes for those who perform a forfeit. The forfeit is known as *wing ma*, which means "horse riding", and the petitioner must run around the *ubosot* three times, straddling a banana tree "horse" and neighing loudly as he goes. An obliging local once demonstrated this for me. It is highly recommended that anyone performing *wing ma* has a group of understanding friends present.

A little further along the bank of Klong Bangkok Noi leads to the railway line. Opened in 1903, it was first built to link to Petchaburi on the west coast of the Gulf of Siam, and then down to Butterworth, in Malaya. A spur was later added to Kanchanaburi, in the west, near the Burma border. The trains had left from Thonburi Station, which was designed by the German architect Karl Döhring and built at the mouth of the Bangkok Noi canal, but as there were no bridges across the Chao Phraya at that time, passengers departing from the Bangkok side had first to take a boat across to the railway station. Rama v had ordered the building of Thonburi Station, filling in

A Japanese locomotive outside Thonburi Station, originally the southern rail terminus.

part of Taksin's moat and moving a Muslim community that lived here, donating land on the opposite bank of the canal for them. An Ayutthaya-era Buddhist temple, Wat Amarintharam, stands on the edge of the station land and lost three of its four assembly halls, consequently becoming known by the locals as *bot noi*, or small chapel.

Following the restructuring of the railway administration system, the decision was taken to build a bridge further upriver, at Bang Sue, and this, the Rama VI Bridge, opened in 1927. It was the first bridge across the Chao Phraya. Trains for the south now departed from Hua Lampong Station, and Thonburi was left to service only the western line. When the Japanese forces occupied Siam in 1941, they used the station as their base for what became known as the Death Railway, the railway line they laid up to Three Pagodas Pass and through to Burma. The Allied forces bombed and destroyed Thonburi Station but after the war it was rebuilt in the same style, a European design in pale red brick with cream detailing and pale blue window shutters, the oblong structure topped with a square clocktower. There were, however, few trains: the line is used by commuters living in the Thonburi suburbs and the neighbouring province of Nakhon Pathom, and by tourists travelling to the Bridge on the River Kwai in Kanchanaburi, but its old status as an important terminus had ended. The station was decommissioned late in 2003, and Bangkok Noi Station, 800 metres down the line, became the terminus and was renamed Thonburi Station. For almost a decade the original station remained empty, with grand plans swirling around for a transport museum and railway park. The station became, briefly, a tourist centre. Then it was used as a setting for a Jackie Chan film, *Around the World in 80 Days*, and the work of the film crew who had transformed it into Agra Station remained visible for several years. The sidings and railway sheds became the haunt of railway anoraks, as there were some picturesque old steam and diesel locomotives in storage there. The market that had grown up next to the station was persuaded to move down the line to the replacement terminus, and the station building became a lonely and abandoned place. No one knew what was going to happen.

But eventually, as is the way in Bangkok, there came a sudden change. Neighbouring Siriraj Hospital had bought up the land, and they have built a new wing and other facilities whilst retaining the old station building, which has become a museum for the hospital, the Siriraj Phimuksthan Museum. The station building is a little difficult to find now, being in the shadow of modern concrete and next to an underpass, but it still faces across the river and Klong Bangkok Noi, and one must be thankful that it has been spared demolition. Sentimentalists such as myself regret the disappearance of the railway land, and the fact that the station no longer looks like a station. But there is an attractive small park on the riverbank, and an old steam locomotive, a Mikado 2-8-2, bearing the number 950 and built by Mitsubishi in 1950, has been moved from the sidings and placed here. The engine had been a non-working one, partially cannibalised to supply parts for the operational steam locos that are still rolled out on special occasions. As for the replacement terminus, it remains in appearance a wayside station, and there is not enough space to store much in the way of railway memorabilia, beyond some decrepit rolling stock that rots away, unloved, amongst the weeds on the canal bank.

Siriraj Hospital takes up a large area of land on the riverfront, and except for the small original building, dating from 1888, is mainly a collection of featureless concrete blocks. The hospital was founded by Rama v as Siam's first modern hospital, and is now one of the country's largest. As part of Mahidol University it is also an important training institute. Few realise, however, that inside this sprawling complex, which is rather like entering a small town, there are at least eight museums, all of them open to the public. Several date back to the early years of the last century, and have grown out of the hospital's educational facilities.

The Parasitology Museum predictably shows various kinds of parasites such as whipworms and roundworms, with models of their life cycles. The Ellis Pathological Museum shows the evolution of medicine in Thailand. At the Veekit Veeranuvati Museum is a display of ancient medical equipment and diagnostic methods, while the Ouy Ketusinh Museum is devoted to Thai traditional medicine, massage and herbal treatments. I especially enjoy the Congdon Anatomical Museum, founded in 1922 by Professor Edgar Davidson Congdon, who was sent to Bangkok by the Rockefeller Foundation to help the Siamese improve their medical skills. The two rooms haven't changed since the 1920s, and have the dusty, cluttered look of an old laboratory: the skeletons of various Siriraj luminaries hang here, presumably donated to medical research rather than to act as a grim warning, as with the highwaymen of old. There are two unnamed corpses, a man and a woman, preserved in ethyl alcohol, and partially dissected to reveal the internal organs. There are Siamese twins preserved in jars. Embryos are to be found at every stage of growth. Someone has reconstructed the entire nervous system of the human body, and it hangs from a hook rather like a giant plant gone to seed. This museum is packed with exhibits, and there simply is not enough display room for everything; once I was startled to see a row of dusty skulls peering up at me from a shelf partly concealed behind a sliding panel. Reputedly the place is haunted, and I'm not surprised.

The most popular museum by far is however the Songkran Niyomsane Forensic Medicine Museum, more familiarly known as "Si Quey's Place". Here the focus is on crime. At the top of the stairs you will see a few skeletons hanging about, grinning knowingly at the visitors. To the rear of the stairwell are a number of cases displaying skulls whose late owners have copped it in violent circumstances, showing just what a machete can do (think boiled egg), and various bullet trajectories. There are severed limbs, one of them bearing a tattoo of an opium-smoking Chinaman. A blood-stained uniform belonging to a nurse murdered by a doctor is on display, as is an impressive collection of murder weapons. There is a preserved head, sliced vertically in half to show the path of a bullet through the brain. No description is given as to the circumstances in which the victim died (the museum is not big on words), but the preservation has been done so well that his hair looks freshly barbered and there is an expression of surprise on both halves of his face. Si Quey himself, however, is the main reason people come here. He was an immigrant from Southern China who arrived in Thailand in 1944, settling in Nakhon Pathom province. Making a living as a vendor, he seemed an ordinary enough member of the community until he abducted a little girl, suffocated her, then cut out her heart and ate it. Si Quey dumped her body near a temple, then fled to Rayong, where he found work as a gardener. This time he killed a small boy. When caught he said he ate the internal organs in the belief that it would promote longevity—a theory he managed to disprove by his own fate. He was hanged in 1958. Si Quey's body was then preserved with paraffin wax, and it stands here in a glass case, black as ebony, and bowing forward with a slightly apologetic air. There is a newspaper photograph of him nearby, and in life he looks a scary enough figure with his big, sharp teeth. In death the teeth are still prominent, and the glass eyes are set at a wicked slant. He is enough to frighten the life out of any recalcitrant child, so if you are having trouble with your offspring I thoroughly recommend a visit.

PART II

BANGKOK

This series of walks takes us through the centre of Rattanakosin Island, inside the inner moat, and around the areas between the centre and the outer moats, before crossing the outer moat to the east into what was originally known as the Sea of Mud, and which formed a natural defence for the city. We explore the Dusit district, built for royalty when the original city became too cramped, and we take three separate walks through teeming Chinatown, reputed to be the oldest Chinatown anywhere. Our walks take us into the former European district, and then following the curve of the river we discover a hidden island covered in jungle and dotted with villages and temples. Our final walks take us through what was known as the Lotus Forest, to the fringe of modern-day Bangkok.

The white elephant, symbol of Siam, as depicted outside the Grand Palace.

The Grand Palace

Our walk takes us inside the Grand Palace and then across the green expanse of Sanam Luang, the old assembly ground, to the remnants of the Front Palace.
Duration: 2 hours

Rama I had a city to build. He had to expunge the memory of an executed king and establish his own royal line, and it had to be done with extreme urgency. King Taksin's reign had ended, and Rama I's reign had begun, on 6th April 1782. Two weeks later, on 21st April, Rama I installed the City Pillar. Made of cassia wood, the Chiang Mai, or New City pillar, is housed inside a shrine and is the abode of Phra Lak Muang, one of the guardian deities of the city. Inside the shrine the king placed the city horoscope, designed to ensure safety from the Burmese, still a threat from the west and the north. Visit the City Pillar Shrine today, and there are two pillars. The smallest of them was erected by Rama IV, a king who had also come to power without much of a power base, having spent the previous twenty-seven years as a monk, and consequently needing to exert his authority. He removed Rama I's pillar, replacing it with his own, together with a new horoscope, this one reflecting concerns of the new threat, that of the Europeans, primarily the British and the French, who were circling the kingdom. The old pillar was propped against the wall

Rattanakosin Inner Island

National Gallery

Memorial of the
Expeditionary Force
37

Pan Pibhop Leela Bridge

Krung Thai
Bank

Ratchadamnoen Klang Road

35

National Museum

Thammasat
University

1

Phra Chan Pier

3

4

Wall of Prince
Prachak's
Palace

2

SANAM
LUANG

Royal Hotel

Earth Goddess Shrine
36

Tanao Road

Amulet Market

Maharaj
Building

5

Wat
Mahathat

6

Prince Surasinghanart
Statue

Bunsiri Rd

Atsadang Road

Ratchini Road

Tha Chang
shopshouses

10

Thawornwatthu
Building

Dusit District
Court

7 **8**

Silpakorn
University

9

City
Pillar
Shrine

34

Chao Phraya River

Na Phra Lan
Shopshouses

Ministry of
Defence
33

Chang Rong Si
Bridge

31

Bamrung Muang Road

Ministry of
Interior

Ratchaworadit
Royal Pier

11

12

Saranrom Palace

30

Wat Ratchapradit

GRAND PALACE AND
WAT PHRA KAEW

32

29

28

Pee Goon Bridge and
Pig Memorial

Ratchakit Winitchai
Throne Pavilion

Royal Survey
Department

26

Hok Bridge

Naval Welfare
Department

Department of
Internal Trade

27

Saranrom
Park

Tha Rong Mo Pier

13

Rama VI
Museum

25

24

Territorial Defence
Department

Ti Thong Road

14

Tha Tian Market

Maha Rat Road

18

Wat Pho

Chetuphon Rd

23

Hor Klong Shrine

22

Ubonrat Bridge

Aurum The River Place
15

Arun Residence
16

17

Chakrabongse House

Department of
Land

19 Museum of Siam

Phra Ratchawang Police Station

Wang Doem Road

Arun Amarin Road

20

21

Charoen Rat 31 Bridge

N

Royal Thai Navy
Headquarters

Chao Phraya River

200m

Tri Phet Road

Phra Pokklao Road

Pinklao
Bridge

Chakrabongse Road

outside, where it remained for more than a century, finally being reinstated during restorations in 1986, and placed next to the Rama IV pillar.

Oddly, before the founding of Bangkok, city pillars do not appear to have been a Siamese tradition: no documentary evidence of them has been found. City pillar shrines were erected in a handful of other provinces during the reigns of Rama II and Rama III, but after Rama IV's pillar the idea died out. Directly after World War II, however, with a government policy of nationalism in full play to mould the image of the country in the wake of the transition from absolute to constitutional monarchy, city pillars were encouraged throughout the country. The idea caught on, although not universally, until in 1992 the Interior Ministry issued a directive to all provincial governors to make sure every province had its own city pillar. There is another shrine next to the main City Pillar shrine, and this one represents all the provincial pillars. Thai people paying their respects almost invariably do so at both shrines.

The land upon which Bangkok was to be built already had a moat, dug in the time of King Taksin, and there was a defensive wall running along its inner bank. Inside the moat were a number of ancient temples, and prior to their relocation, this is where the Chinese community had lived. Far from being just an overspill from Thonburi, they were an organised community, many of them having been encouraged to come from China to Siam by Taksin. Their leader was a man named Phraya Choduek, who was greatly trusted by the king and who handled diplomatic relations with China. Outside of the moat and defensive wall were villages and agricultural areas, marshy ground and creeks alternating with patches of dryer ground, although most of the scattered population lived on rafts or houseboats, tied up at the banks of the river or in the streams.

To expand the size of the fortified city Rama I ordered the digging of a second moat, running parallel to the first, 10,000 Khmer levies being used for the work. The first moat was named Klong Ku Muang Derm (Old City Moat Canal), and the second moat Klong Rop Krung (Canal Encircling City), although in accordance with Siamese tradition different stretches of the waterway were known by names relating to the immediate locality. Two small canals known as *lot*, which means "tube", were dug to connect the two, for transport and for adjusting the water levels.

Using Ayutthaya as the blueprint, land planning for Bangkok fell naturally into three divisions: Inner Rattanakosin, Outer Rattanakosin, and the outlying areas beyond the city wall, which was rebuilt alongside the second moat. The inner island was for the Grand Palace, residences for royalty, royal temples, institutional buildings, and the assembly ground and royal cremation area named Sanam Luang. The outer island was residential, divided by the two *lot* canals, and was for court officials, low-ranking officials, general residents, and foreign communities such as Malays and Vietnamese. Outside the wall, on the riverbank, the Chinese were making their new home. The ox-bow shape of the river protected the city to the west and north, the Sea of Mud was an effective barrier to the east, and anyone making their way up the river from the south would have to pass the forts that Rama 1 began building at the coast and upstream.

Building of the Grand Palace began on 6th May 1782, presenting the king with a problem of where to find sufficient building materials in this flat, muddy delta region. He was also short of funds. Consequently the original palace was made entirely from wood, a collection of structures surrounded by a long palisade, occupying a rectangular piece of land on the west side of Rattanakosin Island, with the existing temples of Wat Pho to the south and Wat Mahathat to the north. On 10th June 1782 the king made a ceremonial crossing of the river to enter the palace, and three days later underwent a brief coronation ceremony. A more solid and palatial palace was needed, and Rama 1 despatched officials and labourers up the river to the ruins of Ayutthaya. There, while leaving what remained of the temples intact, they removed the bricks from the old royal palaces, from the forts and from the wall, and floated them down the river. These bricks were then used to form a new palace, and walls for the city. The timber palace was dismantled building by building as the brick palace complex took shape. Once the ceremonial halls were completed, in 1785, the king held a full coronation.

Cannon at the Ministry of Defence building, with the Grand Palace in the background.

By modelling the Grand Palace on the Royal Palace at Ayutthaya, in the positioning of the courts, walls, gates and forts, the builders could move quickly. Five thousand Laotians were levied from Vientiane and brought to Bangkok, along with local officials to oversee them, and were put to work digging the foundations, building new structures and erecting the new city wall and its forts. Craftsmen and artists from Thonburi, most of them originally from Ayutthaya, fashioned the palatial residences. There were actually two palaces: the Grand Palace, and at the northern end of the inner island, the Front Palace, which was the residence of the deputy king, Rama I's younger brother Bunma, who became Maha Sura Singhanat. A Rear Palace was also built at the mouth of the Bangkok Noi canal for the administration of Thonburi, which remained a defensive line for the city's western side. Prince Anurakthewet, a nephew of Rama I, was installed at the Rear Palace.

The Grand Palace is divided into four main courts, separated by numerous walls and gates. These are the Outer Court, within which were the royal offices and ministries. The Middle Court housed the state apartments and ceremonial throne halls. The Inner Court was reserved solely for women, as it housed the king's harem, and even the guards and internal security personnel were female. The fourth court was for the royal chapel, the Temple of the Emerald Buddha. During the reign of Rama ɪɪ the total area was extended to the south, up to the walls of Wat Pho, and this new area was used for offices for palace officials. New walls, forts and gates were built to accommodate the enlarged compound, which now covers a total of 61 acres, but since that time the palace has remained within its walls. Successive reigns and the growing needs of the nation saw new structures erected within the walls, until it became overwhelmingly crowded, and Rama ᴠ had a new royal district built at Dusit. The Grand Palace is no longer used as a residence, although it is still used for state occasions.

Although usually referred to as the Temple of the Emerald Buddha, Wat Phra Kaew is actually a chapel, not a temple, the difference being that in accordance with Siamese royal tradition, there are no living quarters for monks within the palace precincts. The figure of the Emerald Buddha is housed in the *ubosot*. At first appearing surprisingly small, at about 66 centimetres (26 in) high, the figure is believed to protect the safety of the nation in which it resides, and to give legitimacy to a ruler, which is why it has been coveted and fought over for centuries. No one really knows its origins. There is in existence the *Chronicle of the Emerald Buddha*, which relates its many journeys, but no one knows the origins of that, either. The *Chronicle* states that a Buddhist sage named Nagasena created the image in the Indian city of Patna around 43 B.C. Both Indra and Visnu aided him in creating the figure, and the intention was to encourage the flourishing of Buddhism in lands beyond India. The image was later sent to Sri Lanka, where Buddhism took root in an intensely pure form. When the Burmese requested the image for Pagan, it was loaded onto a boat that never reached the Burmese shore. The image was next seen at Angkor in Cambodia, and after the Siamese invasion of Angkor it was taken to Ayutthaya. So far, so legendary. The Emerald Buddha begins to emerge into history in 1391, when it was carried from the Siamese city of Kamphaengphet further north to Chiang Rai. Both these cities even now have temples named Wat Phra Kaew. In Chiang Rai the image was encased in stucco, as a protection against invaders, until in 1434 the temple in which it was kept was struck by lightning and the stucco was damaged, revealing the image. The king of Chiang Mai directed it be taken to the Lanna capital, but the elephant carrying the image refused to take the trail to the city, and repeatedly tried to take the road to Lampang. This was regarded as an omen, and the image was housed in Lampang for thirty-two years before finally being taken to Chiang Mai, where it was placed inside Wat Chedi Luang, where it remained for eighty years. King Chai Setthathirat, the son of a Luang Prabang king and a Chiang Mai princess, ruled Chiang Mai briefly from 1546–47, and then went back to Luang Prabang, taking the Emerald Buddha with him. Later it was taken to Vientiane, and stayed there for 218 years before King Taksin dispatched Chao Phraya Chakri to quell the Lao rebellion and bring the image back to Siam. It resided in Wat Arun before Chakri, now Rama I, took the image across the river to Bangkok, where it remains to this day, venerated by all Thais. As with its origins, the actual material from which the image is made remains a mystery, for no one has ever tested it. Jasper or jadeite are the two most likely contenders.

The Front Palace, residence of the deputy king, was the second centre of government, and equalled in size the Grand Palace. The two were ready for occupation at the same time, in 1785, when there was a combined celebration. The palace faced east, with its back to the Chao Phraya, and fortified walls surrounded the compound, with a wall along the river serving as the palace back wall. The compound was, like the Grand Palace, divided into distinct sections: an Outer Court for officials, a Middle Court for the royal residence, and an Inner Court for women only. The only difference was the lack of a chapel. The two palaces were connected by one of the very few roads in Bangkok, which ran alongside Sanam Luang.

The position of deputy king was not a consistent one, unlike that of the reigning monarch, and there were times when the Front Palace was unoccupied. Even so, as with the Grand Palace, successive incumbents added new buildings. When Rama III ascended the throne the Front Palace had been vacant for seven years. He appointed an uncle, Maha Uparaja Sakdibalaseb, to the position. There had earlier been a mansion used for housing monks, but it had fallen into disuse and was eventually pulled down, Rama II using the plot of land to breed rabbits. The new deputy king decided the Front Palace had to have a temple, and so he built Wat Bovornsathan Sutthawat on this site. Rama IV decided to elevate the position of deputy king to second king, having the same powers as himself, and his brother, Chutamani, was appointed as Second King Pinklao. This time, the Front Palace had been empty for eighteen years. "I was fine and happy, and then all of a sudden I was made the abbot of a long deserted monastery," the second king grumbled in a private correspondence. Many new buildings were added during this period.

Pinklao died of tuberculosis in 1866, and Rama IV died two years later. Prince Chulalongkorn was only age 15 when he became Rama V, and a regent, Chuang Bunnag, the eldest son of Dit Bunnag, governed Siam. Prince Vichaichan, Pinklao's 30-year-old son, was controversially appointed second king without the full consent of the monarch. Rama V was a reforming king, while Vichaichan was a conservative. A power struggle developed between them and came to a head at the end of 1874 when a fire broke out in the Grand Palace and the blame was directed at the second king's faction. Vichaichan fled and took sanctuary in the British Consulate.

Afterwards, the Front Palace was stripped of its power and after Vichaichan's death in 1885 the title was abolished, Rama V taking the British system of making his eldest son crown prince. The king had the Outer Court of the Front Palace converted into barracks for the royal guards, and today the buildings form Thammasat University. The buildings of the Middle Court became the National Museum. The Inner Court was at first retained for the women, but their numbers gradually dwindled and they were moved to the Grand Palace. The buildings have over the subsequent years either been demolished to make way for roads, or converted into offices.

Along the Riverbank

Along the Rattanakosin Island riverfront we find two universities, a couple of busy river piers, two of the city's leading temples, and some classic late nineteenth century shophouses.
Duration: 1 hour

From Sanam Luang, facing the river, look for the narrow lane named Phra Chan Road, which runs between Thammasat University and Wat Mahathat. Thammasat was founded in 1932 to service the new political system that was transforming the country, and at its core are four old military buildings that once formed part of the Front Palace Outer Court. Linked by a single roof the buildings are topped by an unmistakable tower, the symbol of the university, taking its design from ancient Siamese forms that are to be found in the north of the country. Underneath the tower is a clock, and the room directly beneath the clock was the office of the founder, Pridi Banomyong, who was one of the leaders of the People's Party that overthrew the absolute monarchy. At the entrance to Phra Chan Road is a massive gate, and running along the entire northern side of the road is a white crenelated wall that looks as if it belongs to the Grand Palace but which had originally surrounded the palace of Prince Prachak Silpakorn, a son of Rama IV, who founded Udon Thani in the northeast of Siam at a time when French colonialists were forcing the Siamese to concede large areas of Laos that had been under the rule of Bangkok. The road itself is one of the city's oldest thoroughfares, with little shops on the south side selling temple artefacts, Buddhist amulets and civil service uniforms. On a Sunday morning the street, and indeed the whole of Phra Chan Road, comes alive with vendors selling amulets, and there is no shortage of buyers: everyone from monks to merchants to tourists shops here.

The reason for all this amulet activity is Wat Mahathat, which predates the founding of Bangkok itself, and houses relics of the Buddha, the name translating as "Temple of the Great Relic". Home to Maha Chulalongkorn Ratchawitthyalai University, the country's oldest higher education institute for monks, it is the residence of the Supreme Patriarch of the Mahanikai sect of Buddhism and also houses the Vipassana meditation school, which is free for everyone, overseas visitors included. Prince Surasinghanart, whose statue stands at the main gate facing Sanam Luang and who was a younger brother of Rama I, renovated Wat Mahathat around 1783. Further renovation took place when Prince Mongkut studied here as a young monk, before he became Rama IV. The temple compound is a spacious one, although jammed with school buildings, the monks' quarters and offices, along with what is believed to be the largest ordination hall in Bangkok, and an almost equally large assembly hall. The small Wiharn Noi is the prayer hall used by Prince Mongkut, while the red building known as Akarn Watthu was Bangkok's first library. The most important structure is the *mondop*, or scripture hall, inside of which is the *chedi* in which are placed the Buddha relics. Covered in gold leaf, the *chedi* is a classic example of the early Rattanakosin style, while the main Buddha image, Phra Nak, is made of bronze and sculpted in the Sukhothai style. Somehow, in this crowded temple compound, where there is even a herbal medicine market, there is room for a garden with tall palm trees, and despite the crowds and traffic outside the atmosphere inside is one of peace. It must be the meditation.

At the end of Phra Chan Road is a pier, usually crowded as it is used by students and staff of the immense sprawl of Siriraj Medical School on the west bank, in addition to the Thammasat and Silpakorn universities on the east bank. Pass along Maharat Road,

Na Phra Lan Road building originally used for housing visitors to the Grand Palace.

with the overhanging eaves of Wat Mahathat on one side and some dilapidated shophouses on the river side, followed by the geometric cream-coloured buildings of the Royal Thai Army, and there on the corner, looking diagonally across to the Grand Palace, are the grandest shophouses in Bangkok. Built in the late nineteenth century, they show just how elegant the commercial buildings of that era could be. The Royal Crown Property Bureau owns the building, which has recently been restored. There are thirty-three units encased in gleaming white stucco, with pediments and pillars and green painted shutters and window frames. The splendid premises of the Siam Commercial Bank on the corner retain the style of an old counting house. This area outside the palace walls was assigned for bathing the royal elephants each day. A pier was built here for the mahouts and the area became known as Tha Chang Wang Luang, or "Elephant Pier of the Grand Palace".

Behind the Tha Chang shophouses, almost invisible and accessed by a small gate, is the campus of Silpakorn University. The compound is tiny, crammed with an odd mixture of historic architecture, nondescript buildings from the 1950s and 60s, scattered sculptures, and overhung by ancient trees and thronged with students. Silpakorn was the first university of art in Thailand, and the cradle of modern Thai art. Tha Phra Palace, the architectural centrepiece of the campus, is one of the oldest buildings on Rattanakosin Island. It was built for Prince Kasattranuchit, a nephew of Rama I, and the prince lived here until his death during the reign of Rama II. The king presented the palace to his son, Prince Chesdabodin, who was head of several government units such as the Harbour Department, the Police and the Royal Treasury. Eventually the prince asended the throne as Rama III, and handed over the palace to three of his sons in succession. One of them was Prince Jumsai, who headed the royal craft departments, including the Stonework Department and the Department of Ten Fine Arts Units. Interestingly, then, Tha Phra Palace's connection with the arts dates back to the first half of the nineteenth century.

Rama V handed the palace on to Prince Naris, one of his brothers. Prince Naris, one of Siam's great patrons of the arts, held positions including Minister of Public Works, Minister of the Treasury, and Minister of the Royal Household, serving through five reigns and passing away in 1948. He was the last prince to occupy this palace, eventually moving away from the congestion of Rattanakosin for health reasons, having built Plainoen Palace in the then pastoral surroundings of Klong Toei. After his death the prince's heirs sold Tha Phra Palace to the government, and it was assimilated into the newly founded Silpakorn University.

The palace adjoins the gracious old mansion that houses the Fine Arts Department, and here for many years was a school that taught painting and sculpture to civil servants and other students, who were accepted without fees. In the reign of Rama VI an Italian sculptor named Corrado Feroci arrived in Bangkok to teach at the Royal Academy's Fine Arts section. He was later made principal of the artisans' section of the Fine Arts School. During World War II Feroci took Thai citizenship, adapting the Thai name Silpa Bhirasri. When the school was upgraded to university status in 1943 and named Silpakorn, he became Dean of the Faculty of Sculpture. Professor Silpa Bhirasri, whose works can be seen throughout Bangkok and elsewhere in Thailand, did more than anyone to introduce modern

European ideas and techniques to Thai artists, and today his personality still makes its presence felt throughout the university campus.

Walk through the campus at almost any time of the day, it seems, and there are crowds of students meeting before class, sitting under the trees sketching, eating outside the cafeteria, or just standing and chatting. Tha Phra Palace is a neo-classical style building, very European, its exterior a faded yellow and white. Quite how European it was when first built is unclear. The interior follows a traditional palace plan for its time, but Prince Naris made many Western style changes during the reign of Rama v. During this time he erected three other European buildings in the compound, and used the opportunity to place fluted columns inside the main hall, add shutters and awnings to the windows, and replace the main staircase with a fashionable spiral one that the prince named the "One Slip and You're Dead Staircase".

The Throne Hall, by contrast, is a traditional Thai building with a red-tiled roof. Prince Jumsai had used the Throne Hall as a school for his artisans, and it was a workshop for the carpenters, the woodcarvers, the mosaic artists and the cloth painters who came under the department. A pleasant place for the students to gather is the Music Pavilion, a timber structure built in the time of Rama v. Painted a pale green, the pavilion has lovely fretwork and Western-style wooden railings. Curiously, one side is a solid wall, but the pavilion was originally on the boundary of the outer and inner courtyards, and a stretch of the old wall can be seen up against the Throne Hall. Further into the campus, opposite the Faculty of Painting, Sculpture and Prints, stands a statue of Professor Silpa, and there is a small museum built around what was his study.

Exit through the main gate and into Na Phra Lan Road, and there is another row of shophouses from the time of Rama v, different in style to their Tha Chang neighbours but equally as graceful. Recently renovated by the Crown Property Bureau, a restoration project that received an honourable mention in the UNESCO awards, the building was not initially designed as shophouses but was used for housing foreign visitors to the Grand Palace. On the corner of Na Phrathat Road is the Fine Arts Department, distinguished by the frieze that runs the length of the building under the eaves. Next to this is a building that is a vivid ochre in colour, designed in a Khmer style. It looks as if it should be important, yet there is a discomforting blankness about it, not helped by the parked tour buses that obscure the frontage, belching out diesel fumes as they idle over to keep their air conditioners working. This is the Thawornwatthu Building. Crown Prince Vajirunhis was the first son of Rama V and his highest consort, Queen Savang Vadhana. The king had decided to abolish the position of deputy king and to instead create the position of crown prince, a role that the talented young man seemed destined for, but Vajirunhis died of typhoid at age 16. The king's second son, Vajiravudh, became crown prince and eventually ascended the throne as Rama VI. Rama V decided it would be inappropriate to continue with the old tradition of constructing a large funeral building for a single purpose, and instead ordered Prince Naris to build Thawornwatthu, which after the royal funeral was to be given over for the education of monks and novices. In 1916, under the decree of Rama VI, the Vajirunhis National Library, an amalgamation of three royal libraries, was housed here and made accessible to the general public. Over the years various collections were added to the library until it outgrew its premises. A new National Library building was opened in Samsen Road in 1966, and today Thawornwatthu is home to the Naradhip Centre, a library and research centre for the social sciences.

Maharat Road passes between the palace and the river, a long walk with only the high white crenellated wall on one side and a screen of trees with occasional glimpses of the river on the other. Opposite the fortress-like entrance gate of the palace is the Ratchaworadit Royal Pier and Ratchakit Winitchai Throne Pavilion, built in the reign of Rama IV and used exclusively for royal ceremonies. Next to this, in the curious way in which prosaic buildings are so often found rubbing shoulders with the splendid, are the buildings of the Naval Welfare Department, the Navy Wives Association, the Public Warehouse Organisation, and offices belonging to the Department of Internal Trade. Opposite the southern corner of the Grand Palace wall there used to be a stone-crushing plant, a *rong mo hin*, and the name is remembered in the name of the Tha Rong Mo pier, a concrete structure encased by rickety timber buildings, from which ferries ply across to the Temple of the Dawn. Next to the pier is another handsome parade of Rama v era shophouses, still awaiting the restoration paint but solid enough and with green shutters and fanlights over the windows. This is Tha Tian, the building housing a wet market that is well-known for its salted fish, the name adopted after a fire during Rama iv's reign that completely destroyed the previous buildings, which had been used for accommodating foreign visitors; *tian* meaning "flat" or "clear".

One of the most heartening conservation developments in Bangkok recently has been the opening of boutique hotels in a number of different locations, reviving ancient buildings that were previously looking very sad. Tucked into the lanes immediately behind Tha Tian are a couple of outstanding examples. A four-storey warehouse has been turned into a twelve-room hotel named Aurum The River Place, while an eighty-year-old Sino-Portuguese style wooden house, painted beige, yellow and green, and standing on land owned by Wat Pho, has been transformed into a six-room hotel named Arun Residence. Both of these offer the prospect of waking up to the sight of the Temple of the Dawn, directly across the river.

A few metres further down Maharat Road is an even more surprising development. Chakrabongse House, a palatial residence built in 1908 for Prince Chakrabongse and, except for its three-storey timber tower, formerly invisible behind a high wall, has had three villas in its gardens converted into luxury suites for guests, who also have their own swimming pool. Branded Chakrabongse Villas, it would be difficult to image a more exotic place in which to stay. The prince had been born in 1883, the fortieth child of Rama v, and had been invited by Tsar Nicolas ii, a close friend of the king, to study in Russia. He was later appointed a colonel in the Hussar Regiment, and returned to Siam with a Russian wife. In Bangkok he became Chief of the General Staff of the Royal Siamese Army, and Minister of War, and today is remembered as the Father of the Royal Thai Air Force. The prince's granddaughter Narisa Chakrabongse today owns the house.

The enormous temple that takes up so much space at this southern end of Inner Rattanakosin Island is Wat Pho, aka Wat Phra
Chetun, aka the Temple of the Reclining Buddha. Covering twenty
acres, the temple compound is actually bisected by Chetupon Road,
the more interesting side lying to the north while the southern side
is mostly the monastery and school buildings. There has been a temple standing on this site since long before the days of Bangkok, 200
years before, according to some accounts. Named Wat Phodharam
(which is why the Thais use the name "Pho", not the formal name of
"Chetupon"), it was a centre for studying traditional medicine and
massage, and stone figures and carvings were created showing massage and yoga positions. The temple is considered the first public
university in Thailand, teaching students in the fields of religion, science and literature through murals and sculptures as well as ancient
texts. Traditional massage and medicine is taught at the Traditional
Medical Practitioners Association Centre, a hall just outside the
temple. There is an enormous Reclining Buddha image at Ayutthaya,
and Rama I decided to have another of similar dimensions made
when he enlarged Wat Pho in 1788. At 45.7 metres (150 ft) long
and 15.4 metres (50 ft) high, the Reclining Buddha is a colossal statue plated in gold, the feet and eyes engraved with mother-of-pearl.
Neither resting nor asleep, he is passing into nirvana. Although this
famous image draws the crowds, the temple compound is packed
with other Buddha figures, many of them also brought from the
ruins of Ayutthaya. There are sixteen gates around the temple complex, guarded by Chinese stone figures that were originally used as
ballast in the trading ships plying between the two countries.

From Wat Pho it is only a short walk to the tip of Rattanakosin
Inner Island, where the inner moat meets the Chao Phraya, guarded
these days not by a fort but by the Phra Ratchawang Municipal Police
Station, housed since 1914 in a fragment that is all that remains of an
old palace. On the way there is the Museum of Siam, housed in the
former Ministry of Commerce building designed by Italian architect Mario Tamagno in 1922, which stands at the southern extremity
of the fortress that was built opposite the Wichaiprasit Fort on the
Thonburi bank during the time of Ayutthaya's King Narai.

The Inner Moat

Walking the banks of the inner moat with its historic bridges takes us to temples and palaces, and to a beautiful park that holds sad memories.
Duration: 2 hours

I t is possible to walk almost the entire length of the inner moat on either bank, crossing over via a series of historic bridges placed along its length. At the southern entrance to the moat, opposite the market of Pak Klong Talat, once the largest floating market for the city but now entirely land-based, is Charoen Rat 31 Bridge, built in 1910, the first year of the reign of Rama VI. The king was following a tradition started by his father, Rama V, in building a bridge from his own funds to mark his birthday. Charoen means "growth" or "development", and the 31 refers to the age of the king at the time the bridge was built. An early example of reinforced concrete, the bridge has an elegant plaster balustrade with eighty-eight tigers rampant, and the king's initials displayed in a large sunburst. Beyond this is Ubonrat Bridge, a wide structure with an elegantly curving balustrade, built in 1912 as a memorial to Princess Ubonrat, a consort to Rama V.

A short way along the canal bank is the Hor Klong Shrine, a memorial to an officer of a drum tower that stood near this site, who died in a war during the reign of Rama I. There were three drums used for different purposes: telling the time, warning of fires and the declaring of battles. The drum tower was demolished in the late nineteenth century. Another odd shrine near here is the Pig Memorial. Located on the canal bank, the golden figure of a pig might not seem a particularly apposite gift for a queen, but it was created in 1913 as a birthday present for Queen Mother Sri Patcharindra. The queen had been born in the Year of the Pig, and the memorial was built with donations from her friends. Next to the Pig Memorial is the Pee Goon footbridge, built a couple of years before, when the Queen Mother (she was mother to Rama VI) granted the construction costs to commemorate her fourth-cycle, forty-eighth birthday. The bridge had no name until the Pig Memorial was built, when the name Pee Goon, or Year of the Pig, was bestowed upon it. This small site here is an attractive one, with a garden-like atmosphere, and the bridge itself is one of the most handsome in Bangkok, with its four decorative posts symbolising the birthday candles of the fourth cycle.

The Mon Bridge that takes Charoen Krung Road across the moat has its origins in the earliest days of Bangkok, when a community of Mons who had lived in Ayutthaya settled in this area. They made a living from selling their own distinctive red-clay pottery, and this is symbolised in the wrought-iron design of the bridge, which depicts the type of jar known as a *moh*, and which can also be found rendered in plaster on the neighbouring buildings. Nearby is the Hok Bridge. *Hok* means "lifting", and the platform of this wooden bridge can be lifted up like that of a Dutch bridge. This structure is not an old one, but it is based on the design of a bridge first built in the reign of Rama IV, in the middle of the nineteenth century. There had originally been four of these, but only this one remains. Nearby is Chang Rong Si Bridge, the Elephant Rice Mill Bridge, the name indicating that the original teak structure was strong enough for elephants to cross over to the royal rice mill that was located here. Prince Damrong had the bridge rebuilt in 1910, the Year of the Dog, hence the amusing dog head design. Near to the dog-head bridge is Charoen Rat 34, built in 1913. The bridge has four plaster posts decorated with stucco: look carefully and you will see the Thai figure "4" on each post, standing for the fourth year of the king's reign.

Directly to the east of the Grand Palace, separated from it only by Sanamchai Road, is the long, low, ochre-coloured bulk of Saranrom Palace, a bronze statue of Rama IV standing on a pedestal in front of the Italianate building. The palace was built towards the end of the king's reign, one of the first of the magnificent European designs that were later to come in such abundance to Bangkok, and the king had after the death of Second King Pinklao in 1866 decided to pass the throne to Prince Chulalongkorn and retire to this palace to live in retirement as an advisor on state affairs. However, Rama IV died of malaria in 1868, contracted whilst on an expedition to witness an eclipse of the sun at Hua Hin, and Chulalongkorn became Rama V. The new king gave Saranrom Palace to his brother, Prince Chakrabandhu, and later when the prince attained the age at which he should have his own palace, he moved out and it was handed down to another brother, Prince Bhanubandhu. When in 1884 Prince Oscar, son of the king of Sweden, visited Siam he and his entourage were accommodated at Saranrom. A couple of years later, Prince Devawongse, the Minister of Foreign Affairs, requested permission to open an office in the palace, and for several years it performed a dual function as Foreign Office and state accommodation.

The pavilion in Saranrom Park, where Rama VI enjoyed listening to military bands.

Prince George of Greece stayed in 1890, and the Tsarevitch of Russia in 1893. When the Siamese government was reorganised along Western lines in 1892, the Ministry of Foreign Affairs was greatly expanded and eventually came to occupy most of the building. Directly behind the palace and originally part of the palace complex is a separate building, also European in style, built in 1892 and which used to be home to the Military Academy. This was relocated in 1931, and the building now houses the Royal Survey Department.

Prince Oscar, writing home whilst on his Siamese visit, was greatly impressed by the "beautiful garden and zoo with deer, monkeys, a black tiger, and many other animals and birds". Rama v had in fact designed the gardens specifically with the idea of impressing visiting Western royalty and statesmen, as he manoeuvred to avoid the fate of being colonised by proving to the world that Siam was a sovereign and civilised nation. Henry Alabaster, a multi-talented British diplomat and engineer who had been one of the first to arrive at the court of Siam and who had been engaged as advisor to Rama v, had laid out the gardens, and they remain today a beautifully evocative landscape of the middle years of the fifth reign.

The gardens became Saranrom Park in 1960, a public garden with a botanical park, a large pond, pavilions, and a traditional teak house. Rather strangely, they are set to the side of the palace, but this is explained by the fact that the main entrance was originally on the south side of the building, directly facing the gardens: Rama v, on his first visit to Europe in 1897, had invited many members of European royalty to visit Siam, and in anticipation he had the palace redesigned and the entrance moved to the side, facing the Grand Palace. Entering the gardens today can be via the front, at Sanamchai Road, or through the huge white wrought-iron gates that face the inner moat. Prince Vajiravudh, before he became Rama vi, had stayed at Saranrom for a while and the pavilion where he liked to hear military bands playing is preserved in the park. In the reign of Rama vii, after the 1932 revolution, the reception rooms in the park were used as a gathering place for young intellectuals, and the king also used the grounds for the training of the royal guard. Towards the southern end of the park is a white marble monument, a memorial to Queen Sunantha, the first consort of Rama V, who had drowned with their two-year-old daughter, Princess Kannabhorn, while on a visit to the summer palace at Bang Pa-In in 1880. The royal boat had capsized, and despite help being available, by Siamese tradition no one was allowed, on pain of death, to touch a queen except for the king; not even to save a life. Rama V was grief-stricken. The queen had been only 19 years old, and she was pregnant with their second child, who it transpired would have been a male heir. Saranrom had been her favourite garden and the king had her ashes and those of the young princess buried in this monument. There is another monument at Bang Pa-In, and a third in the form of a granite pyramid placed next to a waterfall at Chanthaburi province, another favourite place of the young queen.

In the northern corner of Saranrom Park is the small temple of Wat Ratchapradit, standing on about three-quarters of an acre of land that was a coffee plantation before Rama IV used his own funds to build the temple in 1864. An immediately striking feature is the grey marble tiles that clad the *chedi* and the *ubosot* and its rounded columns. As the tiles are in both light and dark tones, the effect is slightly chequered. There is also a distinct Khmer influence, with two large *prangs* carrying faces that are in the Angkor style. Inside the *ubosot* the Buddha image is set against a blue mosaic of mirrors, and the ceiling is finished in red and gold with crystal stars. French standing lamps, English street lamps, and a German clock that is still solemnly ticking are amongst the items in this small compound, some of which were gifts to the king, whose seal appears in gilded lacquer on the pediment of the *wiharn*. Wat Ratchapradit was built as the first temple dedicated to the reforming Thammayut sect, the monks being distinguished by their brown robes, rather than the traditional saffron. Rama IV, before he became king and when he was a monk at Wat Ratchatiwat, had founded this sect to restore purity to the interpretation of the Pali Canon. He had subsequently become abbot of Wat Bowon Niwet, in the northern part of Rattanakosin Island, where he continued to promote his reforms. Wat Ratchapradit was the first temple built from new that was dedicated to Thammayut, which following the Sangha Act of 1902 is

The inner moat was part of the original defence works and is crossed by historic bridges.

recognised as the second of Thailand's Theravada denominations. Rama IV died shortly after the temple was completed. Inside the *wiharn* a mural depicts him visiting Wakor district in Prachuap Khiri Khan province in 1868 to observe the total eclipse of the sun, which as a keen astronomer he had predicted two years before the event. The journey had been a state occasion and had included a large number of foreign dignitaries. The eclipse had happened on 18th August exactly when and where the king had calculated it would, and represented an enormous triumph for him in establishing a reputation for Siam as a civilised country, an important strategy to keep at bay the circling colonial powers. But the king contracted malaria on his visit and died six weeks after returning to Bangkok. Prince Chulalongkorn, who had been on the journey with his father, and had also contracted malaria, became Rama V. He ordered the painting of the mural and also had some of his father's ashes buried beneath the Buddha image.

The enormous symmetrical bulk of the Ministry of Defence was completed in 1884, designed in a European style, and originally named Rong Taharn Na, or Front Barracks. On the lawn in front of the building is the Museum of Cannon, displaying a large selection of artillery, including most notably Phraya Tani, the seventeenth century siege cannon that was built by the sultan of Pattani in response to territorial ambitions by the Siamese. Pattani later became a tributary state of Siam, but broke away during the fall of Ayutthaya. Rama I sent his brother, Deputy King Maha Sura Singhanat, to recapture the province. The campaign was successful, and Phraya Tani and a twin cannon, Seri Negara, were both seized. The two cannon were loaded on board a ship, but Seri Negara fell overboard, and lies on the seabed to this day. Phraya Tani is the symbol of Pattani, which remains a restless province, with a largely Muslim population that has more in common with Malaysia, with which it historically has a closer relationship. During a time of recent unrest it was noticed that the muzzles of the cannon on the Defence Ministry lawn were pointing towards the Grand Palace, and they have now been turned to politely point to the south and the north. Phraya Tani and its twin were the largest cannon ever cast in Siam.

In 1887 Rama V issued a decree to establish a War Department, and he began to arrange Siam's military affairs along the Western pattern, to demonstrate that this was an advanced nation and not one that required the civilising intervention of the European powers. He engaged European officers to manage the departments and train the troops, and following the brief Franco-Siamese War in 1893, during which the possibility of Siam being absorbed into the French colonial empire became frighteningly apparent, the department was upgraded to the Ministry of Defence, with the army and navy under its command. Rama VI continued the policy of continually developing the nation's military capabilities.

Much of the Rama VI Museum, situated nearby in the Ratchawonlop Building, which is part of the Territorial Defence Department, is devoted to the king's military interests. As Prince Vajiravudh, he had trained at Sandhurst and served with a light infantry division of the British Army, and as soon as he became king he established the Wild Tiger Corps, a paramilitary force inspired by the British Volunteer Force. During World War I, Siam joined the Allied forces when the United States entered the war in 1917, declaring war on Germany and the Central Powers. Rama VI despatched a force of 1,300 troops to the European front, and they arrived in 1918, flying the new tri-colour national flag. At the end of the war, the Siam Expeditionary Force joined the victory parade in Paris, and they returned to Bangkok in September 1919. They suffered nineteen dead. These men were cremated in Europe, and their ashes were brought back and enshrined in the Monument to the Expeditionary Force, which is set at the northern end of Sanam Luang, a white four-sided structure topped by a small *chedi* and with the names of the dead inscribed on the four sides.

At the northern end of Sanam Luang the inner moat passes beneath Pan Pibhop Leela Bridge, originally built in 1906 for Ratchadamnoen Avenue, and from here the canal disappears under the approach road for the modern Pinklao Bridge, which crosses to Thonburi and has its landing behind the Royal Barge Museum. Die-hard moat followers can find the northern entrance next to the Pinklao Ferry Pier. At the point the canal disappears under the road stands a shrine to U-Toktan, the earth goddess. More than a shrine, it also serves as a public water faucet and was installed in 1872 from the private funds of Queen Mother Sri Patcharintra.

Defending the Realm

Along the bank of the second moat ran the city wall with its
gates and forts, with remnants still in place today, enclosing a
neighbourhood that is known to every backpacker in the world.
Duration: 2 hours

Bangkok's new city wall, its moat and the river made very effective defences, and the Burmese now stood little chance of pulling off a repeat of their attack on Ayutthaya. Gradually the threat of invasion receded, and within a century much of the old city wall had been demolished under the modernising Rama v. Originally there were fourteen forts along the city wall. Today, just two remain: Phra Sumen and Mahakan. Phra Sumen Fort stands at the northern mouth of Klong Rob Krung, the part of the second moat that is more usually known as Klong Bang Lamphu, taking its name from the locality. A hexagonal structure built from brick and stucco, with two levels of battlements and an observation tower topped with a pointed roof, the fort is still a commanding sight gleaming white in the sunshine, even if its cannons threaten only the endless stream of traffic that flows alongside its noble footings. For many years the fort was in a dilapidated condition, having been left high and dry by the demolition of the old wall, but using old photographs as a guide, the Fine Arts Department restored it in 1959 and a second restoration took place in 1981.

Phra Sumen Fort, located at the junction of the second moat and the river.

Around the base of Phra Sumen Fort is a garden, Santichai Prakarn Park, and growing at the water's edge are two lamphu trees, the only ones left of the thick outcrops that once grew so prolifically at the mouth of the canal that gave this district its name. The lamphu tree, *Duabanga grandiflora*, is indigenous to a swathe of Asia running from northeast India across Burma, Thailand, Laos, Cambodia and Vietnam, and as far down as Malaysia. Often found next to waterways, it can grow to a great height, its weight supported by large buttresses that grow at the base of the trunk that provide a broad base and allow the tree to flourish in soft, muddy ground. The flowers it produces are attractive, and the wood makes a robust building material, but perhaps the greatest claim to fame for the lamphu tree is that it is the preferred home for fireflies. Incidentally, if this green little corner at the northern tip of Rattanakosin Island seems unusually lively with birdsong, it is because a renowned owner of songbirds lives on the opposite bank of the canal, and the courtyard of his small timber house is filled with birdcages. He is a regular participant in songbird competitions and as his son shares the same interest it seems likely this area behind the fort will remain melodic for many years to come.

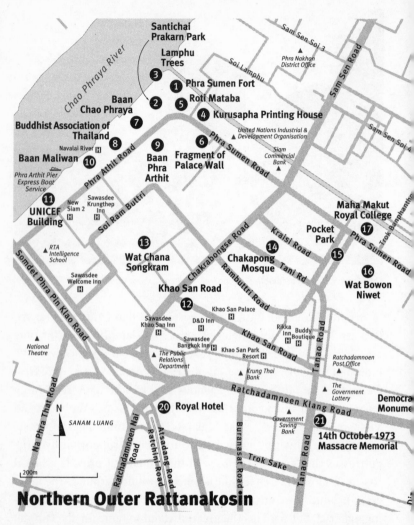

Santichai Prakarn Park

Lamphu Trees

Chao Phraya River

Sam Sen Soi 3

Soi Lamphu

▲ Phra Nakhon District Office

Sam Sen Road

3

1 **Phra Sumen Fort**

Baan Chao Phraya

2 **5** **Roti Mataba**

4 **Kurusapha Printing House**

Sam Sen Soi 4

7

▲ United Nations Industrial & Development Organisation

Buddhist Association of Thailand

8

Phra Sumen Road

▲ Siam Commercial Bank

Navalai River 🏨

Baan Maliwan **10**

9 **Baan Phra Arthit**

6 **Fragment of Palace Wall**

Phra Athit Road

Phra Arthit Pier Express Boat Service

11 New Siam 2 🏨

Sawasdee Krungthep Inn 🏨

Maha Makut Royal College

UNICEF Building

Soi Ram Buttri

Kraisi Road

Pocket Park

17

Phra Sumen Road

Trok Bamphaenthi

▲ RTA Intelligence School

13

Chakrabongse Road

14

15

16

Somdet Phra Pin Klao Road

Sawasdee Welcome Inn 🏨

Wat Chana Songkram

Rambuttri Road

Chakapong Mosque

Tani Rd

Wat Bowon Niwet

Khao San Road

12

Khao San Palace 🏨

Sawasdee Khao San Inn 🏨

D&D Inn 🏨

Rikka Inn 🏨

Buddy Boutique 🏨

Tanao Road

▲ National Theatre

Sawasdee Bangkok Inn 🏨

Khao San Park Resort 🏨

Khao San Road

Ratchadamnoen Post Office

▲ The Public Relations Department

▲ Krung Thai Bank

▲ The Government Lottery

Na Phra That Road

Ratchadamnoen Nai Road

Ratchini Road

Alsadang Road

20 **Royal Hotel**

Ratchadamnoen Klang Road

Democra Monume

N

SANAM LUANG

Buranasat Road

▲ Government Saving Bank

21

14th October 1973 Massacre Memorial

Tanao Road

|200m|

Trok Sake

Northern Outer Rattanakosin

Next to Phra Sumen Fort is a handsome building, plain but well proportioned and painted white, built in 1925 as the Wat Sangwet Printing School. This was the first printing school in Siam, with printing classes in the morning and printing services in the afternoon. In this way, students learned both theory and practice. The school closed in 1946 to focus on printing services, and it became known as the Kurusapha Printing House, an imprint that can be found on many scholarly books about Thailand. The school consists of two L-shaped

buildings, the brick structure at the front and a timber structure at the rear, added in 1933 and made from teak and tabaek. The two-storey brick building, utilising large windows for optimal daylight, a wide entrance for heavy equipment and bulky loads, and topped by a flat roof, was designed by a Siamese architect who combined industrial needs with the residential styling that was then coming into vogue elsewhere in the immediate neighbourhood. The timber building, very attractive when viewed from the little humped bridge that spans the canal, is reputed to be the largest of its kind in Bangkok. The printing school has had no specific use for several years beyond being used for storage by the Treasury Department, but is listed by the Fine Arts Department as a heritage site.

Opposite, curving to follow the route of the moat, is a long terrace of attractive shophouses, several of which have been converted into restaurants, the best-known being Roti Mataba, founded near to Thammasat University and which has been here for thirty years. At the far end of this row is a fragment of wall with a spirit house, and this is all that remains of one of the first palaces to have been built during those earliest days of Bangkok. The palace was the residence of Prince Chakra Chesada. This area around the fort grew into a district of grand houses and palaces, a neighbourhood of nobles and courtiers, and although most of those prior to Rama III's time have gone the same way of Prince Chesada's palace, there are many splendid later

Pleasure launch moored amongst water hyacinth at the entrance to the second moat.

examples still standing along Phra Arthit Road, mostly converted
into offices and restaurants and galleries, their architecture bearing
in many cases the firm imprint of Europe.

Follow leafy Phra Arthit Road as it runs along the riverbank.
The road dates from Rama v's time, the gradual removal of fortifications having provided more space for streets, and conservation
directives protect the architectural beauties along here. Baan Chao
Phraya, directly next to Santichai Prakarn Park, was built in the latter half of the nineteenth century as the home of Prince Khamrob,
who was Director General of the City Police Department. Erected
on the site of an earlier palace, it is very much in the European style,
with fanlights above the windows, a delicate balcony, and a cladding
of cream-coloured stucco. Next to this is the Buddhist Association of
Thailand, housed in the palace of Princess Manassawas Sooksawadi.
Opposite at 201/1 is Baan Phra Arthit, built in 1926 on the site of
a timber palace by Finance Minister Phraya Vorapongpipat. For a
period of about twenty-five years, beginning from 1962, the Goethe
Institute had rented this house, which is now inhabited by a private
company. The house was carefully renovated about twenty years ago,

the architects conserving the original structure and detailing, right down to the original colour specifications of cream walling and green window frames, and there is a pleasant coffee shop on the premises.

Baan Maliwan, now the offices of the United Nations Food and Agriculture Organisation, was built in 1917 to a design by the Italian architect Ercole Manfredi. Originally the home of Prince Naris, a son of Rama IV, Baan Maliwan, as with other houses on the riverfront side of Phra Arthit Road, has its main entrance facing the river, water transport as recently as this period still being a conventional way of accessing Rattanakosin Island. A little further along on the same side of the road is the building housing UNICEF, the United Nations Children's Fund. UNICEF had transferred its Far East headquarters from Manila to Bangkok in March of 1949. For almost ten years the organisation had its offices in the Ministry of Public Health building, but when more space was needed the Crown Property Bureau provided the present site, a compound known as No 19. There are actually three buildings on the compound: a mansion built in the early part of the twentieth century on one side, a nasty 1970s box on the other side, and in the centre, what is referred to as the Middle Building, a former royal palace. Built during the second half of the nineteenth century it is European in style, with shuttered windows and half-moon transoms of filigreed wood above the doors and windows to allow cooling air to circulate. There is a long veranda at the front, overlooking the river and also designed for ventilation, but pleasant though the breezes were, they were not conducive to the stability of office paperwork. In a memoir from those times, an official recalls seeing a big sheaf of pink, yellow and blue papers that had blown out of the window and were floating down the river "looking like pretty lotus flowers, lost forever". Meetings also had to compete with the noisy arrival of squealing pigs being unloaded at a small dock below, bound for the market. Eventually, air conditioning made the palace viable as an office. The palace had also been for a few years the residence of Pridi Phanomyong, who had been a member of the coup that overthrew the absolute monarchy, had become Minister of Foreign Affairs and then Minister of Finance, and during the war had been one of the leading figures in the anti-Japanese Seri Thai movement. In 1944 he had become regent for the young Rama VIII, who was studying in Switzerland, and in 1946 during a time of great political turmoil he became prime minister. A few weeks later the young king, now back in Bangkok, was found shot dead in his bedroom in the Grand Palace. Pridi resigned, but he was a highly controversial figure, rumours being spread that he was part of a conspiracy involved in the king's death, and when a coup ousted the government late in 1947, armoured cars arrived in front of Pridi's residence. When the troops entered they found he had already left, hiding out with supporters and then a week later spirited out of the country by British and American agents to Singapore. The palace's colourful history gave a certain cachet to the offices, and UNICEF staff still show visitors the secret door in the library through which Pridi was said to have made his escape, even though one official has pointed out that the secret door was hard to open and creaked very loudly, and that it would probably have been safer for the fleeing statesman to use one of the ordinary doors.

Enter the narrow little lane opposite the UNICEF building, Trok Rong Mai, and there is a different world. Not that long ago, Khao San Road was a modest thoroughfare that specialised in selling temple accessories, and its only hotel was a small establishment named Vieng Thai, which had opened for civil servants and businessmen in 1962. The area had originally been used for rice growing: *khao san* means "milled rice". Development began to take place in the time of Rama V and initially consisted of wooden shophouses whose residents would have served the mansions of Phra Arthit Road and the government offices that were built on the new Ratchadamnoen Avenue. The opening of the tramline brought more people into the area, and for many years it remained as a middle class district, an unremarkable mix of residences and shops, with a large number of eating-houses for the office workers. Late in the 1970s, so the story goes, with tourism on a roll, young Western visitors were invited to stay at a house on Khao San Road because the owner wanted to improve his English. Word spread, and before long the owner sensed a business opportunity. He started charging his guests 20 baht a day for accommodation, food, laundry and guide services. Others noted his success, and the first commercial guesthouse was opened: named Bonny, it had six bedrooms, and charged 100 baht a day. Thus was born the Place to Disappear, the Short Street of the Long Dreams, the Grand Central of the Banana Pancake Trail. Khao San Road itself is only about three hundred metres long, but is packed with guesthouses and small hotels, bars, restaurants, cafes, gift shops and tour companies. The tide of vest and shorts flows into Soi Ram Buttri, which runs behind Phra Arthit Road and around the walls of the surprisingly large compound of Wat Chana Songkram, a monastery built before the founding of Bangkok, when it was known as Wat Klang Na, or "temple in the middle of the paddy field". Rama I, upon the founding of the city, granted the temple to Mon monks in recognition of the help the Mon had given him in fighting the Burmese, and it became a centre of study for their own sect of Buddhism. Prince Maha Surasee, younger brother of Rama I and known as Phraya Sua, the "Tiger General", had stayed here after winning three decisive battles against the Burmese and had renovated the principal Buddha image. Rama I changed the name of the temple to its present name, which means "Temple of Victory". Because of its association with the Tiger General, many worshippers come here to pay homage in the hope that by so doing they will conquer their own enemies and troubles. Monks and lay workers reside in the teak houses and more modern structures in the leafy courtyards, some of the old buildings having been destroyed by a stray Allied bomb during World War II, intended for Bangkok Noi Railway Station. Inside the *ubosot* are two huge elephant tusks, and a corresponding pair made of ebony, placed in front of the golden Buddha image.

Khao San spreads northeast as far as Tani Road, a Muslim district that derives its name from Pattani, the province in the south of Thailand that has a large population of Muslims. They settled here in the early nineteenth century following the quelling of an uprising by Pattani against Siamese rule. Craftsmen and traders, the immigrants brought with them skills in making gold and silver ornaments, rings, bands and bracelets. They built Chakapong Mosque, which can be seen down Surao Lane, a footpath off Chakapong Road. Tani Road ends at a small square that was until 1963 the terminus for the little yellow tramcars that plied this route. Pocket Park, which forms a pleasant refuge in the square, was laid out in 1976, its odd lozenge shape due to the former canal whose course it occupies.

The canal had run in front of Wat Bowon Niwet, a temple with a dazzling history and a dazzling collection of art and architecture. Built between 1824 and 1832 in the reign of Rama III by Prince Phra Bowon Ratchao on a royal cremation ground, the temple was directly adjacent to Wat Rangsi, built a few years earlier, and the two were later merged. The first abbot of the new temple (its nickname is Wat Mai, which means exactly that) was Prince Mongkut, who took up his position in 1836. Mongkut had been ordained in 1824, at age 20, having been sidelined in his succession to the throne by his half-brother, and as he travelled the country as a monk he became increasingly concerned at the relaxation of the rules of the Tipitaka amongst the Siamese monkhood. In 1833 he initiated the Thammayut reform movement, which aimed to make monastic discipline more orthodox and to remove the animist and superstitious elements that had been assimilated into Siamese Buddhism over the years. As abbot of Wat Bowon he was able to promulgate those ideas, and the temple remains the centre of the Thammayut Nikaya school of Theravada Buddhism to this day, the seat of the Supreme Patriarch. Monks from all over Thailand and from India, Nepal and Sri Lanka all come to study here. During his time as a monk, Prince Mongkut developed what was to be a lifetime interest in Western knowledge, studying Latin, English and astronomy, and becoming close friends with Jean-Baptiste Pallegoix, head of the Roman Catholic Archdiocese of Bangkok, whom he invited to preach Christian sermons in the temple. When, after twenty-seven years in the monkhood, and following the death of his half-brother Mongkut became King Rama IV, his knowledge of the West was to have a profound influence upon the future of Siam, particularly with the signing of the Bowring Treaty, which took place just four years after he had ascended the throne.

Wat Bowon is a royal temple, first class, and has remained an important centre of study for Thai princes over the years. King Bhumibol resided here for a short period after he became monarch.

Within the golden *chedi* are interred the ashes of several members of the royal family. Some notoriety is also attached to Wat Bowon. Field Marshal Thanom Kittikachorn, who oversaw a decade of iron military rule beginning in 1963 before a violent uprising drove him into exile, returned to Thailand in 1976, dressed in the robes of a novice monk, and took refuge in Wat Bowon. His return triggered student protests, which coalesced on the campus of the nearby Thammasat University. Afraid of the spread of communism that had already taken control in Vietnam and Laos, right-wing security forces stormed the campus and massacred many of the protestors before seizing power from the elected civilian government.

There are several entrances to Wat Bowon, but the main entrance on Phra Sumen Road opens directly to the *ubosot*. There are two carved Siew Kang figures on the gate, the Chinese guardian who protects the temple: one carries a trident and a dagger and rides on the back of a crocodile, while the other carries a sword and shield and rides a dragon. The mouths of these two figures appear to seep blood. In the days when there was the Huai Ko Kho, a form of official lottery that was run from a house in Chinatown, gamblers would visit the temple to pray for good luck. Many Chinese were addicted to opium, and devotees thought Siew Kang might appreciate a hit, smearing opium on his mouth and causing the stains that can be seen today. Past the opium-dazed guardians of the gate, the open doors of the *ubosot* reveal not one Buddha figure but two, one seated behind the other. The one to the front is Phra Phuttha Chinnasee, a Sukhothai-era bronze that was brought from a temple in Phitsanulok, while behind it is Phra To, brought from Phetchaburi. In front of the figures are images of three former princely abbots of the temple, and on the walls are murals painted by In Khong, a master painter from Rama IV's reign, of especial interest because this is one of the earliest occasions a Siamese artist had adapted Western-influenced perspective for temple murals. Behind the *ubosot* is the Rama V era golden *chedi*, guarded by ochre and white *bodhisattvas* and with a staircase that leads to an upper level from which can be had photogenic views of the surprisingly Chinese-style rooftops of the Wiharn Keng, a legacy of Rama III's China-leaning influence, the gables adorned with the shapes of humans, flowers, swans and fish, all auspicious symbols of Chinese belief. Around the base of the *chedi* are many Chinese stone figures that travelled in the holds of the rice junks as ballast. Elsewhere in the compound is the Wiharn Phra Satsada, divided into two rooms, one with the Buddha image from which it takes its name, brought here by Rama IV, the other housing Phra Phuttha Saiya, a Reclining Buddha brought here by the king from Sukhothai because he felt it was the most beautiful reclining Buddha he had ever seen. The mural behind the Buddha is also of interest, placing traditional flat-image Siamese groups of monks against a background of Western-perspective trees. Within the part of the compound where the monks live there is a Rama VI era building named Phra Tamnak Phet, Royal Diamond Residence, an audience hall designed in a glorious blending of Siamese and European styles and which once housed one of Bangkok's first printing presses. Flowing through the compound is the old canal that originally divided the two temples, and this is a tranquil place indeed after the madness of Khao San Road.

Opposite Wat Bowon, on Phra Sumen Road, are two very handsome buildings that were erected in 1912 for the Maha Makut Royal College, built as a school for the temple, and a few metres away is the last remaining city gate, from what had been a total of sixteen gates, together with a fragment of the city wall. Where the compound of Wat Bowon ends, Tanao Road begins, a long thoroughfare that leads into the heart of Rattanakosin Island and which is one of the best-preserved streets of shophouses in Bangkok. The road takes its name from Ban Tanao, the name of the settlement around the temple, having its origins in the time of Rama I, who in his campaign to keep the menacing Burmese at bay subdued the strategic frontier town of Tanao Sri, on the border of Siam and Burma. The population was transported to Bangkok and allowed to settle here. They were Mons and Burmese, and many of them had earned their living by lapidary, which is why there are so many jewellery and silverware shops here. Possibly by association, this has also evolved as a street for wedding wear, and shopfront after shopfront displays romantic white bridal gowns. The shops themselves date from the reign of

Rama v, being built to a European style with the sensible precaution of firebreaks at regular intervals. This section of Tanao Road is a brief one, consisting of little more than the elegant curve to align the road at its beginning and then a short, straight burst to reach the intriguing wing-like shapes that have already been glimpsed hovering over the rooftops.

When Rama v built Dusit Palace at the beginning of the twentieth century, he decided to connect Dusit and the Grand Palace with a grand procession route, which he named Ratchadamnoen, which means "royal way". Having toured Europe in 1897 and returned with plans for many gracious European-style buildings and palaces, the king decided to model his new route on the boulevards of Paris. This is a long road, for the Grand Palace is the very heart of the old city, while Suan Dusit, the parkland-like district laid out by the king with many palaces for the royal family, lies on the other side of the third and final moat. The route starts at the gate of the Grand Palace and runs north alongside Sanam Luang and here it is known as Ratchadamnoen Nai, the inner part of the way. The road then swings sharply to the east and cuts directly across Rattanakosin Island in a straight line until it reaches the second moat. This stretch is known as Ratchadamnoen Klang, the central section. Over the canal it becomes Ratchadamnoen Nok, the outer section, and it turns northeast and proceeds arrowstraight to the plaza in front of Anantha Samakhom Palace, where the king had installed a throne hall similar to that in the Grand Palace, where he could grant audiences.

Ratchadamnoen Avenue was the widest road in Bangkok at that time, and was an innovation for a city that had had its first true roads built less than forty years previously. In design it was faithful to its Parisian origins, with the tamarind-ringed Sanam Luang providing a handsome green backdrop early on, the wide central section lined by mahogany trees, and the outer section culminating at the Renaissance-like splendour of the new palace. The king was very open to European ideas, and he and members of the royal family would sometimes organise bicycle processions along the royal route, arriving long after nightfall. He would also organise motorcar rallies along the avenue, something of a foretaste of what was to come.

Siam was to change quickly after the king's death in 1910. Rama v was a great reforming king, but he was absolute monarch. There was no democracy in Siam then. So too was his son, Rama vi, who had been educated in Britain and during his rather short reign (he died in 1925) introduced compulsory education and the Western calendar. In 1912, however, a group of military officers tried to overthrow the monarchy and it was clear that the days of the king as an absolute monarch were numbered. Rama vi's brother, Prajadhipok, became King Rama vii. During his rule, European ideas came home with a vengeance. A group of Siamese students living in Paris became convinced that democracy was necessary for Siam's future, and they mounted a successful coup in 1932. It was a bloodless revolution and Siam became a constitutional monarchy along British lines, with a mixed military-civilian group in power. In 1935 Rama vii abdicated without naming a successor, and retired to Britain. The government placed his nephew, 10-year-old Ananda Mahidol, on the throne: but as the young king didn't return to Bangkok from his studies in Switzerland until 1945, the effective leader of the country was a military officer named Phibul Songkhram. Phibul's government changed the name of the country officially from Siam to Thailand, signifying a new era of nation building, the word "Thai" generally held to mean "free".

This history is symbolised in concrete form at Ratchadamnoen Klang, for as the boulevard approaches the second moat the Democracy Monument has been built right in the centre of the way, forming a massive roundabout at the junction with Din So Road. Whether or not this spot was chosen symbolically, as a huge change in the way of kings, or if it was simply chosen for the majestic views one has of the monument from either side of the boulevard, is unclear. But the entire structure is founded on symbolic values. The Democracy Monument was built in 1939, at the same time as Siam became Thailand. It commemorates the actual date of the political change, 24th June 1932, when the form of government ceased to be an absolute monarchy and became a democracy, with the king as head of state. The height of the four wings is consequently 24 metres (78 ft). The radius of the base is also 24 metres. The seventy-five cannon at the base represent the year 2475 of the Buddhist Era, 1932 by

Mahakan Fort, built to guard a strategic canal junction on the northeastern side of the city.

the Western calendar. The traditional Thai tray and vessel carrying the constitution is 3 metres (9.8 ft) high, representing the month of change, June; the third lunar month in Thai reckoning. There are six ritual daggers, standing for the six principles of democracy: independence, internal peace, freedom, equality, economy, and education. The panels at the base of the four wings depict the roles of ordinary people involved in the revolution. The monument is far more impressive when surveyed on foot, rather than when dashing past in a taxi. Go onto the island, and the bas-relief sculptures tell a story, while the wings soar above and the marble and stone is softened by a blaze of floral colours.

A hundred metres or so is the moat and the only other remaining fort, Mahakan, together with a 200-metre (650-ft) stretch of the city wall. Built of brick coated with cement, as is the fort, the wall is 3.6 metres (11.8 ft) high and a robust 2.7 metres (8.8 ft) thick. Smaller than Phra Sumen Fort, Mahakan has three levels with an exterior staircase for the first two, and six cannon are located between the battlements. The fort protects the city's northeastern flank at the point where the Mahanak canal branches away from the second moat. Directly opposite Mahakan Fort is a large temple that, without

The Metal Castle was built to a design based on now lost temples in India and Sri Lanka.

walls, is set in a green garden compound and has at its centre a structure with towering iron spires, forming a strange pencilled outline against the sky. Wat Ratchanatdaram is set on the intersection of Ratchadamnoen Avenue and Maha Chai Road, and was built by Rama III in 1846, in honour of his granddaughter, Princess Somanas. The central structure is Loha Prasat, the Metal Castle, and the style was adapted from two earlier, and now lost, sanctuaries in India and Sri Lanka. There are five concentric square towers, each taller than the other, and three of them are capped by a total of thirty-seven cast-iron spires, signifying the thirty-seven virtues towards enlightenment. The two towers without spires form walkways, reached by a massive spiral stairway in the central tower, the walkways having shrines along their length. The Rama III Monument nearby was added in 1990. This was a very fashionable part of Ratchadamnoen Avenue. A popular movie theatre, the Chalerm Thai, stood here until it was demolished to improve the setting, and across the canal bridge stands the building that once housed the fashionable John Simpson Store, which sold imported clothing and which now houses a museum dedicated to Rama VII, the last absolute monarch of Siam. Built in 1906 by a Swiss-French architect named Charles Beguelin, and designed to a Neo-Classical style, the building contains a collection of personal belongings and state records that provide both an insight to this young king, who abdicated in 1935 at the age of 41 and died six years later in England, and to the momentous changes that were taking place in Siam at this time.

Although the coup that replaced the absolute monarchy with a constitutional monarchy was bloodless, forty years later there occurred a series of events that will be remembered as one of the darkest episodes in Thailand's history. Field Marshal Thanom Kittikachorn had become military dictator in 1963, but there was growing public discontent over the next decade at the state of the economy, and a growing unrest amongst students, angrily resentful at the replacement of democracy by military rule. In 1973 a number of student activists were expelled for their anti-government activities, and thirteen were arrested. On 13th October there were mass demonstrations for the students to be released and for a return to constitutional government. Students from Thammasat University marched to the Democracy Monument, and other students and members of the public joined in the demonstration, estimates putting the crowds by the following day at more than 200,000. The police lost control of the huge crowd, and the military were brought in, with tanks rolling down Ratchadamnoen Avenue and helicopters overhead. The army opened fire, and the students fought back, and the scene became one of massacre. Dead and injured were taken to the lobby of the Royal Hotel, at the edge of Sanam Luang, while at the other end of Ratchadamnoen, crowds of students gathered in panic at the gates of the royal palace of Chitralada, which were opened, allowing them to flood into the safety of the grounds. King Bhumibol, Rama IX, ordered Thanom and other military leaders to leave the country, and an hour later the king appeared on national television asking for calm, announcing that Thanom had been replaced with Dr Sanya Dharmasakti, a respected law professor who was rector of Thammasat.

A new constitution was drawn up under Sanya, and elections were scheduled for January 1975. An elected government under Prime Minister Seni Pramoj, leader of the centre-right Democrat Party, was established the following month but as there was no clear majority

A fragment of wall once part of a palace built in the first years of Bangkok.

in parliament the government was unstable, and Seni was replaced in April by his brother Kukrit Pramoj, who led the centre-left Social Action Party. Unrest continued amongst the public and the student population, as the economic situation was poor, and there were strikes and rallies. The unions and the Left appeared to have the upper hand, and as this was a time when Vietnam, Cambodia and Laos were falling to communism, many Thais were convinced that a similar fate could engulf their own country. A right-wing coup began to seem likely, and when Thanom returned, undergoing ordination as a monk at Wat Bowon and claiming he was only in Bangkok to pay respect to his dying father, there was a massive demonstration of students at Sanam Luang, which then moved onto the campus of Thammasat University. Early in the morning of 6th October 1976, paramilitary forces entered the campus and opened fire. Hence another massacre took place exactly three years after the first. There is a memorial to those who died in 1973, 1976 and during a further uprising in 1992, set on the corner of Ratchadamnoen Avenue and Tanao Road, a few metres from Democracy Monument.

A Tale of Three Princes

This brief walk takes us through a district that was once the home of royal princes, and which subsequently fell into decay until rescued by residents in one of the city's first conservation movements.
Duration: 1 hour

Rama I, in the year after he founded Bangkok as the capital, ordered the digging of two tube or *lot* canals that would connect the inner moat with the second moat, the latter of which was dug at the same time. The tube canals weren't given official names at the time, and the local people named the waterways after the points through which they passed, so that one canal could have several names. The starting point of the southern tube canal became known as Klong Lot Wat Ratchabophit, after the temple that stands at the canal junction. Only two centuries later, during the bicentennial celebrations, was the entire canal formally given this name for its entire length. The waterway stretches across the outer island to join with Klong Rop Krung, the second moat, at the Damrong Sathit Bridge.

Wat Ratchabophit presents itself as a cluster of stupas and pavilions facing onto Atsadang Road across a low iron fence, forming one of the most pleasant stretches of road and canal on the island. Rama V built the temple in 1869, the first temple commissioned following his accession to the throne the previous year. What is apparent is the

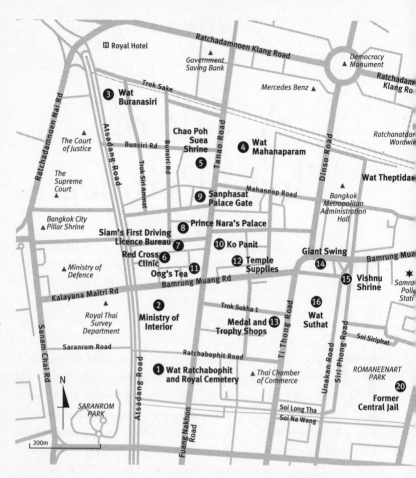

exuberant use of Western forms alongside traditional Siamese forms, indicating the extent to which the relationship with the West was being embraced at this time, less than fifteen years after the signing of the Bowring Treaty. Much of the impetus towards the relationship with the West had come from Dit Bunnag, regent to Rama IV, and his son Chuang, as Sri Suriyawong, had been regent to the 15-year-old Chulalongkorn when he became Rama V, remaining in that position until the king attained his majority in 1873. Wat Ratchabophit therefore marks a significant point in Siamese history, and in the way in which Western architectural styles were absorbed. The stupas that form such a varied frontage along the inner moat are part of the Royal

Cemetery, and along with the familiar bell shapes and Khmer-style *prangs* there are some memorials here that are pure Gothic, rising up amongst the trees like miniature cathedrals. Entering the temple from the north, at Ratchabophit Road, the doors are decorated with cartoonish figures of Western guards. And whereas the traditional temple layout is based upon square courtyards, a circular cloister connects the *ubosot* and *wiharn*, in the centre of which is a golden *chedi*. Because of this layout, the *sema*, the traditional eight boundary stones that surround an *ubosot*, have instead been set on a circle of columns facing in eight directions. Instead of the usual white, the walls of the temple are clad in *benjarong* tiling, the roofs are blue, red and gold, and the interior of the *ubosot* is a lush riot of Italian design. As a contrast, however, the monks' quarters within the temple compound are designed in a Chinese style.

The second tube canal, Klong Lot Wat Buranasiri, is only a few minutes' walk north along Atsadang Road. The temple after which the waterway takes its name is, however, in complete contrast to Wat Ratchabophit. Wat Buranasiri is a quiet temple built in the reign of Rama III by a senior minister named Chao Phraya Sutham Montri, whose daughter Sucharit Suda was to become the first consort of Rama VI. The temple was built on the site of Sutham Montri's birthplace, and reflects the early Rattanakosin era in the design of its *ubosot*, and of its high stupa, which forms a conspicuous landmark here at the junction of the two canals. An interesting later addition, however, is the European-style bell tower, clad in grey stone but topped off with a Chinese roof.

Following Buranasiri Road, which runs alongside the temple, will lead to Wat Mahanaparam, started in 1850 by Prince Udom Rattana Rasri, a son of Rama III, and, after a protracted construction period, completed in the following reign. Inside the compound is a statue of Rama V, placed here in recent years to mark the centenary of Siam's first public school for commoners, which was established in this temple by the king, who hoped to see a system of public schools like those he had seen in Europe. Wat Mahan School was a simple affair with the purpose of teaching children how to read and write, with all ages welcome. Perhaps because of this, the temple compound has evolved into a children's playground: not unusual in Thailand, where temples are regarded as community centres, but in this instance *takraw* courts have been painted in front of the *chedis* and there are always children and young men kicking a *takraw* ball around, in the game in which the woven rattan ball is not allowed to touch the ground. Perhaps because of this, the temple has a strange custom in which devotees offer *takraw* balls to the Buddha image, a 500-year-old figure brought from Sukhothai and named Luang Pho Ruang.

Wat Mahanaparam faces onto Tanao Road, and almost directly opposite is the Chao Poh Suea Shrine, the Shrine of the Tiger God, which although a Taoist shrine, is also one of the most popular places of worship for Buddhists. The shrine is actually dedicated to the warrior god Xuan Tian Shang Ti, who is seated on an altar decorated with embroidered Chinese silk, clad in imperial robes, a sword in his right hand, his right foot resting on a snake and his left foot on a black turtle. So fierce is the god that he has tigers as his servants, and the two stone tigers at the entrance are how the shrine acquired its name. Xuan is believed to have the power of blessing good fortune, and every year on his birthday, thousands of devotees attend the Shrine of the Tiger God, presenting strips of pork, bowls of rice and eggs, and tiny sugar tigers.

Lying between the old inner city moat and Tanao Road is what was once a lively and fashionable area, a home of royalty, which later fell

Renovated shophouses in the quiet square that forms the centre of Phraeng Phuton.

into decline and became sad and neglected, and not a little disreputable. Its buildings crumbled, some burned, some were pulled down, and with the blight of decay on the entire area it seemed ready for the wrecker's hammer. But the residents felt attached to their neighbourhood, and they believed that much of it could be saved. Thus was born one of Bangkok's first urban conservation projects, and it has provided an example and encouragement for many others.

You probably won't find the name Sam Phraeng on the maps, as it refers to the locality, but the name means "three road junctions", the roads being Phraeng Puthon, Phraeng Nara and Phraeng Sanphasat. The area could just as easily have been called Three Princes, for here three sons of Rama IV had their palaces. After the monarch's death, when his son Chulalongkorn ascended the throne, the three brothers built palaces in this neighbourhood. Much of the land was used for the construction of new roads and shophouses, as the city grew and prospered. Built from around 1870 onwards in the style that evolved out of the Straits Settlements, these are amongst the finest shophouses to be found in Bangkok. The grey bulk of the Ministry of Interior stands on the corner of Atsadang Road and Bamrung Muang Road, the latter being one of the first three surfaced roads to have been built in Bangkok (the other two being Charoen Krung and Fuang Nakhon), laid out in 1863. The ministry building is designed in European style, its grey plaster walls rusticated to give the appearance of stone blocks, its window shutters and doors painted a darker grey.

Directly opposite is a small side road that leads into the best-preserved part of the Sam Phraeng community, Phraeng Phuton. This small area demonstrated how far a neighbourhood could fall, declining in importance after the 1932 revolution. It became one of Bangkok's most active, and cheapest, red-light districts. The buildings deteriorated badly, but in the late 1980s the community began to come together with the aim of restoring their neighbourhood. With support from the Fine Arts Department, the Bangkok Metropolitan Administration, and Nippon Paint, who provided materials, the residents put in their own time and skills, and the gracious old two-storey shophouses were carefully renovated, their walls painted a uniform cream and their shutters and timberwork a dark green. The short road opposite the Interior Ministry quickly opens out into the most beautifully proportioned square, its appearance greatly enhanced when the BMA pulled down some latter-era disused buildings in the centre, and laid out a small garden. Next to the garden is the Phraeng Phuton Medical Centre, Bangkok's second Red Cross dispensary, built at the wish of Queen Sukhuman, a consort to Rama V, who passed away in 1927. The cost of the centre was met from donations collected during the queen's funeral ceremony. Patients are treated by any of the sixteen medical staff members that live upstairs in the clinic, and two visiting doctors from Chulalongkorn University. Around this square are craftsmen's workshops, small stores, restaurants, and everything else to keep a self-sustained community on the move. On one side of the square there is parked a number of veteran cars in various stages of repair, the work of Oo Som Rod Gaow, a garage that specialises in old vehicles. This motor shop was one of the first in Siam, and it also served as Bangkok's first Driver's Licence Bureau. Those few Siamese citizens who could afford cars would come here to register them and to get their driving permits. Many of Bangkok's first drivers had to go round and round in this circle to demonstrate that they could drive. The proximity of the Red Cross clinic would have been useful.

The second of the three roads is Phraeng Nara, named after Prince Narathip Prapanpong, and his palace is still standing. Prince Nara loved the performing arts and so decided to build a theatre in the open court behind his residence: it was Siam's first Western theatre and opera house. The prince made some bad investments and he was forced to sell the property. Portions of the palace were subsequently rented out to a law firm, which still operates on the west side of the building. The remainder became Talapat Suksa School, which has now moved on. The palace is not large, but it must have been impressive in its prime: three storeys high, and with a magnificent green-painted timber balcony overlooking the street. Inside the high old rooms are carved wooden panels, and a spiral staircase leads to the top floor. One room has been closed off, and the curious visitor will find it stacked high with cobwebbed tables and chairs, a relic of the school.

And our third prince? Phraeng Sanphasat was the site of the palace of Prince Sanphasat Suphakij, who was chief of the Military Engineers Corps during the reigns of Rama V and Rama VI, and who built his palace in 1906. The prince was responsible for the royal goldsmiths, and this area became known for its goldsmiths and very expensive gold and jewellery stores, prominent amongst the latter being the German company Grahlert, who had a large shop that once stood on the left of the road, decorated with symbols to indicate its royal patronage. Most of the Grahlert goldsmiths lived in a small street nearby, which is still called Company Lane, and there is also a narrow lane here named Trok Chang Thong, the alley of the goldsmiths. This is where much of the splendid gold works commissioned by the Siamese royal family were crafted.

After the prince's death in 1919 the palace was largely redeveloped but the area was completely razed by fire in 1967, and even while the ashes were still smouldering the local population was combing the ruins looking for gold dust and tiny fragments dropped over the course of one and a half centuries. Contemporary reports say their haul was impressive. But nowadays the only indication of royal splendour is the gate of the palace. Having fallen to the flames, the gate was restored by the Fine Arts Department in 1976. A neoclassical structure topped

Veteran cars outside the garage that was originally the city's first driver licence bureau.

with a globe-bearing goddess, it now stands alone as the entrance to nowhere. The replacement houses of Phraeng Sanphasat were built for expediency, and in the rather graceless style from that era that we find all over Bangkok. They act as a salutary reminder that history will owe much to the good people of Sam Phraeng. This area was very much the centre of the gold business, for nearby is Thanon Tee Thong, meaning "the Road of the Gold Beaters", primarily where gold was beaten into leaf for merit making in the temples. Tiny squares of gold, about the size of a postage stamp and no thicker than a piece of paper were placed between pads of buffalo hide and then pounded rhythmically with a heavy wooden mallet, hundreds of times. As the gold became warm under the hammer blows, it would spread to ten times its original area and become of micro-thinness, when it would be snipped into squares with scissors and placed in packets for the faithful. Today, there are no gold workshops in Thanon Tee Thong, but the street has emerged as the city's centre for military insignia and for gold and silver trophies. Shop after shop stand next to each other, packed with medals, badges, buttons, braid, and trophies for every sort of recognition. This street also used to be where court officials and bureaucrats purchased their uniforms, and so these two arcane businesses have simply adapted.

The Road to Golden Mountain

Walking along Bamrung Muang Road will take us through the district that supplies the country's temples, through to the Golden Mount and the village where monks' bowls are made.
Duration: 2 hours

Follow Tanao Road southwards, and we are on one of the last original streets of Rattanakosin, a long line of shophouses on either side, many of them occupied by businesses that have been here for generations. This includes shops selling musical instruments, such as the bamboo flutes made at Ban Lao, a store named Ton Chabub that sells old Thai recordings made on vinyl, and Ko Panit, which sells mangos, and which is easily spotted by the huge heap of the fruit that spills out of the shop and onto the pavement, forming a distinctive yellow landmark seemingly both in and outside of the mango season. A few metres further down, at the circular junction named Si Kak Sao Ching Cha, is Ong Iw Kee, more usually known as Ong's Tea, founded more than a century ago and importing fine teas from China and Taiwan. The shop, with its open frontage, remains unchanged since the day it opened. In the floor tiles can be seen the original logo, a stately teapot, although there is now a more modern sign in use, that of a friendly-faced dragon. Tea purchases will be produced from an ingenious storage area. This takes up an entire wall, where there is a series of sliding glass panels,

A display of fresh mango outside Ko Panit, one of the oldest shops on Tanao Road.

each decorated with motifs of butterflies, clouds, trees and leaves to designate the variety of tea kept behind the panel in its own tiny safe. This prevents the fragrance of the leaves from being contaminated.

Entering Bamrung Muang, we are into a street lined by two-storey shophouses that took their pattern from those built in Singapore. Rama IV had ordered construction of the road, but in the early days nondescript buildings had sprung up. In 1870, Rama V, concerned about the appearance of the fast-growing city, issued a proclamation to widen the road for the greater convenience of the still-novel horse and carriage, and to rebuild the shophouses. Although the Singapore design was followed, with its five-foot covered way, this has long since been filled in and lost. Consequently one is walking in the road, and as a pedestrian is naturally invisible to drivers, so it is rather dangerous to go on foot here until the road widens a little further down. All along the road, on both sides, are shops devoted to temple ware, and anything can be bought here from a giant Buddha image through to small packets of incense. The shops are crammed with every conceivable need, the goods spilling out onto the pavement, with alms bowls, saffron robes, bells, candles of all sizes, shrines, altars, figures of monks, Hindu deities, and Buddha images in every posture. Wander into the alleys that lead off the road, and the workshops where much of this produce is made can be seen, while the courtyard of an old printing works, the business for which this district is also historically known, is used to store freshly gilded Buddha images, row upon row of them. Groups of monks can be seen wandering the street in their saffron robes, window-shopping. Many of them will be from upcountry temples, for this street supplies temples throughout the country. Many of the images are wrapped in transparent plastic sheets, and pickups regularly cruise past with an image loaded in the back, maybe bound for the railway station or a river pier but quite possibly setting out on a long drive to a remote temple with a direct delivery.

The reason for this enormous concentration of temple goods and monks from the provinces is Wat Suthat, a royal temple of the first grade, one of ten in Bangkok, which trains and supplies priests for temples throughout the kingdom. Wat Suthat has enormous significance in the Buddhist cosmos, its name denoting Suthatsa Nakhon, the celestial city of Indra, which sits at the top of Mount Meru, the centre of the universe. Its design reflects this status. Building of Wat Suthat was begun by Rama I in 1807, continued by Rama II, and completed in the reign of Rama III in 1847. The compound is enormous, covering more than ten acres, and within this is Bangkok's longest ordination hall, at 72 metres (236 ft). The principal Buddha image, Phra Sri Sakyamuni, was cast in bronze in 1361 and had been installed at Wat Mahathat in Sukhothai, where it was left when the city was abandoned, exposed for four centuries to the elements when the temple fell into ruins. In 1808 the image was removed by Rama I, who had it floated down the river for installation in the specially prepared *ubosot*. At 8 metres (26 ft) in height, the image was too large to pass through the gate at the landing pier, so a section of the city wall was removed. The king himself helped to haul the image through, and then walked barefoot in the procession that accompanied the image to the temple. He was clearly unwell, and it was noticed that he was so exhausted by the time he arrived that he was staggering. He helped to hoist the image into position, and after this he whispered to his assistants that his work was done. Within a few days he was dead.

Logo on the floor of Ong's Tea Shop, which imports teas from China and Taiwan.

Behind the throne is a gilded limestone bas relief of the eighth-century Dvaravati period, one of the oldest Buddhist artefacts in Thailand, and underneath the throne are the ashes of Rama VIII, who died in 1946 in circumstances that still remain a mystery. A statue of the young king stands in the courtyard. Inside the *wiharn* are exquisite murals painted during the Rama III era, using Western techniques of perspective that were only then becoming understood by Siamese artists, and restored in the 1980s after years of damage from the bats that once hung inside the structure. Outside the *wiharn* are twenty-eight Chinese pagodas, and the surrounding cloisters contain 156 Buddha images, each of which has been adopted by a patron to make merit.

Inside a second *wiharn* is an image of the Buddha, named Sethamunee, and cast by order of Rama III from the tin and lead of opium canisters seized from drug lords, the king saying that a symbol of hope and enlightenment could come from something inherently evil. Around the compound are a great number of grey stone figures, including life-size depictions of European seafarers, carried to Siam from China as ballast in the junks that would return laden with rice or teak.

For all its significance and beauty tourists seldom enter Wat Suthat, their interest usually being confined to the Giant Swing, the huge red frame being visible from either end of Bamrung Muang, and forming the centrepiece of the road junction. The swing was built only two years after the founding of Bangkok, when a Brahman named Kratai asked permission from Rama I to build a temple and ceremonial swing for conducting Brahman ceremonies, and is therefore older than Wat Suthat. It was originally placed in front of the nearby Thewa Sathan Shrine that Kratai built at the same time. Hinduism and Buddhism have always been closely related in Siam, Brahman ceremonies having played a significant part of life in the Sukhothai, Ayutthaya and Thonburi eras, and the king readily agreed. Brahmans believe that Shiva and Vishnu descend from heaven to earth once a year, and amongst the ceremonies was the swing ceremony, or Tri Yampawai, used to give thanks for a bountiful rice harvest and ask blessings for the next. The government official in charge of the rice harvest, accompanied by astrologers, would lead a parade around the city walls and into the shrine precinct. Three teams of young Brahmans would ride on the swing attempting to catch, by mouth, a bag of gold or silver coins held on a pole. Although no one knows how high the original swing was, this was clearly a dangerous practice as a number of injuries and deaths occurred throughout the years. The ceremony was finally abandoned in 1935, although the rice harvest festival is still conducted in December every year. The swing was moved here from its original location in 1920, when the swing structure was rebuilt. Because of continuing deterioration, it was rebuilt again in 1947 and 1970. Today's Giant Swing, which is more than 21 metres (68 ft) high and made from teak, dates from 2006. Wat Suthat remains closely associated with Hinduism, housing the Brahman priests who officiate at state ceremonies. The Thewa Sathan Shrine is on Dinso Road and contains images of Shiva and Ganesh, and there is the small Saan Jao Phitsanu shrine dedicated to Vishnu and standing on the opposite side of Wat Suthat. A few metres away is Bharat Vidyalaya, a school founded by the Hindu community in 1930, originally in Pahurat and moved to the present site in 1948. The school building was erected in 1965, and the Dev Mandir Temple inaugurated on the same site in 1969.

Bamrung Muang Road skirts Wat Suthat and continues east-wards, still with its shophouses selling temple goods and here pass-ing through a district known as Samranrat where, in the lanes to the left, is a small community dedicated to the sewing of saffron robes for monks. The community is housed on land that was once the grounds of the Sommut Amornphan Palace, belonging to Prince Svasti Pravat, a son of Rama IV, and the palace still stands, hemmed in by buildings. Here too can be found Wat Theptidaram, a third-grade royal temple founded by Rama III in 1836 for his daughter, Princess Kroma Muen Apsomsudathep, the only temple in Thailand honouring female dis-ciples of the Buddha, *bhikkhunis*, or female monks. *Bhikkhunis* are highly controversial, going right back to the time of the Buddha himself, and Thailand's Sangha does not ordain them. The Buddhist patriarchs concede that while the Buddha himself ordained women (although, apparently, with reluctance), the monastic rules of Thai Theravada Buddhism require that five ordained monks and five ordained *bhikkhunis* be present for any new *bhikkhuni* ordination. Since there are no *bhikkhunis* in Thailand, the quorum can never be achieved, which seems to be a classic Thai solution. Some other countries do ordain female monks, including Sri Lanka, Vietnam and Taiwan, and any *bhikkhuni* seen inside the temple has been ordained overseas. *Bhikkhunis* are not Buddhist nuns, who are lay persons, non-ordained women who shave their heads, wear white robes and live a monastic life, and who although they are given a great deal of respect, have neither the rights nor the status of ordained monks. Rama III honoured the *bhikkhunis* by installing fifty-two brass imag-es in their own *wiharn*, although they are very small. Here too is an image of Mahapajapati Gotami, the Buddha's stepmother, who was one of his foremost disciples. Because of its association with female monks, Wat Theptidaram is sometimes known as the Angels' Temple.

Wat Theptidaram is in all other respects a conventional enough temple, its architecture displaying the Chinese elements that are so familiar from the reign of Rama III. In the *ubosot* the princi-pal Buddha image is carved from pure white stone and is known as Luang Por Khao, or Venerable White Buddha. The temple does, however, have one other claim to fame, in that this is where Siam's greatest poet, Sunthorn Phu, was ordained and where he spent three years of his life. Sunthorn, who was born at Bangkok Noi in Thonburi in 1786, in the reign of Rama I, was a turbulent poet. He was educated at Wat Si Sudaram at Bangkok Noi, where a statue of him stands on the riverbank. He became a government clerk and fell in love with a girl named Chan. She was a palace lady and forbidden to him, and he was thrown into prison. After his release in 1807 he married Chan, but he had become an alcoholic and she left him for another man. His poetry was becoming recognised and Rama II appointed him as court poet, but he was jailed again after a fight. He began the epic poem *Phra Aphai Mani* while he was in prison, the story of a prince and his wanderings throughout ancient Siam. Rama II was so delighted with Sunthorn's poetry that he awarded him the title "Khun", but during the reign of Rama III Sunthorn was unwise enough to correct one of the king's poems, and was stripped of his title. He became a vagrant, and it was at this time that Sunthorn entered Wat Theptidaram, where he spent three years as a monk, living in the monks' quarters behind the temple, where his room is still preserved and has been declared a national monument. Sunthorn was rehabilitated in the reign of Rama IV, when a daughter of the king read the unfinished Phra Aphai Mani and persuaded the poet to complete it. Rama IV appointed him as director of the royal scribes, and awarded him the title "Phra". Sunthorn spent the remainder of his life in relative tranquillity, and died in 1855. Another statue of him stands in Klaeng, in Rayong Province, where his father had been born and where Sunthorn spent several years living and writing. His birthday, 26th June, is celebrated each year as Sunthorn Phu Day.

The second moat runs alongside Wat Theptidaram, and along here stood the old city wall. Bamrung Muang Road passed through a gate here, a gate that was used for transporting the dead out of the city. The immediate area is still known today as Pratu Phi, the Ghost Gate, and through here the departed were carried over the Sommut Amornphan Bridge on their final journey.

"Opposite the Brahmanee Watt, at the distance of about a mile, are the extensive grounds and buildings of Watt Sah Kate, the great national burning-place of the dead. Within these mysterious precincts the Buddhist rite of cremation is performed, with circumstances more or less horrible, according to the condition or the superstition of the deceased. A broad canal surrounds the temple and yards, and here, night and day, priests watch and pray for the regeneration of mankind. Not alone the dead, but the living likewise, are given to be burned in secret here; and into this canal, at the dead of night, are flung the rash wretches who have madly dared to oppose with speech or act the powers that rule in Siam. None but the initiated will approach these grounds after sunset, so universal and profound is the horror the place inspires... The walls are hung with human skeletons and the ground is strewed with human skulls. Here also are scraped together the horrid fragments of those who have bequeathed their carcasses to the hungry dogs and vultures, that hover, and prowl, and swoop, and pounce, and snarl, and scream, and tear."

Anna Leonowens certainly laid it on a bit thick about Wat Saket, but she had a book to sell. And she was certainly right about the temple being used for cremation ceremonies, which were not permitted inside the city walls. During the frequent outbreaks of plague and cholera the temple was a grisly sight, the corpses frequently stacked in the courtyard. Yet oddly enough, Anna does not mention the outstanding visual feature of this temple, a feature that certainly existed at the time she was writing.

Wat Saket dates back to the Ayutthaya era. No one knows exactly when it was founded, but the temple was used by Chao Phraya Chakri who stopped here on his way back from Cambodia to Thonburi in 1782 to suppress the riots that had erupted in the wake of the apparent insanity of King Taksin. With the king removed and Chakri now enthroned as Rama I, he ordered the temple to be enlarged, and decreed that it should be used for cremations and funeral rites. Rama III decided to build a replica of Ayutthaya's Chedi Phu Khao Thong, the Chedi of the Golden Mountain, in the temple grounds and thus symbolise the city's standing in Buddhist cosmology. As with the original, it was to be a massive structure, an artificial hill that could be seen from all parts of the city. The records have it that the *chedi* was to be fifty fathoms in dimension, and the king asked for donations of logs to act as the foundations. Thousands of logs were laid out in the soft ground in a raft-like fashion, and the structure built upon them. However, the ground proved to be too soft for the weight: the *chedi* tumbled into a heap of mud and bricks, and stayed that way for several years.

Rama IV, the king who employed Anna as a governess, revived the project. Reasoning that the huge mound was best left where it was, he used another thousand teak logs for reinforcement and ordered a small *chedi* to be built on the summit. Anna left Siam in 1868, after the death of the king, by which time Golden Mount had become a prominent landmark. It was the highest point in the otherwise completely flat landscape. The American writer Frank Vincent ascended in 1871, and commented that very little of Bangkok could be seen because of the luxuriant vegetation of the city. It was Rama V, who as Chulalongkorn had been one of Anna's pupils, who completed the *chedi* in the design we see today, a golden bell-shaped structure that houses a Buddha relic from India. During World War II the hill began to show alarming signs of erosion, and concrete walls were added, finally bringing the story of Golden Mount to the present day.

A climb to the top reveals a view that remains one of the most spectacular in Bangkok. There is still something almost rural about the hill, surrounded as it is by trees, and with shrines and gravestones set in its sides. One enters through a small gate and climbs 318 steps that wind around the massive base. The ascent is a gentle one. There are speakers set at regular intervals into the balustrade, and one is accompanied all the way up by a murmuring discourse. On the summit is a light and airy room equipped at the four points of the compass with binoculars. A tiny staircase leads to an observation platform right on top, and there is a small chapel from where one can peer down on the innocent red rooftops of Wat Saket, and across a city that is far from buried in lush vegetation but which from this perspective has a deceptively calm air. Did Anna ever climb this hill? I would like to think so.

Back at ground level, the area around the base of Golden Mount is picturesque. The mount is by the junction of the second moat and Mahanak canal: no sign of traitors' corpses floating in the water here, but the junction is busy with the waterbuses that depart for the journey out to Ramkhamhaeng. The pier is found by entering the gate next to Mahakan Fort, which guards the canals. Spanning the Mahanak canal is a bridge whose panels depict sorrowing figures mourning the loss of Rama v, who passed away in 1910. Vittorio Novi, the Italian sculptor brought out to Bangkok to execute the marble and granite works for the Ananta Samakhom Throne Hall that was then under construction, carved the figures from photographs he took from life models, and the original pictures can be seen in the archives today. Known officially as the Mahadthai Uthit Bridge, but more usually as the Weeping Bridge, the structure was completed in 1914. Continue along Paribatra Road, a leafy street that skirts the base of Golden Mount and follows the second moat, and there is a long-established community of woodworkers that grew up in the wake of the seven sawmills that were working here along the canal-side in the late nineteenth century. The entire street is given over to their businesses, and judging by the spruce appearance of the shophouses, and by the huge amounts of timber stacked in the workshops in the back lanes, they do very well. Beautifully carved doors and panelling, fine window frames and screens with ornate fretwork are all here, along with handsome coffins, a legacy of Wat Saket's original purpose.

In the shadow of Golden Mount is a village that has been there since the founding of Bangkok. Rama i, in building his new capital, had allocated three areas solely for the production of monks' alms bowls, *baat*, which, given the number of temples going up at that time, and the number of monks arriving to live and work in them, must indeed have been brisk business. Today, however, the three districts have dwindled to just this one, Ban Baat, and it is so tiny it consists of only a couple of small alleys lying on the other side of Bamrung Muang Road, and would be easily missed if it were not for a marker board. The way leads between old timber houses and is navigable on foot only, but there is the unmistakable tik-tik-tik of metal being hammered, and heaps of half-finished bowls on the ground, on trestle tables, on pallets... everywhere. There are only half-a-dozen families involved in the production of *baat*, a craft that has been passed down from the Ayutthaya era and which is believed to have come from the Khmer. Each bowl is made from eight sections of metal, representing the eight spokes of the Dharma wheel. The sections have their edges serrated so that they interlock with each other, and then the joints are fused in a wood fire with strips of copper. After filing and polishing, the bowl may be dimpled with a hammer and buffed up to a metallic sheen, or coated with several layers of black lacquer. A craftsman can make one or at most two bowls per day, and factory-made bowls long ago took over as they are faster and easier to make, and cost far less to buy: a factory bowl will cost only 400–500 baht, while a hand-crafted bowl will start at that price and go up to about 3,000 baht for a large one. But although the size of the community has shrunk to the bare minimum, there is still a demand for the traditional bowls. Many temple abbots support the significance of making them from eight pieces of metal, and some, when ordering from Ban Baat, ask for the bowls to be finished with a rubbing of oil, in order for the seams to be more visible. Other than the temples, tourists have become enthusiastic buyers, and the bowls can be bought here from shops or from the craftsmen, the main retailer being Somsak Bupachot, who has a small shop at the entrance to the community, with an attractive selection of bowls on display.

Parallel to the trok of Ban Baat and only a minute's walk is another tiny community, Ban Dok Mai, the Village of the Firework Makers, the Thai name for fireworks being *dok mai fai*, or "fire flowers". Once a prosperous and busy community, for fireworks were as popular in the Rattanakosin era as they are now, this district bears little sign of its former occupation, and is no more than a *soi* and a small alley. The popularity of Ban Dok Mai had continued after the end of World War II, when older inhabitants can remember fireworks being made here and sold for the festivals and also for the rice harvests, when farmers would travel up the canal by boat and collect their supplies. Much went into the art of firework production, the graceful colours and shapes that could be created, rather than the loud bangs. In 1961 there was a serious fire in the community, and after that the government banned production in the city. Manufacturers and traders were forced to move into the provinces. There remain a couple of fireworks shops here, Nai Tuan and Por Pan Chinda, but they are the offices of companies that arrange displays.

A watchtower of the old central prison, now converted into Romaneenart Park.

Ban Dok Mai has given its name to one of the more whimsical of the surviving royal palaces, Ban Dok Mai Palace, which was built in 1902 by Rama v for his thirty-fifth son, Prince Purachatra Jayagara. The prince had been presented with his new home at age 21, but he didn't have much time to enjoy it, for his father packed him off to Cambridge University, in England, where he studied civil engineering. On his return to Bangkok he became head of the railway system, which was then being developed by British and German engineering companies. He expanded the system and built the first bridge over the river, thus allowing southern trains direct access to the capital, and later as communications minister he built the Memorial Bridge.

Prince Purachatra resided at Ban Dok Mai Palace for most of his adult life, leaving it only in 1932, after the revolution that ended Siam's absolute monarchy. A few years previously he had become interested in the potential of radio, and in 1927 had purchased a small transmitter and used it to make experimental broadcasts from his home, before setting up the radio station at Phayathai Palace, on the fringe of Dusit. In 1932, broadcasting was moved to Sala Daeng, on what was to become Wireless Road. After the revolution Purachatra went down to Singapore, where he died four years later. The palace subsequently passed into the hands of the government, and an offshoot of the Ministry of Industry now resides there. At a leafy part of Luang Road, behind a pretty row of shophouses and approached under an inconspicuous archway, the palace backs onto Ban Dok Mai. It is a lovely old structure, more like a country house than a palace, with its fine window detailing and faded-rose stucco. Most striking is the third storey that was added some years after the palace had been completed: it doesn't exactly chime with the original architecture, but in a very distinctive way complements it, adding an eccentric touch that might well have given its original designer hysterics, but on the other hand might have delighted him. As is the way of government departments anywhere, whenever they have the run of a distinguished old building, the palace has been allowed to deteriorate, but even so it still has dignity.

At the junction of Bamrung Muang and Worachak roads is a rather elegant building with a neat pepper-pot tower and, looming behind, two huge water towers. This is Bangkok Waterworks, a project started by Rama V to provide the city with clean drinking water, but not completed until 1914, four years after his death. The waterworks themselves were out at Samsen, next to the electricity station that was built at the same time to provide their power, and the two towers here were built to store the over-supply of water when consumption slackened during the night. They are made of ferroconcrete and are 30 metres (96 ft) high. "A spiral staircase is placed in the middle of each tower, and at the top the visitor finds himself in a circular observation room with windows opening in all directions," reported the *Bangkok Times*, when the towers were completed. "A ladder leads down into the tank, a round and lofty chamber of ferroconcrete, and here is found a very fine echo which makes the climb up the spiral staircase well worth while. Owing to the formation of the chamber a sound is repeated a score of times, thrown back from the wall and roof. To clap one's hands is to set a whole battery of artillery in action," the reporter added, excitedly. A canal ran alongside the waterworks, and across it Prince Bhanurangsi Sawangwongse, a younger brother of the king, and owner of Burapha Palace, built a bridge that he painted black in memory of his deceased wife and son. The bridge was known as Saphan Dam, or Black Bridge, and at each end were mounted the heads of two oxen. In the nose of each ox was a brass ring fitted with a chain and a small metal cup. Any passerby needing a cooling drink of water could press the ox's nose and clean water from the waterworks would gush into the cup. Sadly this fascinating structure has long gone, but the area is still known as Saphan Dam.

Back on Luang Road, and looking towards the second moat, on the far bank can be seen an imposing white façade with green shutters. This is the former central prison, opened in 1890 and closed nearly a century later. Most of the buildings were demolished, but the offices and receiving areas, a cellblock, part of the wall and several watchtowers have been left standing. The offices have been converted into the Corrections Museum, while the interior area has been turned into Romaneenart Park, verdant parkland with fountains and sports courts where human misery once dwelled. Rama V had studied the British prison system and he had the jail based on Brixton Prison in London. He also began prison reform, banning the more barbarous treatment of the inmates. Even so, life in a Siamese prison was not exactly a walk in the park, as it were. The penal system was based on punishment and suffering, and the museum is a gruesome one. The idea for a museum grew out of the training centre that was set up for prison officers in 1939 at Bang Kwang Central Prison, the notorious "Bangkok Hilton", which is located just outside the city at Nonthaburi, so historical authenticity is guaranteed. Of particularly macabre interest is the recreation of the execution chamber, set up in one of the blocks. When decapitation was replaced by machine-gun fire, in 1934, a neat way was found to obviate the Buddhist strictures against killing. The prisoner was strapped to a frame, and a blanket marked with a target was hung between him and the gun. The executioner was therefore simply indulging in a little harmless target practice.

Statue of King Taksin at Wat Intharam.

A traditional Teochew house on the bank of Klong Bangkok Yai.

ABOVE AND LEFT *The exuberant Chinese architecture of Chee Chin Khor Temple.*

RIGHT *Windsor House, a classic example of the gingerbread style of architecture.*

LEFT *Ordered from Britain in the 1820s and originally intended for the Grand Palace, this distinctly un-Buddhist fence was eventually used at Wat Prayoon, which locals immediately dubbed "Iron Fence Temple".*

RIGHT AND BELOW *The pastoral surroundings of Wat Thong Thammachat, even though the main road is only a two-minute walk away.*

TOP AND ABOVE *Princess Mother Memorial Park is laid out on the streets that Princess Srinagarindra knew as a child.*

ABOVE *Old Thonburi Station, originally built as a terminus for the southern line, was later used by the Japanese armed forces as their operational base for the Death Railway.*

BELOW *One of the last smithies working at Ban Bu, the village of the bronzesmiths.*

ABOVE *A vendor at Wat Rakhang sells turtles for release into the river, a traditional Buddhist act of mercy.*

TOP AND ABOVE *Bells are everywhere at Wat Rakhang, the Temple of the Bell.*

An unusual gift for a queen: the Pig Memorial presented to Queen Mother Sri Patcharindra, who had been born in the Year of the Pig.

The inner moat.

Bridges across the inner moat: TOP *the Hok Bridge;* ABOVE LEFT *Pee Goon Bridge;* ABOVE RIGHT *Chang Rong Si Bridge.*

RIGHT *Cast-iron Roman galleys feature on the uprights at Phan Fa Lilat Bridge.*

LEFT *Memorial at Saranrom Park to 19-year-old Queen Sunantha and two-year-old Princess Kannabhorn, who drowned in a boating accident in 1880.*

ABOVE *More than 130 years later, offerings of soft foods and toys are left at the memorial for the spirit of the little girl.*

LEFT *The Earth Goddess Shrine at Sanam Luang is also a public drinking fountain.*

BELOW *Antique cannon outside the Ministry of Defence.*

Phra Sumen, the larger of Bangkok's two remaining forts.

Wat Sangwet Printing School, the country's first college of printing.

A new lease of life for this old wooden house in Khao San Road.

Originally a fashionable department store selling imported clothes, this building on Ratchadamnoen Avenue now houses the Rama VII Museum.

Mahakan Fort, the smaller of the city's two remaining forts.

ABOVE *Rama III Monument, with Loha Prasat, the Metal Castle, in the background.*

RIGHT *Gardens at Loha Prasat.*

BELOW LEFT *A rallying point for change: the Democracy Monument.*

BELOW RIGHT *A memorial to those killed during the uprisings in 1973, 1976 and 1992.*

RIGHT *Gate to nowhere: all that remains of the palace of Prince Sanphasat.*

BELOW *European-style door guards at Wat Ratchabophit.*

An unchanged design for Ong's Tea Shop: the tea is kept in safes behind the panels.

The Weeping Bridge, its panels signifying a mourning nation following the death of Rama V.

European Gothic designs abound amongst the traditional Thai memorials at the royal cemetery at Wat Ratchabophit.

Everything a temple needs, from Buddha images to monk figures and incense sticks, can be found at Bamrung Muang Road. Much of the temple ware is made in workshops in the alleys behind the shops.

Monks from temples throughout Thailand visit the Bamrung Muang shops to order images, furnishings, bells and other goods for temples, schools and religious institutions.

ABOVE *Classic 1920s shophouses built near the Memorial Bridge.*

RIGHT *A market porter handles durians at Pak Klong Talat, Bangkok's largest fruit, vegetable and flower market.*

BELOW *Shrine for the market workers at Pak Klong Talat.*

LEFT AND BELOW
*Pottery motifs
at Ban Moh, the
potters' village.*

*At first sight a classic late nineteenth-century mansion, this structure at the
foot of the Memorial Bridge is actually a façade.*

ABOVE *A fresco at St Francis Xavier Church.*

RIGHT *Ban Duriyapraneet, a home to traditional Thai music for more than a century.*

RIGHT *Rama V so admired this statue when he saw it in a Florence foundry that he had it shipped back to Bangkok, where it stands now in the grounds of St Francis Xavier Church.*

ABOVE *Wat Uphai, built by Vietnamese refugees.*

LEFT *Italian styling is apparent on the main gate at the royal crematorium, Wat Depsirindra.*

LEFT *Stylised curtains at the doors and windows of Wat Kanikapon, built by Chinatown brothel owner Madame Faeng.*

ABOVE AND LEFT *Fund-raising day at Wat Kanikapon.*

BOTTOM LEFT *A statue of Madame Faeng.*

BELOW *A mansion for a departed soul: a shop making funerary offerings near to the Poh Teck Tung Foundation.*

This shop in Chinatown sells Thai and Chinese styled Buddha images,
and also acts as a neighbourhood shrine.

Shrine at Peiing School. The school was built by Chinese merchants
and originally provided tuition only in the Teochew dialect.

Luang Kochaid Sahark Mosque is the only mosque in Chinatown, built for Malay and other Muslim traders.

Riverside shrine for workers on Songwat Road.

Wat Sampeng, marking the official eastern boundary of Chinatown.

TOP LEFT *A Chinese door guardian at Wat Sampeng.*

TOP RIGHT *Monks' living quarters.*

ABOVE AND RIGHT *Recycling old vehicle parts at the Siang Gong Zone helped Thailand to develop after World War II.*

ABOVE *The house of a prosperous merchant, converted by The Oriental hotel into a Chinese restaurant.*

ABOVE *The Chinese junk-shaped chapel built by Rama III at Wat Yannawa.*

RIGHT *Tugboats like this one, passing beneath the Memorial Bridge, guide shipping through the notorious mudbanks at the mouth of the Chao Phraya River.*

TOP *Overshadowed by modern buildings is the mansion of Luang Sathorn, the first private developer to fund construction of a road and canal when he built Sathorn Road in about 1890.*

ABOVE *Soi Pradit Market, with the Meera Suddin Mosque in the background.*

RIGHT *Wat Khaek, the oldest Hindu temple in Thailand, built by immigrants from Tamil Nadu.*

LEFT AND ABOVE *Mon-style* chedi *and golden Buddha statues at Wat Songtham, in Phra Pradaeng.*

BELOW *Monk statues at Wat Songtham.*

Not forgotten: the Buddha image at this abandoned chapel in Bang Krachao is still visited by devotees.

Wat Bang Krachao Klang, a rural temple only minutes away from the city.

A lone artist paints a fresco at Wat Bang Krasop, at Bang Krachao.

ABOVE *Triple eaves adorn the temple of Wat Bang Krasop.*

LEFT *A stupa made from clay bricks at Wat Chak Daeng, Bang Krachao, symbolising the pottery-making heritage of the Mon people.*

RIGHT *Samray Church, the first Presbyterian church built in Bangkok.*

ABOVE *Rice barges pass in front of Wat Bukkhalo, the only temple in Bangkok to have a chapel on top of a three-storey building.*

ABOVE *Footballer David Beckham makes a surprise appearance as a deity at Wat Pariwat.*
BELOW *A coastal freighter moored at Rama III Road, with Bang Krachao in the background.*

An unusual design for Wat Hua Lampong, with both its ordination hall and chapel built on a single-storey platform.

Designed by Mario Tamagno, Hua Lampong Railway Station shows the influence of the architect's Turin background.

Offices of the Railway Police at Hua Lampong.

ABOVE *An intense swirl of colour, music and incense smoke at the Erawan Shrine.*

LEFT *Flowers for devotees outside the Erawan Shrine.*

BELOW *Fertility symbols at the Tuptim shrine beside the Saen Saeb canal.*

The Potters' Village

*A potters' village founded by Mon immigrants, the city's biggest
flower market, Little India, the first modern school, and a Japanese
ossuary that was the hideout for an army officer on the run, are all
to be found in this colourful district.*

Duration: 3 hours

With the siege of Pegu in southern Burma in 1757 and the subsequent fall of the city to the Burmese King Alaungpaya, the last independent Mon kingdom vanished. The Mon had once been a great people, the first recognisable civilisation in Southeast Asia. They are believed to have originated in eastern India and to have migrated eastwards across Burma and the central Siam plains, bringing Buddhism with them. The Khmer empire and the rise of the Tai had seen them pushed back into Burma, where they settled throughout the south. Now that Pegu was in Burmese hands, the Mon were a people without a country. A large number of Mon had migrated to Ayutthaya during the second half of the sixteenth century, during a time of great internal turmoil in Burma, and they had joined the Siamese in fighting the endless Burmese wars of this period. Now a new wave of migrants followed, being welcomed by the king of Ayutthaya as staunch enemies of the Burmese. But of course, Ayutthaya itself had only a decade left before it too fell to the Burmese, led now by Alaungpaya's son Hsinbyushin. As with most of the other survivors, the Mon moved down the Chao

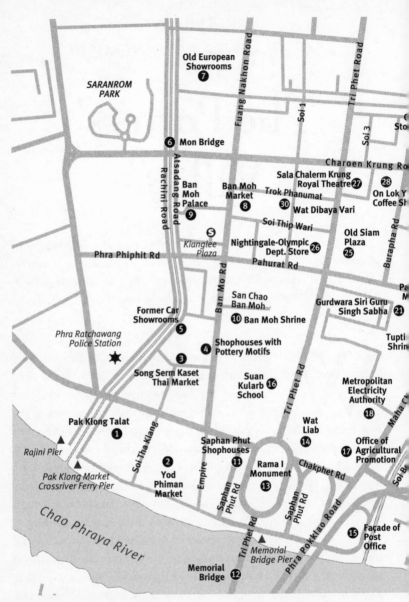

Phraya River. Some settled on Koh Kred, about twenty kilometres north of Bangkok, where an earlier canal cut to straighten the course of the river had created an island. Here they made their own distinctive pottery from baked unglazed red clay, carved and moulded with intricate

Maha Chai Road

Baribatra Road

Sam Yot
Plaza

am Yot

24
iri Chan
uilding

▲ Saphan
   Lek Square

S Pirom Plaza

H Grande De
      Ville Hotel

Chakkrawat Rd

hong
1

23

**Damrong
Sathit
Bridge**

Yaowarat Rd

oyal India
estaurant

kKrawat Rd

N

200m

**South Outer
Rattanakosin**

patterns. Other Mon refugees sailed further down the river and eventually formed a community in a small nook of Rattanakosin Island, at the junction of Klong Lot Wat Ratchabophit and the inner moat. Mon traders would sail their boats along the moat and tie up at a spot where a bridge had been built. This structure became known as Saphan Mon, or Mon Bridge, and by the time of Rama III, in the 1820s, it was a handsome teak structure. The main business of the Mon at this settlement was pottery, and in particular the conical-lidded traditional cooking pots called *moh*, which they made here and also imported from Koh Kred. The area became known as Ban Moh.

A visit to this area today won't reveal many cooking pots, but what can be found is an area of crumbling and stately shophouses, amongst the finest on Rattanakosin Island, together with an oddly rural atmosphere, for traffic bypasses this sliver of land and the canal is quiet and leafy. There is a river pier, serving the busy market of Pak Klong Talat, and a sluice gate at the mouth of the canal protects the water level when the Chao Phraya rises. The shophouses were built in the late nineteenth century, after the Mon had given up their pottery trade, but look up at the pediments on the corners of this big, old development and it can be seen that the architect has placed replicas of the *moh* on each one to represent the original activity of the area. Follow the canal further and the motif is reproduced elsewhere, and it becomes an intriguing little search to find pottery designs, one of the most inventive being the abstract design woven on the corner of Ban Moh Road and Phra Phitak. Near here is the modern-day Saphan Mon, a prosaic enough concrete structure, but having an elegant pottery theme worked into the wrought iron railings. The rather grand sweep of buildings on Atsadang Road, facing the canal, were shops selling luxury imported goods and included Siam's first motor showrooms. The shophouses on the corner of Soi Phraya Sri are outstandingly handsome and prosperous looking, and they were at one point used as a commercial store run by German and English owners. This street takes its name from a prominent *phraya sri*, or senior court minister, of Rama III's time: the minister's residence stood on this spot. Ban Moh does in fact have a strong connection to the royal family of this era, for almost invisible behind a wall on Ban Moh Road is one of Bangkok's oldest palaces. Ban Moh Palace was the residence of Prince Phithak Thewet, the twenty-second son of Rama II. He was born in the Grand Palace in 1798. When he was 12 years old, he was given his own palace on the bank of the moat here, near to the homes of his brothers. But in 1832 a fire razed the area. The prince then built this present structure. During the reign of Rama IV the prince was promoted and given command of the cavalry and elephant brigades. The canal-side location of his palace was important, because a bathing place was needed for the elephants. As an example of early Rattanakosin architecture the palace is outstanding, although unfortunately it is not open to the public. The design was a fairly standard one for princes of this rank: a single-storey building, raised high above the ground to be away from the flooding, with a wooden frame and walls, and a roof of unglazed tiles. Prince Phithak Thewet lived at Ban Moh Palace until his death in 1863. He was the founder of the Kunjara na Ayutthaya family, who retain the palace to this day and use it as a private home.

Pak Klong Talat ("market at the canal mouth") was formerly a floating market, the waterways filled in many years ago and the

Shophouses built in the late nineteenth century on the site of the old pottery village.

market activity now taking place in the streets and in the narrow *sois*. It was closed in 1893 when the area was being developed and the vendors moved to a market at Hua Lampong. In the years immediately following World War II the population of the city began to grow rapidly and the existing markets proved to be not enough to supply demand. The government provided the land to once again become a market, and placed it under the control of the Market Organisation. There are actually three separate markets wedged in here, although they all deal in flowers, fruit and vegetables, and collectively Pak Klong Talat is the most important wholesale flower market in Thailand. Dawn is the best time to visit, when the flowers arrive by boat and truck from all over Thailand and florists come to collect their supplies for shops, stalls and markets elsewhere in the city. The people who make a living by stringing and selling flower garlands also come here to buy sacks of jasmine and marigolds. As well as wholesale the market here is retail, with shops and stalls in the streets and alleys, and all offering flowers at low prices.

The market stretches all the way along the riverfront to the Memorial Bridge, a distance of around 200 metres (218 yards), the bridge itself being important to the transportation of market produce. On the corner of Saphan Phut Lane is a block of tall, imposing shophouses built in the time of Rama VII. They are different in style to the shophouses that were being built in Rattanakosin only a few years earlier, reflecting the changes in fashion and building technique heralded by the 1920s. Gone are the old sloping roofs, and in has come what must have been a very smart concrete parapet with a deck roof. The walls and windows are largely unadorned, letting the bulk of the building with its smoothly curving frontage speak for itself. Look a little closer and it can be seen that the design was originally for three storeys, and that a fourth has been built up over the roof deck at a later date. These shophouses face the piazza at which sits a statue of Rama I, the bridge having been built to commemorate the 150th anniversary of the Chakri dynasty. The statue was installed at the same time the bridge was opened in 1932: the design was by Prince Naris, while the statue was moulded and cast by Corrado Feroci. It is, however, a fanciful likeness, as are any of the first three Chakri kings and of King Taksin, images of the Siamese monarchs having been forbidden until the reign of Rama IV, the first of the great modernisers, when in 1856 an unknown photographer was allowed to photograph the king alongside Queen Dhepsirindhara.

On the other side of the piazza is the approach road for the Pokklao Bridge, which was opened to traffic in 1984, and next to this can be found a curious structure, a beautiful mansion painted yellow and white, set amongst trees and with a spacious forecourt protected by an elegant fence. There is a functioning clock in a central tower, and a Thai flag flies from the roof. There are no signs of life here, and when examined from the rear, the house, although it has an attractive leafy back garden, proves to be only a façade. When the bridge and roadworks were being constructed, Bangkok lost one of its architectural gems. Siam had issued its first stamps in 1883 and opened its first post office the same year, housed inside a mansion belonging to Phra Preecha Kolkarn. Almost exactly a century later, in 1982, the old mansion was demolished to make way for the approach road. Although it had ceased to be the postal headquarters in 1927, when the General Post Office opened on Charoen Krung Road, the building with its symmetrical Rama V-era façade and its tall clock tower was still firmly associated with the postal service and featured on a centenary stamp the year after its destruction. As part of the

The Memorial Bridge, originally a bascule span powered by electricity.

conservation plan for Rattanakosin, the frontage of the house was rebuilt to a smaller scale near its original site in 2004.

At the foot of the Memorial Bridge is Wat Ratchaburana, one of the oldest temples in Bangkok, having been built late in the Ayutthaya era by a Chinese trader named Liab. Initially known as Wat Cheen Liab (*Cheen* meaning "Chinese") it later became known as Wat Liab and gave its name to the power station that was built here on temple land. Electricity had been introduced to Siam in 1884 by Field Marshal Chao Phraya Surasakdi Montri, who had served as charge d'affaires at the Siamese Embassy in Paris and been greatly impressed with the illumination of the city by electric light. Returning to Bangkok, he attempted without success to raise interest in the possibilities of electricity. Realising that electric light had to be seen to be believed, he decided to introduce lighting to the army barracks, which is now the Ministry of Defence building and which was then being constructed on a site next to the Grand Palace. Selling some land he had inherited from his father to raise the finance, the field marshal commissioned one of his military trainers, an Italian named Mayola, to visit England and purchase the equipment. Mayola bought two generating sets and the necessary cabling, spending 14,400 baht, and had everything shipped to Bangkok. The generators were installed at the barracks, and a cable was strung across to the Grand Palace. Surasakdi Montri hung lights from the cable and switched them on for the king's birthday, 20th September. Thereafter, electricity was installed for lighting at the royal court and in the houses of the aristocracy, and eventually on selected streets. (Surasakdi Montri also imported the first motorcar into Siam, around the year 1900, and consequently has much to answer for.)

In 1887 the government had granted a concession for a horse-drawn tramway to a venture led by John Loftus and Andreas du Plessis de Richelieu, the trams running from the Grand Palace all the way to Bang Kolaem, at the southern end of Charoen Krung Road. The venture was not a success and was transferred to a Danish company, Bangkok Tramways Company, whose chief engineer and later managing director Aage Westenholz was able to harness the modest power supplies available to provide an electric tram service, beginning in January 1893. They were the first electric trams in Asia. In 1898 Richelieu obtained a fifty-year monopoly concession to provide electric power to Siam, and established the Siam Electricity Company. Westenholz was placed in charge and a power generating station was built on land owned by Wat Liab. The tram company was absorbed into Siam Electricity, and new tramlines were opened in other parts of the city. By the early 1920s there were seven lines covering almost fifty kilometres. Siam Electricity therefore owned

The **prang** *of Wat Liab, a temple that was almost obliterated during World War II.*

both the generating plant and the trams. In 1912, another generating plant was opened at Samsen by the Public Works Department to serve the northern side of the city, much of the output being used for the newly constructed Bangkok Waterworks and the new Dusit district built on what had been open land and orchards.

The Wat Liab power station, as Bangkok's primary source of electricity, was a distinctive landmark with multiple tall chimneys. The boilers were fuelled by paddy husk (there was an oil reserve on standby) transported direct to the plant in boatloads of ten tons at a time, the boats using a small inlet from the river to moor directly alongside. Suction pumps were used to unload the husk, the pumps being powerful enough to unload two boats in forty-five minutes. The husk was stored in a shed and transported to the boilers by means of four screw compressors. There were ten boilers, feeding steam to six turbines, each turbine driving an alternator that generated alternating current at 3,600 volts and 50 cycles. From the alternators the current went through a switchboard that distributed it via high-tension underground cables to feeders and thence all over town, providing lighting for streets, houses and offices, and power for installations such as the city waterworks and the Memorial Bridge lifting mechanism. The feeders supplied current to the generating plant for the tramways, where there were three electric motor generators that supplied the necessary 550-volt direct current for traction; from 1926 onwards, when it was electrified, they also supplied the Paknam Railway that ran the 21 kilometres (13 miles) from Hua Lampong to Paknam, the town at the mouth of the Chao Phraya.

Wat Liab, although continuing to be known as such, had officially been renamed Wat Ratchaburana in the reign of Rama I, when it had been designated as a royal temple, first class, the name being taken from a prominent temple at Sukhothai. Rama II built a cloister to enshrine some of the 162 Buddha images that he brought in from the provinces, eighty of which he placed in a new *wiharn*. Rama III added a *prang* that was decorated with coloured ceramic tiles, and in the reign of Rama IV the master artist Khrua In Khong, a pioneer in using European perspective in traditional Siamese art, added murals to the *ubosot*. In 1935, something very curious was added to Wat

Liab. The number of Japanese citizens in Bangkok had been increasing, and after making numerous requests they were finally given permission to build an ossuary in Bangkok to house the ashes of their dead. A monk named Fujii Shinsui, who was from the Shingon sect centre at Mount Koya and was then studying in Bangkok, conceived the idea of a three-storey concrete ossuary based on the Temple of the Golden Pavilion in Kyoto, and was given permission to build it in the grounds of Wat Liab. Funds were raised through the Japanese Association of Siam. A Buddha image was sent to the ossuary from a temple known as Ni Thai Ji, or Japan Thai Temple, in Japan's Nagoya province. Monk Fujii, still in Bangkok at the outbreak of the Pacific War in December 1941, was sent as a military chaplain to serve with the Japanese army during the invasion of Burma, leaving the ossuary in the care of an elderly monk named Chino and a student named Sasaki Kyogo. With the Japanese army occupying Siam, the electricity generating station at Wat Liab became a primary target for Allied bombers, and in April 1945, in the final stages of the war, the temple itself was hit and so badly damaged that it was deleted from the official list. Only the *prang* and, ironically, the Japanese ossuary survived.

In June of that year one of the most notorious Japanese military commanders arrived in Bangkok. Colonel Tsuji Masanobu had played a significant role in the massacre of Chinese in Singapore and in the Bataan Death March in the Philippines. In Burma he had been complicit in the execution of an Allied airman, whose liver was removed and cut up, and then roasted on skewers during a mess dinner. Although the other Japanese officers were unable to eat their portions, Tsuji finished his with great enthusiasm, declaring that it helped him to hate the enemy even more, and thus adding cannibalism to the list of war crimes that he faced upon the Japanese surrender by Emperor Hirohito on 15th August 1945. Tsuji had been in Bangkok to quell a likely uprising by the 150,000-strong Siamese army and police force, which was being kept in check by a garrison of only 10,000 Japanese. Now he was a fugitive. On August 17th he removed his uniform and went to the bombed-out ruins of Wat Liab, where at the ossuary he found the monks Chino and Sasaki. Disguising himself as a Buddhist monk and acquiring an identity card in the name of Aoki Norinbu, Tsuji took shelter in the vault. He wasn't to stay there for long. In the middle of September the British entered Siam. They heard rumours that Tsuji was disguised as a monk, and began searching for him. In the early hours of the morning on 29th October, Tsuji left the ossuary and made his way to a rendezvous with members of Chiang Kai Shek's Blue Shirt Society, who were operating out of an office on Surawong Road. Two days later, now disguised as a Chinese merchant in a white jacket, black trousers, white pith helmet and tinted glasses, he boarded a train at Hua Lampong and accompanied by two escorts made his way to Ubon. From there he crossed the Mekong in a canoe and went to Vientiane. He then made his way to Hanoi and on over the Chinese border to Chungking, the temporary capital and seat of Chiang Kai Shek's government. Tsuji arrived back in Japan in 1948, and managing to evade war crimes charges he became a prominent politician. He disappeared while on a trip to Laos in 1961, and was officially declared dead seven years later.

Wat Liab was rebuilt from local donations and in 1960 restored to its former prominence, the *ubosot* featuring very fine stucco mouldings undertaken by Sanga Mayura, who was one of the artists who painted the murals in the ordination hall of the Temple of the Emerald Buddha during the reign of Rama VII. The Japanese ossuary remains to this day, and since the war has always had a resident monk from the Mount Koya Shingon centre, usually sent on a three-year mission, and given a second ordination according to Thai Theravada Buddhist law in order to undertake religious ceremonies with the Thai monks. Sasaki Kyogo went on to become a respected scholar and university professor in Kyoto. His son Koden and grandson Kojun have both spent three-year residences at the ossuary. The Wat Liab generating plant had been put out of action in the April 1945 air raids that destroyed the temple, and to keep the trams running two Mitsubishi submarines that the Siamese had purchased in the late 1930s were moored in the river and their engines connected to the tram sub-station at Bangkok dock to run the generators. This was not very effective, but the Wat Liab plant was working again within a few months, and continued working until well after Siam Electricity's half-century concession

Suan Kularb School, designed for a new generation of administrators and leaders.

expired, after which both plants were taken under the wing of the new Metropolitan Electricity Authority (MEA), a state enterprise under the Ministry of Interior. A few years later, in 1961, the generating side of the business was transferred to a new organisation that later became the Electricity Generating Authority of Thailand, leaving the MEA in charge of distribution. The Wat Liab plant was closed down in 1965 when power generation was moved to the outskirts of the city, and the present MEA offices and a carpark were built on the site.

There are some districts of Bangkok so poetically named that one goes there full of anticipation, only to find something completely different. Suan Kularb, or the Rose Garden, is one. Although adjacent to the city's largest flower market, it has nothing to do with roses. What will be found is a handsome colonial style building occupying an entire block: the orange-ochre frontage with its regularly spaced green shutters seems to go on forever. This is Suan Kularb School, and it was the first educational institute in Siam to offer a modern curriculum.

Rama V, who realised that if his country was going to survive in the modern world it had to have a modern educational system, founded the school in 1882. Up to that time, schooling had been by monks in the temples. But Suan Kularb changed all that, training the new generation of civil servants, professionals and merchants who were to take Siam through an era of extraordinary growth and prosperity. The original school was not on this spot, however. It was located in the grounds of the Grand Palace, just a short distance away, on a plot of land in the compound named Suan Kularb. So the school took this name, and retained it when the move was made to these premises, built on land belonging to Wat Liab in 1910. The school is still known to students as "the long building" because for many years it was the longest building in Siam. Near the main entrance is an image of a many-armed elephant named Luang Phor Pu that is believed to house the protective spirit of the place, known to one and all affectionately as "Grandfather", and to whom the students make daily offerings of garlands. The school emblem depicts a book with a ruler, pen and pencil, a royal headdress and the initials of Rama V along with a bouquet of roses, and a gracious rose design is woven in amongst the lettering on the school gates. Suan Kularb, a male-only school, counts some of Thailand's greatest leaders in politics, law and business amongst its former pupils. This immediate locality has evolved into something of an educational district; Siam's first school of arts and crafts, Poh Chang College, opened directly next door to Suan Kularb in 1913, where it flourishes to this day, while directly across Tri Phet Road is the Rajamangala University of Technology and also a sizeable school belonging to Wat Liab. On the corner directly next to the temple stupa is a very unusual three-storey building with broad verandas and orange-painted balustrades. Originally the residence of Chao Phraya Rattanathibet and built in the latter years of Rama V, it was for many years used by the Ministry of Education. This well-maintained building is now home to the Agricultural Promotion Department.

There are several Indian communities in Bangkok, most notably around the junction of Silom and Charoen Krung, where they are prominent in the jewellery industry, and along the stretch of Sukhumvit Road from Soi 4 down to the 20s, where they invested in land when the road was little more than an elephant trail and where they now have vast property holdings. Nowhere, however, is there a greater concentration of Indian families and businesses than at Pahurat, the square of land bounded by Pahurat, Chakraphet, Tri Phet and Charoen Krung roads.

The Indians were not the first occupants of this area. When Bangkok was first established, and the Chinese merchants moved a little way downriver to what is now Chinatown to make way for the new construction work, the area that was to become Pahurat was stagnant, marshy ground. Around this time internal convulsions in Vietnam resulted in a large migration of Vietnamese to Siam, and while the Christian immigrants settled in the Portuguese Catholic community the Buddhists made this wilderness their home. For a while it was known as Ban Yuen, the Vietnamese village, but in 1898 came a fire so devastating that it completely cleared the land. A few years earlier, Princess Pahurat Manimai, the first-born daughter of Rama V and Queen Saovabha Bongsri, had died at the age of eight. The little girl had already been allocated properties under the royal patronage, and these were donated by her grieving parents to the building of a new road, one of many that were being built in Bangkok at this time. Pahurat Road ran ten metres wide across the land and was originally intended as a residential area for members of the royal court, who lived on its south side. A large number of Chinese shopkeepers and craftsmen, mainly jewellers, settled here to serve the community. On the northern side of the road, where the China World department store now stands, was Wang Burapha, a palace and fort built in the time of Rama I as part of the city's eastern defences and greatly enlarged in the 1820s. In the 1870s, with invasion from the east no longer a threat, the palace was rebuilt again, this time as a courtly residence for Prince Bhanurangsi Sawangwongse, a younger brother of Rama V, who was commander-in-chief of the Royal Siamese Army and founder of the Thai postal service, but who is probably best remembered by history as the father of the famous racing driver, Prince Bira. Alongside was a market named Ming Muang, which made fine quality clothing. To service this market a number of textiles suppliers began to move into the area, predominantly Indians, who have had a long trading history with Thailand.

Amongst the Indian immigrants were a large number of Sikhs, who began arriving in the final years of the nineteenth century, and who in their homeland have a special affinity with textiles. The first is recorded as Ladha Singh, who arrived in Bangkok in 1890, and by 1912 the community had grown to a size where, rather than holding prayers in their own homes, they established their own temple, or gurdwara. For this they rented a wooden house in Ban Moh, but this proved inadequate and in the following year the community leased a larger wooden house on the corner of Pahurat and Chakraphet roads, where they could conduct prayers and other ceremonies on a daily basis. By 1932, the Sikh community had become large and successful, and had raised 16,200 baht to purchase a piece of land on which to build a new gurdwara. A further 25,000 baht went towards the construction of a three-storey building, which opened in 1933 and was named Gurdwara Siri Guru Singh Sabha. During the World War II bombing by Allied forces, two 1,000-pound bombs aimed at the nearby Wat Liab power station and the Memorial Bridge missed their target, and fell through the roof of the gurdwada. Several hundred Sikhs were inside at the time, but miraculously the bombs failed to explode and no one was hurt. Other bombs exploding in the vicinity did, however, cause cracks to the building, and although they were patched up the decision was taken in 1979 to demolish the structure and build a larger one. The present gurdwara was completed two years later and is a six-storey structure standing on an area of 1,440 square metres (15,500 sq ft). It is the second largest Sikh temple outside of India. Although the golden dome and white upper storeys can be seen sailing above the rooftops, the building is completely hemmed in by the surrounding buildings and labyrinth of lanes, and unlike the traditional four entrances of a gurdwara, it has only three, the fourth being impractical because of the India Emporium, which adjoins the structure on the eastern side. The gurdwara is more than a temple, it is a self-contained community centre that includes a clinic, kindergarten, function rooms, and the traditional *langar* hall where vegetarian food is served as an act of hospitality and freely available to anyone.

Although the Sikhs form the majority of the population in Pahurat, which is now regarded as the centre of Thailand's wholesale and retail textile business, this is also the home of Hindus and Muslims, and is one of the most densely packed districts in Bangkok. The pavements are almost impassable at weekends, but even the pavements seem relatively clear when the alleys that run through Pahurat market are explored. Lined on both sides by textile shops and stalls, some are barely wide enough to allow two people to pass. But here one is in an Indian bazaar. There is Indian music, the smells of Indian spices and cooking, and of course the textiles and garments that can be purchased are dazzling in their variety and cheapness. Here too is chunky Indian jewellery, pictures of deities, and household shrines. Tiny restaurants serve food at prices that are next to nothing, and Bangkok's oldest Indian restaurant, Royal India, opened here half a century ago in the alley opposite the shrine to the Chinese goddess of mariners, San Chao Mae Tuptim, built by Fukkien Chinese who plied between Bangkok and South China. First registered as a place of religion in 1917, the shrine was destroyed during the Allied bombing and rebuilt in 1955.

A remnant of the original days of Ban Yuen is still here. Wat Dibaya Vari, to be found down a small alley behind the Nightingale-Olympic Department Store, was built in 1776 by Mu Thien Su, an ethnic Chinese immigrant from Vietnam. The temple was later abandoned, after the Vietnamese had left, but was renovated by a group of Chinese immigrants who settled here in the time of Rama v. A fire later badly damaged the temple and it was rebuilt after World War II. In the past few years it has been completely rebuilt, and given its cramped surroundings is surprisingly large, rising to a height of four storeys. Inside is an image of Kuan Yin, the goddess of mercy, and figures of several other Chinese deities. The name of the temple means "holy water" after the well above which it was built.

Wang Burapha fell into disuse in the 1940s and was pulled down in 1951, but this district, which to this day is known as Burapha, had in the preceding decade emerged as one of the trendiest spots in town. Ming Muang Market had developed into a popular public market for textiles and clothing: it took the form of a large square bordered on all sides by shophouses, with the open area covered by a roof, and hairdressers, clothes shops and restaurants all doing a thriving business. Thailand's first modern department store, Nightingale-Olympic, opened its doors opposite the market in 1936, occupying the first two floors of what was at the time the tallest building in the city, its frontage taking its design theme from an abacus. Today the store remains in a time warp, with aged mannequins and no air-conditioning, but

These craft are part of a fleet that keeps the canals and river clear of weed and litter.

still stocked as it always has been with imported products such as cosmetics, sporting goods and musical instruments. The store had been opened by a Chinese immigrant's son named Matti Niyomvanich, and remains family-owned to this day. In its prime the store employed almost a hundred staff and served the most affluent sector of society, being so well known and respected that it even had a mail order service for customers in the provinces. Today, once fashionable sportswear and equipment moulders in cabinets, none of the fashions seem to be later than the 1960s, and some of the goods have such a museum aura around them that they are no longer for sale. Most of the business now comes from the cosmetics, especially the Merle Norman brand, which started out in Los Angeles only a few years before Nightingale-Olympic opened, and on which some of the store's early fame was built.

The year 1932 saw the building almost opposite of the Chalerm Krung Royal Theatre, decreed by Rama VII as one of the landmarks to celebrate the 150th anniversary of the founding of the city. An imposing Art Deco structure, it was the first of its kind in Southeast Asia to have air-conditioning, and was fully equipped for the new talkies. Renovated in recent years, the theatre today specialises in the staging of *khon* masked performances, and is used for live concerts and classical plays. Also dating from the 1930s is the nearby On Lok Yun coffee shop, completely unchanged by its very elderly owner who has sought to retain the original ambience when this was one of the coolest hang-outs in town for young people shopping in the market and enjoying the theatre. Burapha remained a fashionable district through the 1950s and 60s, when the clearance of the old palace allowed the building of three new cinemas, the King, the Queen and the Grand, all showing the latest Hollywood films. Also dating from the early post-war years were the Merry King department store, and the opening of many new shops selling famous brand-name goods of the day, along with fashionable electric lighting and other interior décor products and consumer goods. Eventually, in the 1960s, Burapha was eclipsed by the construction of Siam Square, which became the trendy hangout of the day (a position it retains even now). Ming Muang Market was cleared away, and Old Siam Plaza built on the site. Originally the Plaza was meant to be a centre for jewellery and gold shops, of which there are many in this immediate neighbourhood, some being run by Chinese descended from the shopkeepers who moved in when Pahurat was built. This didn't work out but today Old Siam is a thriving shopping mall for clothes, so the spirit of the old market lives on.

Although there is much in the Pahurat area to tempt buyers, local and foreign alike, there is one thriving little district of shops where you almost certainly won't be able to buy anything. Along Burapha Road, east of the Chalerm Krung Royal Theatre, are a great number of gun shops. Anyone wishing to legally purchase a gun in Thailand will come to one of these shops, which also sell accessories and ammunition. Most of the guns sold are imported, as Thailand does not have a significant legitimate firearms industry, and there is a heavy import duty. Thais can buy guns, of course, but much official documentation is required, including proof of income, employment and address, along with fingerprinting and a background check for a criminal record. A foreign purchaser will need to supply the same information. Given that the whole purchasing process takes about a month, and that prices are deliberately high, there are few foreign customers. But for Thais with the right money and background, wishing to defend themselves and their homes, or who shoot as a hobby, this small area is where almost any kind of gun can be purchased.

Beyond the City Wall

In this neighbourhood, in what was once a forest temple, Prince Mongkut founded the Thammayut Buddhist movement, and nearby are two villages that housed Khmer and Vietnamese Christians who had fled their homeland.
Duration: 3 hours

Next to Phra Sumen Fort there is an alley, and a tiny bridge that leads over the second moat into the northern reaches of the old city, beyond the wall, where in the sunny little lane that runs behind Wat Sangwet stands a modest house, half brick and half timber, from which each weekend emanates the sound of traditional Thai music. Ban Duriyapraneet, or Bang Lamphu House as it is also known, is a music conservatory that has been in existence since 1898, established by Souk Duriyapraneet, a master of Thai traditional music, and still in the hands of the family today. Souk was from a family that included two other masters of music, and he studied under both of them. He married a girl named Thaem Choeiket, who was a member of a dance troupe that performed for the royal courts, and initially the couple lived on a raft house moored in the canal near to the fort. When they could afford to buy a house on land, they moved into this property at 83 Samsen 1, and the house remains little changed to this day. Souk was renowned for his skills on the xylophone and with various woodwind instruments, and he was part of the Royal Orchestra that

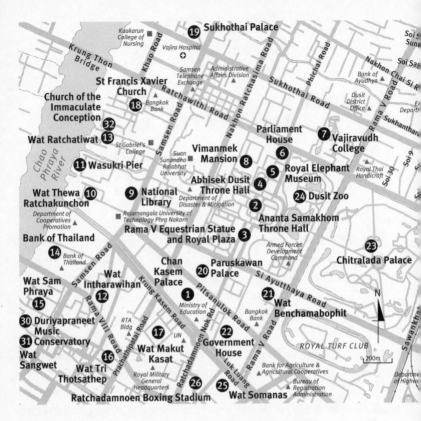

was formed in the reign of Rama VI. The couple had many children, and taught them all music, and from this grew the conservatory. The house has become a historical place for Thai music and musical instruments, and the Duriyapraneet Foundation was formed in 2003 to continue the traditions of Thai music and dance. This includes lessons every weekend, when children as young as six through to teenagers can participate. Classical dance lessons take place in the morning, while traditional Thai music lessons take place during the afternoon.

Wat Sangwet dates before the Bangkok era, although no one knows when it was built. The temple's original name was Wat Samcheen, which would indicate that three Chinese funded the building. Extensive renovations were carried out in the first, third and fourth reigns, and it was after the latter that the temple name

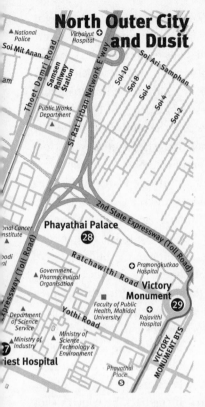

North Outer City and Dusit

▲ National Police
Soi Mit Anan
Vichaiyut Hospital
Soi Ari Samphan
Thoet Damri Road
am
Samsen Railway Station
Soi 10
Soi 8
Soi 6
Soi 4
Soi 2
St.Rat Urban Network E'way
Public Works Department ▲
2nd State Expressway (Toll Road)
nal Cancer nstitute
Phayathai Palace
28
bodi al
Ratchawithi Road
Government Pharmaceutical Organisation
Pramongkutkao Hospital
Victory Monument
xpressway (Toll Road)
Department of Science Service
Yothi Road
Faculty of Public Health, Mahidol University
29
Ministry of Industry ▲
Ministry of Science Technology & Environment
Rajavithi Hospital
7
iest Hospital
Phayathai Place
VICTORY MONUMENT BTS

was changed to Wat Sangwet. A quiet neighbourhood temple, a royal temple third grade, it has the unhappy distinction of being set on fire in 1869 when a blaze that started in a nearby noodle shop devastated the area. Rama V ordered the reconstruction, which is the form the temple takes today. Threading our way through these little lanes will take us to Wat Sam Phraya, the name indicating this temple was built by three noblemen. Another temple that dates back to the late Ayutthaya era, it was restored in the time of Rama III and has a particularly fine Chinese-style gable decorated with porcelain to form a floral design, and a Reclining Buddha image in the *ubosot*.

To complete a trio of threes, three members of the royal family built Wat Tri Thotsathep, on the other side of Samsen Road. Prince Supradit, a son of Rama IV, intended to build this temple, which was to be located near his palace. He passed away in 1862 before the work could begin, and so Prince Nopphawong, another of the king's sons, took it up. He passed away in 1867, before the building was complete, so Rama IV himself completed the work. The temple name translates as "Temple Built by Three Deities". There are three Buddha images in the *ubosot*, the two standing figures having been supplied by the king; the clothes they are wearing belonged to the two princes. The temple is royal third grade, and it has splendour in the marble and granite used in the construction, the soaring golden *chedi*, and ornate golden detailing to the roof and the window frames. The murals have recently been painted by national artist Chakrabhand Posayakrit.

Follow Samsen Road northwards and under the elevated expressway is a temple that because of the highway structure and the surrounding buildings is almost obscured. Only by entering the slip road on the right does Wat Intharawihan become visible, which is odd, really, as the temple's main attraction is an immense Buddha figure in the compound, standing 32 metres (105 ft) high, and under other circumstances it would be dominating the landscape. Popularly known as Wat In, the temple dates back to the late Ayutthaya period, when it was known as Wat Bang Khunphrom Nok, after the name of the locality in which it stands. Rama I provided land in this area for the settlement of Lao prisoners of war, and the temple was renovated by a nobleman named Chao Inthawong, who also arranged for a priest from Vientiane to be installed as abbot. The temple took its new name from Chao Inthawong. Building of the Buddha figure began in 1867 but the work was not completed for another sixty years, in 1927. The idea of building the enormous structure, which is made of brick and stucco, was that of the temple's abbot, Ajarn Toh. He was already elderly when the work began, and died at the foot of the image when he had gone to inspect it one night in 1871. A bust of the abbot, now encrusted with gold leaf, is placed near the entrance to the temple. The Buddha is a standing figure, holding an alms bowl, and there is a structure at the back by which devotees can climb and add pieces of gold leaf to the body. The image is named Luang Phor To. The flame-like topknot contains relics of the Buddha, which were donated by the government of Sri Lanka and placed there in 1978.

In 1982, when the city of Bangkok celebrated its 200th anniversary, restoration works were carried out and the image was decorated with Italian golden mosaic tiles. Every day worshippers visit the temple complex to make offerings, traditionally bringing gifts of mackerel, a boiled egg and a garland of flowers to place at the enormous toes of the statue. The *sema* boundary markers around the *ubosot* are unusual in that they are supported by small *nagas*. Inside the *ubosot* are wall murals depicting scenes of daily life in Siam, and the area behind the *ubosot* has statues of Hindu deities and of Chao Mae Kuan Yin, the goddess of mercy. This, incidentally, is one of the

The building of the enormous Buddha image at Wat In took sixty years to complete.

centres in Bangkok for making and selling amulets, a practice that appears to have started as a way of funding the construction of the image, as Wat In is a civil, and not a royal, temple.

Our way now takes us across the third moat, the final line of defence around the city, although when it was dug in the time of Rama IV in 1851, the threat of invasion had almost vanished and the canal was primarily for transport and drainage. At the mouth of the canal, on the far bank, is Wat Thewa Ratchakunchon, a temple with an outstanding sky-blue fresco in the *ubosot*, angels floating in the firmament around the golden Buddha image that almost fills the small hall. The temple has some particularly fine residential architecture in its grounds, and is also home to the Golden Teak Museum, a structure brought down from the north, and whose glowing golden teak interior forms an exhibition area for the display of Buddhist artifacts from Sri Lanka and sculptures of renowned monks from the Rattanakosin period.

Rama IV planned to build temples all along the bank of the outer moat, as had been done in Ayutthaya. Wat Makut Kasat and Wat Somanas were therefore built as new temples and are the only two temples in Rattanakosin that have two rings of *sema*, or boundary

Wat Ratchatiwat, where Prince Mongkut resided before he became Rama IV.

stones. The first ring, called the *maha sema*, is placed within niches in the temple walls, while the second ring, the *khantha sema*, surrounds the *ubosot*. In temples that have two rings of *sema*, the monks can perform religious ceremonies in both the *ubosot* and the *wiharn*. At Wat Makut Kasat, the gables and the door and window frames are decorated with the royal crown insignia of Rama IV. The murals inside the *ubosot* depict scenes from stories in the Pali Canon about the Buddha's male and female disciples, along with illustrations of meditation techniques and commandments, while Khmer incantations are inscribed on the door and window panels. Rama IV dedicated Wat Somanas to Queen Somanas, his consort, who had died at the beginning of his reign aged only 17. Wat Somanas stands on twelve acres of land, with moats on three sides and the outer city moat in front of the compound. Both of these temples have the same distinctive layout, with the *ubosot, wiharn,* cloister and *chedi* located in the middle, and two clusters of monks' dwellings one on each side.

The murals at Wat Somanas omit the life story of the Buddha and instead depict a literary masterpiece from the time of Rama II, and are considered to be amongst the finest works from the fourth reign, using European techniques to portray the sky, trees, and the lives of ordinary people.

A little way further along the riverbank, on the other side of a small inlet that runs beside the National Library, is Wat Ratchatiwat, its magnificent teak sermon hall regarded as being one of the finest examples of teak construction in Thailand. Originally an Ayutthaya-era temple named Wat Samor Rai, this was a forest temple in the time when the area was woodland and marshy ground, and Prince Mongkut came to reside here when he was a monk. Mongkut began his reform movement known as Thammayut Nikaya at this temple. He had entered the priesthood in 1824 and spent several years in different parts of Siam, becoming aware that there were serious discrepancies between the rules given in the Pali Canon and the actual practices of Siamese monks. Taking up residence at this then-remote temple, in 1833 he founded the Thammayut movement that endeavoured to purify monastic discipline and remove all non-Buddhist elements, such as animism and superstitious beliefs. Monks of this sect are expected to eat only one meal a day, the food being gathered during the traditional alms round. The temple is regarded as the birthplace of Thammayut, and Mongkut continued to promote the reforms when he became abbot of Wat Bowon Niwet, in the northern part of Rattanakosin Island, in 1836. When he became Rama IV he founded the first new temple to be devoted to Thammayut; named Wat Ratchapradit, it is a small temple in the corner of Saranrom Park, opposite the Grand Palace, and the king financed its construction from his own funds. The passing of the Sangha Act of 1902 has established Thammayut as the second of Thailand's Theravada denominations. Wat Samor Rai was renamed as Wat Ratchatiwat during the fourth reign, the name meaning "temple where the king resides". In the time of Rama V the temple structure had deteriorated, and so the king directed Prince Naris to reconstruct the Khmer-style *ubosot*, but retain the original walls because of the significance of the building in the history of the Thammayut sect. The murals were done using the European fresco technique and depict the story of Phra Vessandara, the Buddha's tenth reincarnation. Prince Naris prepared the drafts and Carlo Rigoli, an Italian artist brought out to

Siam to paint the frescoes inside the dome of the Ananta Samakhom Throne Hall, followed his designs to create a work that evokes the frescoes that can be found in European monasteries, using light and form to give a realism to the scenes and images. The *sala karn prian*, or sermon hall, situated on the other side of the access lane is constructed entirely of teak and can accommodate up to one thousand people. Wat Ratchatiwat retains something of its former rural charm, the temple being set in garden surroundings on the bank of the river, with the graceful buildings of the temple school in the leafy grounds.

Along the riverbank in front of the temple, running northwards from the landing pier, is a footpath that takes us over a small canal and past a carefully tended Christian graveyard. Following the lane around the cemetery brings us to the rear of a Romanesque church, but before going to the front, pause and examine the small building on the right. It is a chapel with three windows and a gabled roof, a plain structure with elements of Thai and European styles blended, and looks as if a congregation of twenty would fill the building entirely. This is the oldest Catholic church in Bangkok. The Church of Immaculate Conception was built in 1674, during the time of Louis Laneau, the first bishop of Siam. This was the height of the Ayutthaya period, and King Narai was following a policy of closer relationships with the European powers. Bishop Laneau was head of the Roman Catholic mission in Indochina, and was headquartered at Ayutthaya. A large number of Catholic priests, many of them Portuguese, were travelling to and from Ayutthaya during this period, and a group of them founded a small community on the bank of the river, where they built the small chapel that we see today.

At that time there were only about 600 Siamese Catholics, according to Catholic records, but there were many more of other nationalities within the country, including the Portuguese and other Europeans, along with Vietnamese, Japanese and Chinese. This was, of course, before the founding of the Portuguese Catholic community at Thonburi, and so it represented a firm foothold for the lower Chao Phraya region. The Catholic priests had reason to believe they could greatly increase their number of Siamese converts, and this

The Church of Immaculate Conception, founded by Portuguese missionaries.

small community was near to the garrison town of Thonburi and to numerous other scattered settlements, and conveniently on the route to Ayutthaya.

The French precipitating the siege of Bangkok in 1688 was an enormous setback for the Catholic missionaries and for Europeans in general. They were no longer welcome in Siam, except for the Portuguese, who were so well assimilated that they were regarded almost as Siamese. The era of King Taksin still saw a rocky relationship with the Christians, again except for the Portuguese, and so the small Immaculate Conception parish on the riverbank continued, and was known as the Portuguese Village, Ban Portugal. In 1785, just three years after Bangkok had been founded, there was a persecution of the small community of Christians in Cambodia, and a number of them fled to Siam, where Rama I granted them sanctuary and directed that, as Christians, they should settle in the Christian district of Ban Portugal. Catholic records state that in 1785 there were 379 Cambodian Catholics at the Church of Immaculate Conception, a sizeable community, large enough for the village to become known as Ban Khmer, the name by which it is still known today. Eventually the tiny chapel was inadequate for the congregation, and Monsignor

Jean-Baptiste Pallegoix built a second church in 1832, rebuilding it as the present structure in 1847. The original chapel is known as Bot Noi, or Small Chapel, and it has been used as a storeroom and as a museum, although following a recent restoration it is unclear what the next phase is going to be. The people of Ban Khmer are a mix of Portuguese, Khmer and Thai blood, and their heritage can be traced in certain types of food they eat and words they use that have migrated into their dialect.

Retracing our steps past the cemetery brings us to the rear of another Christian church, this one far larger. This is Ban Yuen, the Village of the Vietnamese, and St Francis Xavier Church. There have been several Vietnamese settlements named Ban Yuen, but this is the largest and most enduring of them all. During the time of Rama I there had been a significant migration of Vietnamese to Siam, both Christian and Buddhist, and while the Buddhists settled in the Pahurat district, on the fringe of Chinatown, the Christians had settled on land adjacent to Ban Khmer. In 1835, about 1,500 Annamite Christians fleeing persecution in Vietnam sought asylum in Siam, and joined the Yuen village next to the Khmers. Rama III granted permission for them to build a church, and in 1834, under the direction of Msgr Pallegoix, a bamboo church was erected and named St Francis Xavier Church, although it was perhaps inevitably known as Wat Yuen. Msgr Pallegoix lived at the Immaculate Conception Church, where he had established a friendship with the princely monk Mongkut, who resided at the neighbouring Wat Samor Rai. Pallegoix had a deep knowledge of science, mathematics and languages, and the monk had an insatiable desire to learn all he could of the West. At the same time, Pallegoix wanted to learn all he could of the Siamese and Pali languages, and the two men enjoyed a mutually rewarding intellectual friendship that endured for many years. When Mongkut became King Rama IV he was happy to donate more land to Ban Yuen for the building of a larger church, and the St Francis Xavier that we see today was completed in 1867.

The community of Ban Yuen today still has a distinctive quality. This is partly due to the size of the church and its bell tower, and the surrounding church buildings, especially the Coupeau Building,

A statue of the founder of St Gabriel's College, Brother Martin de Tours.

designed in a European style and used as a gathering place for priests and for religious ceremonies. Rama V purchased the bronze statue of Jesus giving sight to the blind man, when on his Europe visit in 1897 the king had visited the foundry in Florence where it was cast. He at first placed it in the Chakri Throne Hall, and when Amphon Throne Hall in Dusit was complete he moved it there. In 1945 the statue was moved out onto the lawn, and then in 1949 transferred to St Xavier. Many of the houses in Ban Yuen are very old, with a mix of timber and stone, and there are several restaurants and food shops selling Vietnamese food. As with the Khmer community, members of the Ban Yuen community feel themselves to be Thai but are aware of their Vietnamese heritage.

One thing very much apparent in these two Christian communities is the way in which the missionaries established schools, because the two neighbourhoods together have a large number of schools and colleges, along with a school for ballet, a school for piano lessons, and a number of kindergartens. Walk through the lanes of this area in the late afternoon, and you will be in a sea of schoolchildren and college students of every age and stage and grade. Conception School, St Francis Xavier Convent, Joan D'Arc School,

St Francis Xavier Church, in the centre of Ban Yuen, the Vietnamese village.

and on Samsen Road, the handsome pink building of St Gabriel's College, with the statue of its founder almost certainly the only statue in Bangkok that wears a pair of genuine spectacles. At the back of the nearby carpark is a stretch of ancient walling that was once the garden of an old palace, long gone, and the nearby Suan Sunantha Teacher Training College was originally another palace.

Almost Heaven

*Dusit, built for the royal family when the centre of
Bangkok became too congested, is a remarkable blending of
European and Siamese design, created largely by a team of
Italian architects and engineers.*
Duration: 3 hours

Since 1782 and the founding of Bangkok as the capital, the
monarchs of the Chakri dynasty had resided at the Grand
Palace. The palace had been the first building erected in the
new city, and all else had stemmed from there. Many of the
buildings within the palace compound, and the palaces built nearby, also housed government departments. Bangkok was not a large
city. Most of the transportation was by canal and river, as the first
roads were not built until eighty years after the city was founded.
For the first four kings the Grand Palace had served as an effective
residence and centre of government. During the reign of Rama v,
however, many new structures were built inside the palace walls,
both to accommodate the increasing needs of state and to house
the growing population of the royal court. As a result the palace
grounds became very crowded, and stiflingly hot during the summer months, with the passage of air being blocked by the closely
clustered new buildings. Sanitation was a significant problem, and
epidemics spread easily within the crowded compound. Siam was
developing and any further works were clearly not possible.

Rama v made his first visit to Europe in 1897, the first European visit by any Siamese monarch. He became convinced that a new palace needed to be built, along with a series of other palaces to house members of the royal family and the ministries of state. For this he would need an area of land outside the city, and he would also need foreign expertise in architecture and engineering. The king, to escape the confines of the Grand Palace, had been fond of visiting the area between the third moat, dug in his father's time, and the Samsen Canal, to the north of the city, which at that time was orchards and rice fields. The king bought land in this locality, using money from the privy purse, and himself cut down the first trees in 1899 to inaugurate building work on what he named Suan Dusit, the Celestial Garden. To link the Grand Palace and Suan Dusit, the king directed the construction of Ratchadamnoen Avenue, a leafy European-style boulevard with offices and shops on either side. Bicycles had been introduced into Siam at this time, and Rama v was a keen cyclist: cycling trips were undertaken by the king and members of the royal family during the cool of the evening to inspect progress, and with the first temporary buildings in place only a year after work had begun, the king soon began to enjoy staying at his new royal garden. As motorcars began to arrive in Siam, the processions of bicycles soon became processions of cars, much to the amazement of local residents.

The first permanent structure at Suan Dusit was Vimanmek Mansion, a marvel of design built entirely from teak, with not a single nail being used. Originally used as a summerhouse on the island of Sichang, just off the coast of Chonburi, where the king enjoyed spending time with his family, the structure had been known as Pha Chuthathut Palace. During the Franco-Siamese War of 1893, which led to Siam ceding Laos to France and thus greatly expanding the Indochine territories, the French had briefly occupied the island. The summerhouse was abandoned, and fell into disuse. In 1900 the king had the building dismantled and re-erected at Dusit, where it was renamed Vimanmek and used as a royal palace for five years until the completion of Amphorn Satharn Villa in 1906. Vimanmek Mansion has an elaborate architectural style that reflects a Western influence. The building has two right-angled wings, each being 60 metres (196 ft) long and 20 metres (65 ft) high, with the structure being three storeys in height except for the part where the king resided, which is octagonal and has four-storeys. Vimanmek is today a popular museum, with thirty-one exhibition rooms, many of which maintain the atmosphere of the past, especially the bedrooms, the audience chamber and the bathrooms.

Suan Dusit reveals an extraordinary flowering of architecture, combining Thai and European styles and utilising materials and techniques that were just coming into use at that time in Europe. More than any other nationality, however, it is the Italians who have left their indelible stamp upon this garden district. It doesn't appear to have been planned that way, but to have evolved by chance, starting several years before the king's first visit to Europe, where he was to become enamoured by the artistic and architectural genius of the Italians. In 1890 a young civil engineer and architect named Carlo Allegri had arrived in Bangkok to work for the building firm Grassi Brothers. There were few Italians in Siam at this time, and Allegri quickly befriended a Piedmont nobleman named Colonel Gerolamo Emilio Gerini, who had a few years earlier been appointed by Rama V as a military instructor for the Royal Guard. The engineer was thus drawn into royal circles, and when he was offered the position of assistant chief engineer with the newly-created Ministry of Public Works, under the direction of Prince Naris, he readily accepted. There had been no government agency responsible for public projects before that time, foreign contractors having carried out projects on an ad hoc basis.

Allegri now found himself in what must have been an exhilarating position, although not at first an easy one. He was the sole Italian amongst a number of British and German engineers, and spoke, literally, only phrasebook English. But the scope of the work more than compensated. The king, as absolute monarch and with a very clear vision of what he wanted, was decreeing an endless stream of grand projects: palaces, villas, bridges, roads and railways. Within two years Allegri had been appointed chief engineer, where he was involved in all the major building projects during the second half

Venice of the East: Italian bridges span the canal at the Marble Temple.

of the fifth reign. Along with the best materials from Europe he was also able to hire architects, engineers and craftsmen, and the number of Italians working in the departments responsible for engineering, architecture, sculpture, marble work and fresco painting grew to around forty. Of these, there are several names that can be attached to some of the most outstanding buildings and monuments in Bangkok today. Mario Tamagno, who arrived in 1900 and stayed in the city on a twenty-five year contract. Annibale Rigotti, who arrived in 1907 and spent two periods in Siam, the second in the mid-1920s. Ercole Manfredi, who arrived in 1909 and who was to remain in Bangkok for the remainder of his long life, passing away in 1973 at the age of 89. Most enduring of all the names, perhaps, is that of Corrado Feroci, who was invited to Siam in 1923 to teach sculpture at the Fine Arts Department, and who designed and sculpted many of Thailand's best-known monuments. Feroci stayed in Thailand for the rest of his life, becoming a Thai citizen during World War II to avoid arrest by the occupying Japanese army. He was known thereafter as Silpa Bhirasri. He founded Silpakorn University and is regarded as the father of modern art in Thailand. His birthday, 15th September, is observed each year as Silpa Bhirasri Day.

The best known of all the works in Dusit was also one of the first. Wat Benchamabophit, Temple of the Fifth King, the Marble Temple, so named for the gleaming white Carrara marble with which it is clad, is a remarkable blending of Siamese and Italian art forms. A Buddhist temple laid out in Christian cruciform plan, Wat Ben as the Thais know it was begun in 1900, and followed the tradition that a Siamese king should always have a royal temple adjacent to his palace. There had been a small temple in the Dusit area, Wat Laem, but this was demolished to make way for the garden development. Rather than replace it, the king decided upon a completely new temple that was in grandeur to equal the palaces. Prince Naris, who was artistically gifted, created the design, and Mario Tamagno was the architect. Allegri came up with the idea of white Carrara marble cladding and pillars, and the marble courtyard. The red-painted iron bridges that arch so elegantly over the canal are stamped with the name of their Italian manufacturer, and even the streetlamps have a Venetian touch to them.

Unlike the older temple complexes in Bangkok, the Marble Temple has no central *wiharn* or *chedi*, having instead many smaller buildings that combine European influences such as stained-glass windows with traditional Thai religious architecture. The main *ubosot* contains a golden Buddha statue against an illuminated blue backdrop, and the ashes of Rama v are buried beneath the image. Beyond the *ubosot* is a cloister containing fifty-two bronze Buddha images in many different styles, representing various Buddhist countries and regions, and behind the cloister is a large bodhi tree, grown from a cutting brought from Bodhgaya, where the Buddha found Enlightenment. Unlike other temples, monks do not go out seeking alms but are instead visited by merit-makers at dawn each morning.

As the architectural splendours of Dusit began to rise out of the alluvial mud, orchestrated by Carlo Allegri at the peak of his creative powers, his personal life was unravelling. Two of the children he had by his Siamese wife died young, one of malaria and one by drowning in the little stream that flowed through the grounds of their house on Surawong Road. His wife died soon after of fever. Allegri began a long slide into opium addiction, frequenting the divans on

Chinatown's Sampeng Lane. The project that, by his own account, was to bring him back out of his decline was Rama v's grandest of all: the Ananta Samakhom Throne Hall was to be a majestic throne hall that would rival the Renaissance buildings he had so admired on his two visits to Italy. Working to Indian ink drawings supplied by the monarch, Allegri as chief engineer along with Tamagno and Rigotti as architects drew up the plans for a baroque structure with a Latin crossplan, topped with a central cupola clad in copper and placed at the point where nave and transept intersected. The site, like much of Dusit, was a swamp. Allegri had decided that in engineering terms the massive structure had to be floated, and he devised a series of caissons that were combined with hundreds of piles created by drilling ten metres below the surface using a special drill named a Compressol, supplied by a French firm, and filling them with concrete.

The foundation stone was laid in the early morning of 11th November 1908, the opening day of the fortieth anniversary of the fifth reign. The materials began to arrive from Europe: marble, granite and ironwork from Italy, bronze and copper from Germany, and textiles and carpets from England, much of it being unloaded at the new Wasukri Pier that had been built in 1909 as a landing stage for the royal barges. Many of the elements were prefabricated, and in late 1909 Rigotti went back to Italy to coordinate the production and delivery. A year later Galileo Chini, a Florentine painter and ceramist, was engaged to execute the monumental frescoes for the interior. Within days of Chini signing his contract for the thirty-month job, there came dismal news. Rama v had always known that the Ananta Samakhom Throne Hall was going to take many years to complete. He had made it a practice to carefully monitor the progress, frequently visiting the site and chiding anyone he felt was being tardy. He had joked to Chao Phraya Yomarat, who was supervising the works, that if it were completed in ten years he would relinquish the throne and become a grass-gatherer on an elephant trail. A year later he was dead, passing away at the Amphorn Sathan Residential Hall in Dusit on 23rd October 1910 of kidney disease. Chini arrived in a very subdued city. Work continued under Rama vi, but slowed

The Ananta Samakhom Throne Hall, centrepiece of Dusit, was built on swampland.

down after the outbreak of World War I, which delayed shipments from overseas, and the Ananta Samakhom Throne Hall was completed in 1916.

On 24th June 1932, the Equestrian Plaza in front of the throne hall was the rallying point for thousands of supporters of the People's Party, following the bloodless coup two days previously that had terminated the absolute monarchy and declared a constitutional monarchy. The first constitution was signed in the Ananta Samakhom Throne Hall on 10th December the same year. The equestrian statue of Rama V had been erected in 1908 from funds raised by the people and had been cast in Paris by a French craftsman. Now a plaque was affixed to the ground commemorating the date of the rally. The Ananta Samakhom Throne Hall was appropriated as the permanent meeting place of the National Assembly, until in 1970 a plot of land was requested for the building of a new legislature, as the throne hall was no longer large enough to accommodate the growing assembly and its secretariat. Rama IX granted land immediately north of the throne hall for the building of the new Parliament House, and with the completion of this building the Ananta Samkhom Throne Hall was returned to the king. It is today still used for the ceremonial opening of parliament. Thus did Suan Dusit pass naturally from the seat of the absolute monarchy to the centre of the constitutional monarchy and the democratic government of modern-day Thailand.

Rama VI expanded Suan Dusit further eastwards by the laying out in 1913 of another garden called Suan Chitralada. Within this garden he had a two-storey residential villa built and named it Chitralada Royal Villa. During the reign of Rama IX, the villa became the primary residence of the king and the royal family. Known generally as Chitralada Palace, and surrounded by high walls and a tree-shaded moat, this is a working palace, for within the four-square-kilometre (980-acre) compound a host of royal projects have been initiated. There is a small dairy farm, a fish farm, a demonstration paddy field and a rice mill. Agricultural research centres have been founded, and sustainable production methods explored, along with ways to improve poor soil and to protect endangered plant species. This part of Suan Dusit has retained its pastoral quality more than any other, enhanced by the greenery of the Royal Turf Club on the other side of Si Ayutthaya Road. A railway line runs alongside Chitralada from the confluence of lines slightly further north at Bang Sue, and the palace has its own private station, a modest rural halt with an Italian design, built in 1920 to replace an original wooden structure that had been built under the direction of Rama V.

Carlo Allegri returned to Italy in 1916. This, however, was not the end of the Italian story, for Tamagno and Manfredi stayed on, while Rigotti later returned to Bangkok on another contract. One of the most spectacular buildings during this time was Norasingha Mansion, commissioned by Rama VI in 1923 for Chao Phaya Ramarakop, one of the leading figures during the sixth reign, who was head of the army and the navy. Today it is Government House, containing the Prime Minister's Office. The king wished it to be based on the Palazzo Ca' d'Oro at Venice, and the classic Venetian styling can be seen in the cloverleaf design over the windows and galleries, the marble pillars and bronze sculptures in the arcade, the Gothic motifs of the arches, and the symmetry of the inner courtyard. Rama VI passed away two years after the work had started, and Rigotti, his contract finished, went back to Italy in 1926. This

highly ornate and complex work, which consists of three separate mansions, halted and it remained unfinished for several years.
Work resumed in the early years of the constitutional monarchy,
under Field Marshal Plaek Phibunsongkhram, the prime minister,
with Manfredi responsible for the architectural design and Corrado
Feroci executing the interior designs and the sculptural work. The
rooster motifs that can be found in the windows and under the eaves
of the Thai Khufa Building, which had been named by Field Marshal
Plaek and forms the front of the structure, refer to the Year of the
Rooster, the prime minister's birth year. Government House is one
of the great defining works of Suan Dusit, yet it has attracted con-
troversy over the years for the perceived transplanting of a classical
Italian style into an entirely different culture. One of the main critics
was its architect. Late in his life, still in Bangkok, Ercole Manfredi
gave an interview to a local newspaper. He was always regarded as
an eccentric, even his daughter Maly remarking that he was "an odd
number", and he tended to be cantankerous and bluntly spoken. He
was dismissive of his work on Norasingha Mansion. "I built it in the
Venetian style because I thought that Bangkok was the Venice of the
East," he told the Bangkok Post during the 1967 interview. "Now I
am so ashamed of it. It is just not right for this climate."

Many of the other royal palaces and mansions of Dusit have been
given over to government use or are used by the armed forces, but
many have become museums. One of the first permanent works to
be completed at Dusit was the Abhisek Dusit Throne Hall, a single-
storey ornate building with carved floral motifs on panels adorn-
ing the gables and eaves. Completed in 1904, it was used for official
receptions of foreign dignitaries. The hall fell into disuse after 1932,
but after decades of neglect it was restored in the late 1980s and
became a museum dedicated to Thai handicrafts. Suan Dusit's former elephant stables have been converted into the Royal Elephant
National Museum, with displays on the use of elephants in war, and
the ceremonies that have surrounded the fabled white elephants.
Chan Kasem Palace, built in 1909–11 for Crown Prince Vajiravudh,
who succeeded his father as Rama VI before he had time to take up
residence, now houses the Ministry of Education. Paruskawan Palace,

built in 1905 for Prince Chakrabongse, is now the headquarters of the Metropolitan Police Bureau and the National Intelligence Agency. Ladawan Palace, built in 1907 for Prince Yugala, who was the Prince of Lopburi, fell into a sad state of repair in the 1990s after years of neglect, but it has recently been restored by the Crown Property Bureau, who use it as their headquarters. Sometimes known as the Red Palace, because of the crimson wall that encircles the estate, Ladawan was designed by one of the lesser-known Italian architects, G Bruno, and is a two-storey villa surmounted by a four-storey octagonal watchtower. Upon Rama v's return from his second European tour in 1908 he expanded the palace northward, creating an additional private garden called Suan Sunantha, in honour of his first consort Queen Sunantha, who had drowned in a boating accident in 1880, at age 19. The garden became the setting of residential houses belonging to the king's consorts and children and is now the campus of Suan Sunantha Rajabhat University. The Chulachomklao Royal Military Academy, once a training school for army officers, has been absorbed into the Royal Thai Army's headquarters and, with the academy now relocated outside of Bangkok, the premises have become the Royal Thai Army Museum. Directly opposite is Ratchadamnoen Boxing Stadium, built by order of Field Marshal Plaek Phibunsongkhram during changes that were being made along Ratchadamnoen Avenue to create more office space. Work began in 1941 by an Italian contractor named Imprese Italiane All' Estero-Oriente, but the stadium was delayed by the war and the subsequent lack of building materials. Completed in 1945, the stadium has become a national institution for the staging of Muay Thai contests.

Royal buildings that were not palaces but residential halls, mainly for the female members of the family, have been successfully converted into a number of specialist museums dedicated to subjects that include the prehistoric pottery of Ban Chiang, a collection of ancient fabrics and silk, the personal clothing and belongings of Rama v, the photographic work and oil paintings of Rama ix, a display of antique clocks and timepieces, a large display of pottery retrieved from Chinese and Vietnamese junks wrecked off the coast of Rayong and Chantaburi between the fifteenth and eighteenth centuries, and a collection of royal carriages that evokes the brief era between roads being built in Bangkok, and the advent of the motor-car. The most popular and successful of all the conversions is that of Khao Din Wana, originally a botanical garden established by Rama V, which was given to the government in 1938 by Rama VIII to create Dusit Zoo, a favourite place for Bangkok families, with its extensive animal collection, picnic areas, playgrounds and lake with pedalos.

On the western fringe of Dusit, next to the river, behind a very long, handsome and ornate fence, is the Bank of Thailand. The offices are housed in a modern building, but behind this are two palaces that the bank inhabited from 1945 onwards, soon after it was founded. Bangkhunphrom Palace was the residence of Prince Paribatra Sukhumbhand, the thirty-third son of Rama V. Mario Tamagno was in charge of the architectural design while Carlo Allegri was chief engineer and Emilio Gollo, who had joined as his deputy in 1899, was responsible for the structural engineering. Construction of the main building, Tamnak Yai, started in 1901 and was completed in 1906. Tamagno has used rococo and baroque styling, with a variety of window shapes and exuberant stucco mouldings, topped with a mansard roof into which dormer windows have been set.

There is a second building, Tamnak Somdej, which was built later, around 1913, for the prince's mother Queen Sukhumala Marasri. This time German architect and engineer Karl Dohring provided the design, although Italian artist Carlo Rigoli created the interior frescoes. During Prince Paribatra's thirty years of residence, Bangkhunprom Palace became a salon for artists, writers and musicians. After the 1932 revolution, the prince went into exile in Bandung, Indonesia, where he enjoyed gardening and music until his death. The palace was turned into government offices and became the office of the central bank in 1945, and since 1992 has housed the Bank of Thailand Museum. The second palace behind the bank premises is Devavesm Palace, initially the residence of King Rama V's younger brother Prince Devawongse Varophakarn, and designed and constructed under the supervision of British architect Edward Healey. The main mansion is neo-classic, using elements of Greek and Roman architecture. After the revolution the Ministry of Public

Health was based in the palace before it was taken over by the bank, which now uses the building for official receptions and as office space for the museum.

Northwards along the riverbank is Sukhothai Palace, the residence of Prince Prajadhipok, before he became King Rama VII. The prince was the seventy-sixth son of Rama V, and had been born in the Grand Palace in 1893. He was sent to study military science in England. When he returned to Bangkok, he became a lieutenant colonel in the Royal Guards, and later was appointed head of army general staff. His father being dead by this time, the prince's brother had become Rama VI. The king granted the prince a parcel of land out on Samsen Road, near to the green fields of Bang Sue, on the bank of the Samsen canal where it joins the Chao Phraya River. The prince's mother, Queen Saowabha, built a mansion on the land as a wedding gift for her son's marriage to Princess Rambhai Barni in 1918. It was named Sukhothai Palace after Prajadhipok's title, the Prince of Sukhothai. The prince took up residence and lived there happily until 1925, when his brother died and he somewhat unexpectedly became King Rama VII. He then moved to Amphon Sathan, one of the earliest works in Dusit, and also one of the few not to have been designed by Italians, the architect having been a German named C Sandreczki.

Sukhothai Palace does not look especially palatial. It is a two-storey brick-and-mortar building with English-style gables and eaves, and is flanked by two smaller mansions. Covered pathways connect the buildings, and the whole effect is more of a country estate than the residence of an heir to the throne. Although, of course, when it was built this was countryside, and Prince Prajadhipok was happily contemplating a military career that was to take him to the rank of commander of the Second Division, before his brother passed away and duty called. The king was not many years into his reign when, in 1932, the monarchy was overthrown in a coup and he found himself no longer absolute ruler but a constitutional monarch. He went to Britain for medical treatment in 1933, and in 1935 he abdicated. He died in Britain in 1941, at the age of 48. After his death, the Ministry of Health used the palace for a while. When the king's widow, Queen

Rambhai Barni, returned to Thailand many years later, the palace was returned to the royal family.

Phayathai Hotel is not a name that has become part of the classic Bangkok fabric, like The Oriental or the Royal, but such a hotel did once exist. Very palatial it was, too, and for good reason: it had originally been built as a palace. The story behind it is almost lost, but it's an intriguing one. When Rama v built Dusit Palace and laid out the surrounding area he had several new roads constructed. One of these was Ratchavithee Road, which ran through orchards alongside the Samsen Canal to an area of rice fields known as Thung Phayathai. The king thought it would be pleasant to have a country residence built here, and in 1909 he bought forty acres of land and had a royal mansion built. He named it Tamnak Phayathai. Here, the king and Queen Saowabha spent happy weekends, planting experimental crops, and growing rice and vegetables. The queen loved the palace so much she often stayed on for many days, the king commuting between Phayathai and Dusit in his yellow motorcar. Their country idyll was short-lived, however. Within a few months the king had passed away. After some hesitation his grieving widow decided to move into Tamnak Phayathai, and here she remained until her own death ten years later. During this time her son, Rama vi, continued to build on this area of land. A small canal, Klong Phayathai, was cut through the grounds to link Samsen with the canal that ran along Ratchavithee Road. To the east of this waterway were Tamnak Phayathai and a single-storey throne hall built for official audiences. To the west were mansions for the ladies of the inner court, the kitchens, and houses for attendants.

When the queen died, Rama vi had the palace dismantled. Part of it was rebuilt at Vajiravudh School, and other parts became living quarters for the abbot of Wat Ratchatiwat; these buildings can still be seen today. In its place Rama vi built a far more extensive royal residence, in a more European style. The centrepiece was the Phra Thinang Phiman Chakri, a two-storey masonry building with an unusual Gothic tower. In its main hall the king gave audiences or dined privately. European visitors must have felt at home here although slightly bewildered by the ornate fireplace that was one of the main design features. Echoing the architectural form of this building was the smaller Phra Thinang Srisutthiniwat, on the other side of Klong Phayathai and linked to the main building by a covered walkway. This was used as a reception hall for female members of the royal family. Next to this, on the bank of the canal, was a small teak building named Phra Tamnak Mekalaruje. Looking like a rustic summerhouse, it was used by the king after the royal hair cutting ceremony. To the rear was a model city, covering about half an acre. Named Dusit Thani, it had originally been a smaller venture at Dusit, and here the king enlarged the concept, the idea being that it could be used for training in how a city should be run. The miniature buildings were replicas of actual structures, with temples, shops, theatres, hotels and private houses. There were dwarf trees, a special grass imported from Japan, and a little river running through this Lilliputian paradise. There was even a city newspaper, to which the king was a regular contributor. Rama VI passed away in 1925, just three years after moving into his royal residence. This was at a time when Thailand's national railway network was opening up the country, and the State Railway of Thailand asked Rama VII for permission to turn the palace into the Phayathai Hotel. Later, when radio broadcasting was introduced, it briefly became Bangkok's first radio station.

Walk westwards from Victory Monument along Ratchavithee Road today, and needless to say there is no sign of any orchards or rice fields. Samsen Canal is hemmed in by buildings and shaded by overhanging trees. There is a small temple, Wat Aphai Thavaram, on its bank. But along this humdrum thoroughfare there is a green expanse, and there is the Gothic turret of Phayathai Palace. What happened was that after the building ceased to be suitable for radio broadcasts it was presented to the Royal Thai Army to be used as a hospital. After that it became part of King Mongkut Hospital. All those featureless 1970s-style buildings in the neighbourhood, and on the other side of the road where the Rong Na, the royal barn, once stood, are medical buildings of some kind. Wander the grounds of Phayathai Palace now, and there is still much to be seen. The original mansion in which Queen Saowabha spent her final years has disappeared under the extensive front lawn, but the magnificent single-storey wooden throne hall is still there. Klong Phayathai still runs through the grounds, its flow aided by what appear to be the original water wheels. The whimsical little teak house where the king would relax after the hair-cutting ceremony is still perched on the water's edge, but sadly, the model township of Dusit Thani has gone. Outside Phayathai Palace, on the lawn the visitor is likely to see elderly folks in wheelchairs, and attendant nurses, watched paternally by the statue of Rama VI, placed there in 1971.

On the eastern edge of Dusit, near to the Bangkok Fire and Rescue Department, with its striking lookout tower, is the Priest Hospital. Established in 1949 to care for ailing Buddhist monks and novices, the hospital is an all-male institution, monks being unable to come into contact with women, and provides a support system for medical care of the monastic order throughout Thailand. Further along Si Ayutthaya is Suan Pakkad Palace, which in contrast to the palaces of Dusit is one of the best examples of traditional domestic architecture in Bangkok. Laid out on the site of a former cabbage patch (hence the palace name), are eight teak pavilions that had been assembled as the home of Prince Chumbhot and his wife Mom Rajawongse Pantip. Most exquisite of all is the Lacquer Pavilion, a seventeenth-century house from Ayutthaya, which was dismantled, rebuilt and painstakingly restored in Suan Pakkad in 1959. The residence was converted into a museum in 1952, and displays an extensive collection of family heirlooms and artworks along with a display of artefacts from the prehistoric settlement of Ban Chiang, housed in a recently built pavilion.

Victory Monument, although not part of Dusit, is one of the most famous works created by Corrado Feroci and was erected in 1941 as a memorial to fallen servicemen and civilians. The monument consists of an obelisk ringed by six statues representing the army, navy, air force, police and civilians, a tribute to the casualties in the Franco-Thai War (November 1940–January 1941), over the disputed provinces of Battambang and Siem Reap, in what is presently Cambodia, and territories along the Thai-Laos border. In 1940, following the defeat of France by Nazi Germany, Thailand under Phibun Songkhram tried to reclaim border territories lost in 1893, when the French navy had blockaded the Chao Phraya. Thai troops advanced into the area west of the Mekong River opposite Luang Prabang and Champasak in Laos and Battambang and Siem Reap in Cambodia. At sea, there was also a naval engagement between the Thai and French navies near Koh Chang, in the Gulf of Thailand. Accounts of the engagement differ, but it appears that three Thai ships were sunk with a loss of sixty sailors. The French navy returned unscathed to Saigon in spite of being pursued and bombed by Thai aircraft. Japan, already in North Vietnam at that time, intervened and forced a ceasefire in January 1941. A treaty was signed in March 1941, allowing Thailand to retain the disputed territories, but after World War II, Siem Reap and Battambang were returned to France as part of the reparations for Thailand's wartime collaboration with Japan. The names of the 656 fallen servicemen and civilians are inscribed around the base of the monument, which has become a major transportation hub for buses and which is a busy stop on the BTS Skytrain line, which loops around the monument.

Not all the works undertaken by the Italians in Bangkok were to a palatial scale. Many of them were modest. But even in the smaller works, in the private projects and in the detailing of engineering projects or renovations, the Siamese and Italian cultures can be seen meeting in a surprising harmony. Phan Fa Lilat Bridge, which takes Ratchadamnoen Avenue over the second moat, has cast-iron Roman galleys decorating the uprights. The Red Cross Hospital has a barrel vault ceiling that evokes the image of a European railway station. Wat Depsirindra, on the bank of the second moat at the eastern side of the city, was built as a royal crematorium; traditionally the fire is lit by magnifying sunlight onto a candle, and this has been symbolised by a neoclassical gate with a marble candle, more Catholic than Buddhist. The Royal Mint, which is today the National Gallery, is now bereft of its reflecting *klong,* but has a classical majesty enhanced by its creamy yellow-and-white Florentine colours. The Siam Commercial Bank, tucked into a leafy corner of Talat Noi, is a stately Italian villa. During what was a very brief period, little more than half a century, Italian culture permeated Siamese culture and created works that are a delight to us today.

The Shady Ladies of Sampeng Lane

This walk will lead us through the original Chinatown thoroughfare of Sampeng Lane, once a hotbed of gambling, opium dens and brothels, ending at a temple with a murky past. Duration: 2 hours

Although Yaowarat is the main thoroughfare of Chinatown, and the name that all taxi drivers will recognise (many are bewildered if you ask for "Chinatown"), anyone wanting to seek out the origins and authentic atmosphere of this district should head for Sampeng Lane.

When Rama 1 moved the settlement of Chinese merchants and workers from the land he needed to build the new capital, he offered them land further to the southeast, beyond the second moat and the new city wall, and stretching between two existing temples, Wat Sampluem and Wat Sampeng. There was a canal next to Wat Sampluem, and this became part of the second moat. Siam had not yet reopened to the Western nations, and China was essentially the only trading partner. The Chinese junk trade grew very quickly after Bangkok was founded, the ships mooring along the middle of the river and small boats transporting goods to and from the warehouses on shore. Sampeng Lane therefore grew as a thoroughfare parallel to the river, with narrow lanes running down to the water's edge on one side, and out to the muddy limits of the settlement on the other,

Chinatown

beyond which was a waterlogged area that marked the beginning of the Sea of Mud, a large stretch of estuary country that formed an effective eastern defence for the city. Although the Siamese were used to aquatic living, and happy enough to set up home on boats and stilt houses, the Chinese were a land-based people, and Sampeng quickly came to resemble a typical southern Chinese settlement.

To help build the palaces and temples of Bangkok and to dig the canals, thousands more Chinese were imported as labour, and to the merchant class were added craftsmen: blacksmiths, goldsmiths and silversmiths, carpenters, brickmakers and builders. Along with the Chinese came opium and the secret societies. There came also the world's oldest profession: prostitutes, mainly from southern China. Sampeng Lane became Bangkok's first red-light area, although the brothels that were opened along the narrow lanes off Sampeng were identifiable by a green light above their doors. These were legal, and they were not all simple bawdy houses: many vied with each other in the quality of their decor and the sophistication of their girls. The brothel owners prospered: one madame, a Mrs Faeng, famously built a temple from her earnings. But a slang phrase for a woman of loose morals entered the Thai language at this time: *ae Sampeng*. Sampeng Lane also has the reputation of being the starting point for big-time gambling. The Chinese brought with them their fondness for gambling, one of most popular games being *huey*, which involves betting on a letter of the alphabet. In the early 1830s, in the reign of Rama III, Bangkok and its environs suffered bad flooding. The market gardens and rice fields were wiped out, and the king was forced to buy rice from overseas. The amount of money in circulation dropped, and the people suffered great hardship. An influential Chinese named Chao Sua Hong managed to persuade the king that a form of lottery, based on *huey*, would release more money into circulation and raise tax revenue. The office, Rong Huey, was set up near Sampeng Lane in 1835, next to the bridge over the canal. Chao issued one letter of the alphabet for betting every morning, plucked at random from a large bag. He quickly prospered. A nobleman named Phra Sri Viroj thought this was such a good idea that he also opened a Rong Huey, issuing a letter of the alphabet every evening. Other huay offices followed. Gambling fever took hold of the capital, and quickly became a serious problem. Despite the efforts of the next two monarchs it remained so for many years. A survey of 1888 found that there were 403 registered gambling houses in Bangkok, and it wasn't until 1916 that Rama VI managed to abolish them. This he achieved only by establishing a government lottery.

It was the Bowring Treaty of 1855 that changed the direction of Siam's trading towards the West, for other treaties quickly followed and the Siamese enthusiastically embraced European produce and ideas. Goods from British India began to arrive in Bangkok, and a large community of Indians evolved. The Chinese of Sampeng Lane, however, readily adapted: they became merchants dealing with the Europeans.

A visitor to Sampeng Lane today may be surprised at how narrow it is, but it was built (or, rather, evolved) long before there were any roads in Bangkok. The entrance is at Saphan Han, the bridge that was originally a turntable structure to allow vessels to pass up the newly built canal. *Han* means "to turn", and the bridge had revolved around a spigot. This was replaced in the reign of Rama III by a structure that had roofed shops built upon it, but this again was replaced and the current bridge is a prosaic enough crossing, almost invisible amongst the cluster of vendors. Narrow though it is, both sides of the lane are lined with shops, with their goods displayed out front. There is room enough for probably only three people abreast, but the thoroughfare has become more comfortable in recent years, with the addition for part of the way of a plastic roof, the air-conditioning inside the shops keeping the interior reasonably cool, or at least not as stiflingly hot as it used to be.

Anyone confronted by Sampeng Lane for the first time will see only a long, long line of shops, but as is so often the case in Bangkok, the lane falls naturally into a number of sections selling similar goods. From Saphan Han to Chakrawat Road are outlets for fabrics, household decorations and jewellery. From Chakrawat to Ratchawong Road are traditional medicine shops, and leatherwear and fabric shops and wholesalers. Ratchawong to Trok Issaranuphap is for wholesalers and retailers of gifts and stationary, while the final stretch is for garments, hats, shoes, bags and luggage, and umbrellas. Around the middle of the stretch is the fresh market of Talat Kao (Old Market), occupying the lanes to the left, while on the right is Talat Mai (New Market), which is actually the oldest market in Chinatown and sells dry foods. At the junction of Sampeng and Mangkon Road are two ornate commercial buildings dating from the early years of the twentieth century, their facades being European in style, although Shanghainese craftsmen fitted out their interiors. Bangkok Bank is on one side of the way, while Tang To Kang gold shop, on the other, is reputed to be the oldest gold trader in the city. Both businesses have their origins in Chinatown, although they didn't start out in these premises. The alleys leading off Sampeng often have names that indicate their original purpose: Trok Khao San was where rice milling companies had their offices; Trok Rang Katha was where metal pans were made; Trok Tao was where the stove makers had their workshops; Trok Rong Khom was where paper lanterns were made and where calligraphers and artists worked; and Trok Vet had the unhappy distinction of leading down to an area of the riverbank that was used as a public latrine.

Wat Sampluem still stands at the entrance to Sampeng Lane, although it was renamed Wat Chakrawat in the reign of Rama III. Chao Phraya Bodindecha had led a military campaign against Laos, and returned with the Phra Bang Buddha image that he installed in the temple. Phra Bang (literally "Delicate Buddha") is a cast-bronze, gold-covered standing Buddha, 83 centimetres (32.6 in) in height, its hands facing forwards, and was, along with the Emerald Buddha, considered to be an exceptionally powerful talisman. The image, which is believed to have originated in Sri Lanka, had arrived in Laos in 1353 from Angkor, the Khmer deploying it in an attempt to spread Buddhism in the new kingdom of Lan Xang and to give legitimacy to the first king, Fa Ngum, who was the son-in-law of the Khmer king. In 1545 it was taken to Vientiane, which was being prepared as the kingdom's next capital. When the Siamese under King Taksin invaded Laos in 1778, Chao Phraya Chakri took both the Emerald Buddha and Phra Bang back to Thonburi, thereby relieving Laos of its spiritual protection and its sovereign independence. However, political problems that arose in Siam were attributed to the image and in 1782 it was returned to the Laotians. In 1828 the Siamese captured Phra Bang again when Vientiane was sacked, and General Bodindecha renovated Wat Sampluem to house the image, as it was thought to be inauspicious to have both the Phra Bang Buddha and the Emerald Buddha both within the confines of the old city.

The *ubosot*, rather than facing east, as is traditional, actually faces west, to align the Phra Bang image with that of the Emerald Buddha, in Wat Phra Kaew. Nonetheless, the image once more seemed to bring political misfortune and Rama IV returned it to Laos in 1867. Since that time it has been kept in Luang Prabang, the town that takes its name from the image. A Buddha image named Phra Nak was moved from a shrine in the Grand Palace as a replacement. Today, Wat Chakrawat is probably best known for its crocodiles. General Bodindecha had cut a small waterway from the river to create a pond in the temple grounds, and the practice of keeping the reptiles here began about half a century ago when one was found in the river outside the temple. The original was stuffed and is displayed

Chinese door guards at Wat Sampeng, site of a royal execution.

in a glass case beside the pond, where a couple of live ones are kept. To the right of the compound, just inside the gate, is a small *wiharn* with an outer wall decorated in a very unusual black-and-gold pattern, the kind of styling more commonly found on interior walls or roofs. Next to the black *wiharn* is a larger *wiharn* in a more traditional style. On the left of the entrance is a stairway leading to a platform containing a *mondop* topped with a rather understated *prang*, its plainness drawing emphasis to the standing Buddha images facing out from the four sides of the *prang*. The temple's large, all-white *ubosot* is located opposite. A grotto in the grounds has a black shape referred to as the Buddha's shadow, possibly a reference to the departed Phra Bang, and worshippers place gold leaf offerings on the shape. In a neighbouring niche is a small image of a fat monk, commemorating the legend of the monk who was so handsome that the girls wouldn't leave him alone, and in order to discourage them he ate himself spherical.

At the end of Sampeng Lane is the temple that originally gave the thoroughfare its name. Wat Pathum Khong was originally known as Wat Sampeng, and dates back to the Ayutthaya era, although no one knows when it was originally built. There is a melancholy history attached to this temple. Kroma Luang Rak Ronnaret, the fifteenth son of Rama I, had risen to a very high position in the court of Rama III. He is said to have been a forceful man, highly versed in Buddhism, and when he was appointed supreme judge over the priesthood he exerted a corrupting influence. The prince had been a close friend of Rama III before the king had ascended the throne, and when he did so, the king gave him great powers that in some areas almost equalled his own. These he abused with dangerous enthusiasm. A lengthy account published in the *Singapore Free Press & Mercantile Advertiser* at the time of the prince's downfall records that he was the prime mover in establishing the legalised gambling establishments "which have caused so much misery in Siam", recommending gambling to the king as a proper business to be licensed for the purpose of collecting revenue. He organised for himself a concession for the sale of strong spirits. He imposed double labour and taxes on the Mons, and when they complained to the king, the prince sent enforcers into the Mon villages. The king had at first treated Rak Ronnaret with indulgence, but gradually the prince became a grave liability, the great power he wielded at court putting him beyond mere dismissal. Serious irregularities in the royal accounts appear to have been the final impetus for the king to take action, and in November of 1848 a detachment of the royal guard was sent to the prince's palace to arrest him. Investigations appeared to reveal that the prince was plotting to dethrone the king. There could only be one course of action in the light of those findings, whether they were true or not, and on the morning of 12th December the prince was taken to Wat Sampeng, a royal temple conveniently outside the city walls. There a velvet sack was placed over his head, his head was laid upon the execution stone and he was beaten to death with a sandalwood club. His body, the *Singapore Free Press* reports, was thrown into the river. The Thaen Hin Paraharn Kabot, the Rebel's Execution Stone, can today be found behind the *wiharn* of this riverside temple.

On the Waterfront

With its busy shophouses and godowns, its shrines and its narrow lanes, this area of Chinatown along the riverbank is the most picturesque part of the district granted to the Chinese by Rama I.
Duration: 2 hours

Ratchawong Pier is the point at which the Chinese immigrants landed in those early days before the city had spread eastwards and it also marked the northern end of the Chinese harbour, being the main port for junks plying to and from China and from Chonburi, Surat Thani and other Siamese provinces. The condition of the riverfront in the pre-road days may be imagined from the original name for the nearby Wat Bophit Phimuk, which was Wat Lain, or the Temple of Mud. This was a civil temple, so it probably had no formal name, and it had been built of timber during the late Ayutthaya period. Rama I gave the temple its present name. During the reign of Rama II the temple gained some notoriety when a cholera epidemic killed a large number of people and the corpses had to be piled up in the courtyard. Rama III replaced the wooden structure with a stone building, and Rama IV added a teak pavilion, decorated with the king's emblem, the crown guarded by mythical animals. Today, Wat Bophit Phimuk is a royal temple, second grade.

Road building in Bangkok did not start until the 1860s, and even then it was slow to progress as most commercial needs were still served by the river and the canals, rice and timber forming the bulk of exports. Construction of the roads began in earnest only in the 1890s, as international trade grew in the wake of the Bowring Treaty, and rice mills, shipping, warehousing, trading houses, factories and distribution centres all began to require more efficient transport. Sampeng and Bangrak were amongst the first districts to have modern road systems, the roads being built initially as feeders for the canals and the river, and at the start of the twentieth century, for the railways. At the same time the population of Bangkok was growing quickly, much of it by Chinese immigration. Yet one more reason for building roads was that the Privy Purse Bureau, the largest landowner in Bangkok, was beginning to appreciate that roads meant houses, and that houses meant revenue. Yaowarat Road was started in 1892, running parallel to Charoen Krung, and Ratchawong Road was built in the same year to link the two. The older buildings on Ratchawong Road and Songwat Road, which runs along the riverbank, date from this time. And very handsome many of them are, too. Take a look at the building on the corner of the two roads: it has been sadly neglected, but its delicately arched windows and projecting upper storey with filigree woodwork are classic for this period.

A little further along Ratchawong Road is an archway marking the entrance to a narrow little thoroughfare, the wording in Thai and Chinese only. Dr Sun Yat-sen came to Siam for the first time in 1903, entering the Chinese community through the secret societies, introduced by Zheng Zhi-yong, who owned the largest sweepstake business in the country. Sun was looking for support to overthrow the Qing Dynasty and was travelling through Southeast Asia attempting to raise funds, but at that time Zheng was supporting the Chinese emperor, and Sun had little success amongst the Chinese in Bangkok. Chinese secret societies, collectively known in Siam as Hongmen, had started to form in the early days of Bangkok and were influenced by the Chinese fraternal organisation known as Tiandihui, which had originated earlier during the Qing period. By the time Sun arrived in Bangkok the Hongmen had become a number of distinct groups, essentially separated by the main dialects of Teochew, Cantonese, Hokkien, Hakka and Hainanese, but with further complex groupings

Songwat Road is a place of traders, unchanged since the late nineteenth century.

beyond that. The main purpose of the secret societies was to help and support their members and give them protection in what was a harsh world, but they were also closely associated with vice, extortion and violence. There was often intense rivalry amongst them: in 1889 gang war had erupted in Yaowarat and the army was called in to restore order. Sun understood the complexities, and he studied the situation patiently, coming to Siam on three more occasions, once in 1906 and twice in 1908. He gained the support of Xiao Fo-cheng, a Chinatown publisher who had been born in the Straits Settlements and whose British citizenship afforded him protection from the Siamese author-ities, and Xiao played an important role by publishing newspapers that argued the case for revolution in China.

Chinese opinion in Bangkok began to change in support of Sun, and in 1908 he stood on the balcony of a building in Chinatown and gave a final impassioned speech. From that time onwards Siam's Chinese community became an important component of Overseas Chinese support for Sun's revolution, raising immense amounts of money, not just through individual donations, but with merchants and even rice mills putting up collateral to raise loans through the banks. A photograph exists of Sun addressing the crowds in

Chinatown. The location is at the junction of Soi Phalittaphon and Mangkon Road, and Sun is standing on the third-floor balcony of one of the corner buildings, which still exists. In 2004, Soi Phalittaphon was renamed Soi Sun Yat-sen during a ceremony that was celebrating Chinatown's 222nd anniversary and which was attended by Queen Sirikit and Princess Maha Chakri Sirindhorn, and the archway was placed over the entrance to the lane.

Turning right into Songwat Road just after leaving Ratchawong Pier takes us through a part of Chinatown that is possibly more how we feel Chinatown should look, rather than the cramped alley of Sampeng or the honking, fume-laden Yaowarat Road. Here are shophouses functioning in exactly the same way they did when they were first built, with trading companies stacking the ground-floor of the premises with goods, and using the upper storey for either offices or living accommodation. The architecture, other than occasional infill where buildings were damaged during World War II, is original. The traffic in this narrow street is almost entirely pickup trucks. Songwat shophouses follow a style that had been influenced by the Straits Settlements and are frequently ornate, with decorative stucco, scrollwork on windows and ventilation grilles, and painted floral mouldings. A short way along the street, on the left, is an elaborate Chinese archway, and in the courtyard beyond is a Chinese temple; behind this can be seen, intriguingly, what appears to be a European mansion. This is Peiing School, built in 1920 by the Chinese community, and initially providing tuition only in the Teochew dialect. The school's architecture was influenced by the neo-Renaissance style then in vogue, and the building has been beautifully preserved. A few paces further down from the school is a narrow little alley that opens out unexpectedly to reveal another European mansion, which is even more surprisingly a mosque. The Luang Kochaid Sahark Mosque is the only mosque in Chinatown, and takes its name from a native of Pattani province in Southern Thailand, who worked as a Malay translator in Bangkok and who built the mosque for Muslim traders from the southern provinces and from British Malaya.

Beyond the mosque is the turning for Yaowa Phanit Road, which leads into a network of lanes that have been paved over to form a

Walking Street (try telling that to the pickups and motorcycles) and which again form a far more quintessential image of Chinatown. If the walker follows the trail, he will come to Wat Samphanthawong, the temple that has given its name to this immediate district. The temple pre-dates the founding of Bangkok and originally stood on a mud bank surrounded by water, which is why it was originally called Wat Koh, or Temple on the Island. Rama I renovated the temple in 1796 and upgraded it to royal status, and the king's son, Prince Samphanthawong, renovated it in the reign of Rama III, whereupon the temple took the prince's name. The image in the *ubosot* is made from a hollow log with a covering of lime, and its wooden arms have a gold layer. There is an outstandingly beautiful teak house in the grounds.

As we head eastwards back towards the river we pick up Songwat Road again, passing Wat Pathum Khong and, next to an attractive terrace of timber shophouses, we find the Siang Gong Shrine, a name that translates roughly as "god uncle". Immediately beyond the shrine sprawls a district of streets and alleys that has become known as the Siang Gong Zone and which is remarkable for the fact that it looks like a breaker's yard. Street after street is piled high with engines, crankshafts, gearboxes, and everything you will ever find in the innards of a motor vehicle. This had originally been a district of Hokkien blacksmiths and tinkers. Directly after World War II, with a large amount of vehicular scrap in Bangkok and with shortages of new parts to build or repair vehicles, agricultural equipment and boats, a few industrious Chinese families began to dismantle abandoned military equipment and sell the components. The scrap that couldn't be used was melted down and used to make other components. Thailand was industrialising fast, and demand began to exceed supply, so Siang Gong began to import used car parts from Japan. Engines, transmission shafts and spare parts were sent all over the country, the extraordinary junk yard supplying the nation's buses, trucks, riverboats, tractors, generating sets, refrigerators, pumps, pile drivers, and, yes, the famous little tuk-tuks that have become a symbol of Bangkok. This recycling of old equipment has kept costs down and been effective in helping the country develop.

Siang Gong Zone is where old vehicle engines and transmission systems are reborn.

Siang Gong these days also takes pride in its craftsmanship, building engines that save fuel and cut down on emissions, and technical college students are frequent visitors to the workshops here to learn, and also to collect components for their own projects. So successful has been the Siang Gong Zone that other districts have grown up, often under the auspices of the same families, and propagating the name: in the Wang Mai district, behind Chulalongkorn University, is Siang Gong Suan Luang; there is a Siang Gong Rama III, a Siang Gong Rangsit, and, the largest of all, at 33 acres and more than 1,200 units, Siang Gong Bang Na.

The Siang Gong Zone stands at the entrance to Talat Noi, the Little Market, which occupying the corner of land formed by the river and Rama IV's Klong Padung Krung Kasem, the third and final moat, became a thriving market in the middle of the nineteenth century. These days, Talat Noi is a pleasant blending of old and new architecture, residential and commercial, culminating in the River City shopping complex, which specialises in fine art, antiques and curios, and next to which is the busy Siphraya Pier, serving riverboats and ferries. Chao Sua Son, a member of the influential Chao family, was a prominent landowner here and along the narrow Soi Wanit 2 and down the even narrower Soi Chao Sua Son is the family house, one of the few remaining Chinese courtyard houses in Bangkok. The courtyard is entered under an arch and the house is built around the three remaining sides. It is still occupied by the family.

Given the rarity of Chinese courtyard houses in Bangkok, it is rather surprising that two should be next door to each other. The neighbouring Soi Duangtawan also leads down to the river, and here can be found the Sol Heng Tai Mansion, built by the wealthy Sol clan in the very early days of the founding of Bangkok. The Sols were one of the very few Chinese families to have entered Siam in the last days of Ayutthaya, a wooden tablet in the house recording the birth of a son in 1776, at the start of the Thonburi period. The family were Hokkien, and they made their fortune from trading, money lending and land holdings, in the 1840s being awarded the royal licence to collect swallows' nests for the famous delicacy of bird nest soup. They owned a large area of land in and near Talat Noi and also established a small trading port in front of their residence.

The house, although following the traditional courtyard design, is unusual in that it has two storeys, rather than one. Construction is of teak timbers assembled by wedge connections, with the external walls and the entire first floor made of brick. Female members of the family lived in one wing, and male members in the other. The family stored rice, fruit, and their money in the house, the latter being mainly gold bars kept in metal safes, so heavy that over the years the floor sank under them. The presence of so much gold attracted the attention of thieves, who applied some ingenious ways of breaking into the gold room, in one successful heist tunnelling upwards and using vinegar to eat away the seashells and sugarcane that formed the binder for the walls. The house has passed down through female descendants of the family and is occasionally open to visitors. Another way to get in is to join the diving school operated by one son, who has built a swimming pool in the courtyard for training purposes. The house has also provided a backdrop for several Chinese-themed films and television dramas.

Following Soi Wanit 2 will soon lead into an attractive paved area, with foodstalls and shade trees, and to one side is a European-style archway that is the entrance to the first local commercial bank in Thailand. Two foreign banks opened late in the nineteenth century: Hongkong & Shanghai Bank was the first, in 1888, occupying a house that stands where the Royal Orchid Sheraton now stands, and printing Siam's first banknotes; while the Chartered Bank, the forerunner of Standard Chartered Bank, opened in 1894 next to The Oriental hotel. Prince Mahisara Ratchaharuthai, a brother of Rama v, realised it would be difficult for Siam to develop its economy without the firm foundation of a national banking system, and in 1904 he founded as an experiment a bank that he, rather oddly, named the Book Club. Located in a shophouse on Ban Moh Road, its articles of formation specified it would carry a selection of books to read on the premises or to borrow. Nonetheless, the Book Club was a working bank, with manager Phra Sanpakarn Hirunyakij overseeing a staff of eighteen Siamese and four Chinese compradors. Cash deposits enjoyed an interest of 7.5 percent per annum, and the volume of deposits quickly allowed the Club to extend loans. The following year, with healthy cash flows, the prince decided to introduce cheque withdrawal services.

In 1905 the Club opened a foreign trade and exchange department, headed by a German banker. It was time for the Book Club to declare that it was no longer a library. Siam Commercial Bank Company was inaugurated in 1906 under royal charter, which allowed it to use the king's crest. It was time too to move out of the cramped Ban Moh shophouse, and Italian architect Annibale Rigotti was commissioned to design a building on the riverbank at Talat Noi.

The new premises opened in 1908, and remain unchanged to this day, a lovely example of an early twentieth century bank. The building has its own garden with a big old bodhi tree. Pick up one of the leaves and it will immediately be seen where the bank derived its distinctive logo. This is still a working bank, although the headquarters is now over on Ratchadapisek Road. No one minds if you step inside and look around. Everything here is original: the grilles behind which the tellers sit, the tiles on the floor worn by a century of bank customers, the quaint old light fittings. There is a big vault

Warehouses on the bank of the outer moat at the eastern end of Chinatown.

under the floor where the money was stored, and almost poignant in its simplicity, the prince's office can be seen to the side of the banking hall. Siam Commercial Bank is today one of Thailand's big three banks, with the country's largest network of ATMs. The English language name was registered as the official name, although the Thais know it as Thanakhan Thai Phanit.

As we have seen, the Portuguese formed the earliest European community in Ayutthaya, and in Thonburi, having travelled down from the destroyed city and established themselves on a parcel of land on the riverbank granted them by King Taksin, who had been grateful for their support, and where they built Santa Cruz Church. In 1786, Rama I granted the Portuguese community an area of land at his new capital, at the far end of the land he had granted the Chinese, just beyond Wat Sampeng. The Portuguese built Holy Rosary Church in 1786, and they founded two schools, Kularb Wattana and Kularb Wittaya, the word *kularb* being Thai for "rose", the name deriving from the church name. Thais know the church as Wat Kalawan, the Thai pronounciation of "Calvary". The building that stands on the site today is the third Holy Rosary Church, and dates from 1898. A Gothic, cream-coloured structure, it has a high façade and a spire, and outstandingly beautiful Romanesque stained glass windows.

At the same time as the Chinese and the Portuguese were settling into their new land along the Bangkok riverbank, a Vietnamese prince arrived in Bangkok, pleading for military assistance from Rama I. Nguyen Phuc Anh was a nephew of the last Nguyen lord who had ruled over southern Vietnam, and his family had been slain in the Tay Son revolt (1771–1802). The Siamese king granted him a large fighting force, and the prince returned to his own country. His first attempt to destroy the rebellion failed, but he later succeeded and eventually founded the Nguyen Dynasty, the last of the Vietnamese dynasties, unifying Vietnam after centuries of warfare. A number of Vietnamese refugees who had travelled with the prince to Bangkok stayed in the city, the Catholics settling down in the Portuguese community and the Buddhists nearby, where they built their own temple, Wat Yuen Talat Noi—*yuen* being the Thai word for Vietnamese. The temple, distinctive with its Chinese roof, was later renamed Wat Upai Ratchabumrung. The bodhi tree in the forecourt, with the gold silk draped around its trunk, has grown from a sapling presented by Rama V.

Along the Dragon's Back

Our walk through the newer part of Chinatown takes us from the temple that houses the world's largest solid gold Buddha, to a temple built by a famous brothel owner, and finishing at the smallest temple in the district.
Duration: 2 hours

While Sampeng Lane represents the origins of Chinatown, and Songwat Road represents a more picturesque version, Yaowarat Road really is the artery. But it is not a pretty street, its fascination lying in the sheer vitality and industry of the Chinese, the teeming life in the side streets and the markets, the enormous vertical signboards, the regional foods in the restaurants and noodle shops, and the endless, endless goldshops that line both sides of the way—representative not just of the Chinese cultural affinity with gold but a legacy of the time when few Chinese were allowed to buy property and so gold became the secure investment. Rama v built Yaowarat in 1892, after a fire had devastated the shantytown that lay to the north of Sampeng. The Department of Public Works announced on 30th January of that year that His Majesty had commanded the building of a new road between Charoen Krung Road and Sampeng Lane, to run from Mahachai Fort in a southeast direction and join Charoen Krung Road at Wat Samcheen Bridge. "This road is to be 1,430 metres long and 21 metres wide, with a 14-metre roadway and

The Jubilee Gate, representing the head of the dragon at Yaowarat Road.

with a 3-metre pavement along both sides," said the announcement in the *Royal Gazette*, adding: "His Majesty the King has graciously named it Yaowarat Road".

Much to the delight of the Chinese residents the new road materialised in a slightly curvy form, rather than the straight line that typifies most of the other roads being built at that time, and they pronounced it to be in the form of a dragon: a lucky omen, indeed, although the shape was due to the road having to avoid property holdings, which is why it took ten years to build. The head of the dragon is where Yaowarat meets Charoen Krung Road in a large traffic circle, known as the Odeon Circle, after a cinema that was built here. The centre of the circle formed a small garden that became the haunt of derelicts, and in 1999, to mark King Bhumibol's seventy-second birthday, the Jubilee Gate was erected here to signify the eastern entrance to Chinatown. More usually known as the Odeon Gate, and designed in traditional Chinese architectural style, the gate carries four Chinese characters on its arch that mean "Long Live The King" and are in the handwriting of Princess Maha Chakri Sirindhorn, who is fluent in Chinese.

A few metres from the Odeon Gate is the most famous place in Chinatown, Wat Traimit, formerly known as Wat Samcheen, the original name meaning "three Chinese", commemorating its founders. The temple itself was an obscure one. Were it not for a strange act of fate, those tour buses parked outside today would have never bothered to stop there.

Wat Phraya Krai had been built near the riverfront downstream in what was to become the Yannawa district at some time during the early days of the founding of Bangkok. In the time of Rama III the temple had been renovated in honour of the king and came under royal sponsorship with the new name of Wat Chotanaram. During the reigns of Rama IV and V the temple had been abandoned and fallen into ruin. In 1931, the East Asiatic Company applied for permission to rent the monastery estate, and they cleared the land except for the remains of the ordination hall, in which there were two Buddha images, one of plaster and one of bronze. The Buddhist Ecclesiastical Committee directed that the nearby Wat Phai Ngoen Chotanaram take the bronze image and Wat Samcheen take the plaster image. Thus did Wat Phai Ngoen Chotanaram, buried obscurely in the back lanes of Bang Kolaem district, narrowly miss out on world fame. The two temples took delivery of the images in 1935, a local newspaper recording that a large truck was used to move the plaster image along Charoen Krung Road to Wat Samcheen, and that telephone lines and the electric lines for the trams had to be held up with large poles to allow the image to pass beneath without becoming entangled.

Wat Samcheen installed its plaster image in a corrugated iron lean-to by the side of a dilapidated *chedi* on the east side of its ordination hall. The temple was located in a low-lying area next to the canal, and the grounds were prone to flooding, and no one paid much attention to the image. The temple was renovated in 1939, when a new ordination hall was built and the temple name changed to Wat Traimit, but the image stayed where it was for another fifteen years, until a new *wiharn* was built to house it. On 25th May 1955, a lifting crew placed ropes around the image and, using a pulley and manpower, began to heave. The crew worked from early morning until late afternoon, manoeuvring the heavy figure, but then a rope gave way and the image thudded hard against the ground, chipping the plaster and revealing the glistening of gold beneath.

The course of events that led to the Gold Buddha arriving at Wat Traimit and becoming one of the country's great visitor attractions, and one of the world's most revered Buddha images, have been established with reasonable certainty. During the Sukhothai era, the city-state's most revered king, Ramkhamhaeng the Great, had made a series of inscriptions on an upright stone slab that set out details of his kingdom. The Ramkhamhaeng Stele, which is now in the National Museum, describes in lines 23–27 how, at Wat Mahathat, in the middle of the city, was a gold Buddha image. There is no other information, but as there are no other gold Buddha images it would appear to be the one that is now in Wat Traimit. That would date the figure to around the year 1280, at least. The form of the image is classic central-era Sukhothai, a time when the Siamese identity was first blossoming. The head of the image is almost egg-shaped, the nose is long and tapering, the eyebrows curved, the hair tightly curled, the lips smiling, and detailing to the body, robe and base all place it during the period of Ramkhamhaeng. The Sukhothai kingdom lasted exactly 200 years, and it is not known when the image was encased in plaster. When Sukhothai was absorbed into Ayutthaya the image was moved and installed in the new city. Centuries later, the attacking Burmese ignored the plaster Buddha image and it was left in the Ayutthaya ruins for several years until Rama I, in 1801, decided to move many of the images down to Bangkok. The most significant images were housed in Wat Pho, while the plaster-covered gold image along with the bronze Buddha were placed in Wat Phraya Krai, where they remained as the temple fell into ruins around them.

For many years, despite the full knowledge that this was the world's biggest solid-gold Buddha, the image remained housed in the same modest chapel that had been built to hold the plaster image. My own first view of it was thirty years ago, and I was surprised at the lack of security, although, reasoning it through, I realised the image would have been very difficult to steal. The image was cast in nine sections that fit smoothly together and a key was discovered in the base that can be used to dismantle the figure for transportation:

but first, of course, the figure has to be lifted so that the key can be reached. In recent years Wat Traimit has undergone substantial renovations and rebuilding to reflect the reputation of its illustrious image, which resides now on the top level of a magnificent building clad in white marble and topped by a gold spire. There is a museum here that details the finding of the image and includes the old pulley and ropes that were used on the fateful day in 1955, along with fragments of the plaster casing. An attempt has been made to establish a date for the plaster using carbonation techniques but the casing proved to be highly porous and less than an inch thick, and so no results were obtained. Radioactive dating was attempted on the black lacquer on the casing, but that doesn't appear to have yielded any results either. Varying measurements have been given for the height and width of the figure, which is seated in the Subduing Mudra position, but it is certainly over 3 metres (9.8 ft) high and 2.5 metres (8.2 ft) across the lap. The weight is 5.5 tons, give or take half a ton. Is it really solid gold? Yes, but different sources claim different purity: one source says it is 18 karat, another says that the sections from the base to the neck are forty percent pure gold, from the chin to the forehead 80 percent, and the hair and top-knot ninety-nine percent. Like all the best stories there remains considerable mystery about the Gold Buddha, but the image has a Mona Lisa quality in that it seems to have an internal life and to be quietly appraising the viewer with a sense of amusement.

On the other side of Yaowarat Road, and looking like the entrance to a Chinese shrine, is a large gate, raked at an odd angle to the road for feng shui purposes. This is not actually a shrine but is the premises of the Thian Fa Foundation, founded in 1902 by the five main language groups in Chinatown in an early move to unite the essentially disparate community. Traditional Chinese medicine was offered free of charge to poor Chinese immigrants, and today modern medicine has been added to the services provided by the foundation. In the forecourt of the hospital is a 3-metre (9.8-ft) gilded wooden image of Kuan Yin, the goddess of mercy, who presides over the premises. Carved from a single piece of sandalwood, the image was brought from China and is believed to be 400 years old. The image has been

The Poh Tek Tung Foundation is a charity that collects unclaimed bodies.

in the possession of the foundation since 1958. Thian Fa works closely with the Poh Teck Tung Foundation, a charity organisation that collects the bodies of accident victims and if the deceased has no known relatives, arranges burial. The tradition is an old one in China, based on the work of a Song dynasty monk named Tai Hong, who became greatly revered. Chinese immigrants in Bangkok raised a statue to the monk in Wat Liab, and when a plague descended on the city, many devotees went to the statue and asked for blessings, donating money and coffins, and funding a graveyard. In 1909 these efforts came together under a group of twelve Chinese merchants who established the foundation, hiring employees and engaging volunteers to go out and collect unclaimed corpses. The foundation bought land on Plub Phla Chai Road where today the offices stand, opposite a shrine dedicated to Tai Hong, whose followers are of the Mahayana school of Buddhism, rather than the Theravada school that is dominant in Thailand. A new graveyard was opened outside of Bangkok about twenty years ago, and the bodies are buried there in numbered graves. Photographs are taken of the corpses so that any families recognising the deceased can have the remains disinterred and buried elsewhere. Members of the public can make donations to purchase a coffin, at a cost of 650 baht. Poh Teck Tung has a fleet of well-maintained ambulances and fire engines in the car park of its modern office building: the Chinese character above the door is *shan*, which means "to perform a meritorious deed". The shops immediately surrounding the foundation have large displays of fake money, clothes, houses and cars that are burned to provide for the souls of the dead.

The temple mentioned earlier as having been built by a famous madame is Wat Kanikapon, erected in 1833 during the reign of Rama III, and located adjacent to the Tai Hong Shrine. She was known as Khun Yai Faeng, which means "Grandmother Faeng", and the house of prostitution was located in Trok Tao, just off Sampeng Lane. Madame Faeng was a devout Buddhist of the Maha Nikaya sect, and she and her girls raised the funds to build the temple. As was often the case in that era, the temple was not given a name and was simply known as Wat Mai Yai Faeng, the New Temple of Grandmother Faeng. She was the founder of the Paorohit family, and when Rama V ascended the throne her descendants carried out some renovations and petitioned the king to name the temple. The name he selected was Wat Kanikapon, which means "temple built from the earnings of prostitution".

The temple is a relatively plain one, and appears to have undergone few substantial changes since it was built. Many original objects and buildings can still be found in the compound, including the principal Buddha image, the *wiharn*, a cloister with several Buddha images, one small stupa, several lacquered gold-leaf painted cupboards, and the bell tower. Roses decorate the entrance arch and the gable ends, and the detailing around the window frames evokes the image of green curtains, symbolising the temple's origins. Madame Faeng invited Father To, a renowned monk who later rose to the ecclesiastical title of Somdet Phra Phutthachan, to deliver a sermon for the temple's opening, and although his remarks do not appear to have been particularly flattering and he is reported to have said that funds raised in this way through sin were worth less in terms of merit making than were more legitimately raised funds, a statue of the monk was placed in the courtyard. The temple founded and runs a primary school, which comes under the auspices of the Bangkok Metropolitan Administration. A bust of Grandmother Faeng can be found in a niche behind the *ubosot*, although it's not a very good one and looks like it has been made from a mould used for monk images, to the extent that the poor lady has to have a wig to hide her bald head.

Another lady commemorated in a temple, although in a completely different context, can be found at Wat Kanma Tuyara, whose name translates as "Temple of Kan's Mother". Kan Sakhonwasi had been a courtier at the time of Rama iv and his mother, Klin, lived in a house on this site. The temple, a civil temple of the Thammayut Nikaya sect of Buddhism, founded by Rama iv, was built in the garden in 1864. Today, the large gateway dominates narrow Mangkon Road. The *ubosot* is tall and narrow, a style of the time but also being practical in the confined space, and there is a distinctive bell-shaped pagoda that takes its design from Thammekka Pagoda in India. The principal Buddha image is of gilded bronze and is enshrined in a wooden image house that is covered with gold leaf and decorated with chips of coloured glass. As a neat domestic touch, the temple window frames are painted with four floral patterns in a vertical row consisting of figures of fruit trays surrounded by bunches of flowers.

One of the larger Chinese shrines in Bangkok is the Li Thi Miew Shrine further down Phlab Phla Chai Road, near the police station. This Taoist shrine has a large roof, on which two dragons are playing with a pearl, and there is a courtyard with a figure of Kuan Yin, the goddess of mercy, set against a water cascade. Nearby in Charoen Krung Road is the Kwong Siew Hospital, founded by another charitable foundation, and next to this is the only Guangdong shrine in Bangkok, built more than 130 years ago by Cantonese immigrants, using building materials and images brought from their homeland. The gods represented here include those who have an influence on education, craftsmanship, handicrafts, and morality.

The oldest Chinese shrine in Bangkok predates the city itself, showing there was a thriving Chinese community in what was later to become Chinatown, separate to that which occupied the area where the Grand Palace now stands. The Leng Buai Yia Shrine is in a courtyard reached by walking down the narrow alley of Yaowarat

Soi 6. There is a plaque inside with an inscription stating it was built in 1658, a century before the Burmese razed Ayutthaya. Built by Teochew immigrants, the shrine is a traditional one with a roof made of glazed tiles adorned with two ceramic dragons. The shrine contains an altar dedicated to Leng Buai Ia and his wife. To the left and right there are altars to the deity Kuan Yu and the Queen of Heaven, Tianhou. Near the entrance is an ancient bell attributed to the Emperor Daoguang, who ruled towards the end of the Qing Dynasty. Other items inside the shrine include three plaques from the reign of the Qing Dynasty Emperor Kangxi, and a container for incense sticks given as a gift by Rama v.

The largest Chinese Buddhist temple in Chinatown is Wat Mangkon Kamalawat, the Dragon Lotus Temple, more often known to local residents as Wat Leng Noei Yi, which means the same in the Teochew dialect. Founded in 1871 on land donated by Rama v, construction took eight years and was financed by wealthy Chinese merchants and government officials. The temple is set in a courtyard off Charoen Krung Road, opposite Phlab Phla Chai Police Station. The architecture is traditional Chinese, with a multi-tiered tiled roof decorated with animal and floral motifs, and Chinese dragons tussling with a pearl of wisdom. A temple of the Mahayana Buddhist sect, with three Chinese-style gold Buddha images in the *ubosot*, Wat Mangkon nonetheless encompasses other beliefs: the entrance to the *wiharn* is flanked by large statues of the four guardians of the world, the Chatulokkaban, clothed in warrior costumes, while elsewhere there are shrines dedicated to a variety of Buddhist, Taoist and Confucian deities and religious figures, all important in local Chinese beliefs. At the rear of the temple stand three pavilions, one dedicated to Kuan Yin, one to the temple's founder, Phra Archan Chin Wang Samathiwat, and one to the saint Lak Chao. The front courtyard includes a furnace for the ritual burning of paper money and other offerings to ancestors, and near the rear of the courtyard is a case containing fifty-eight bronze Buddha images. All this helps to make Wat Mangkon a very popular temple and it is believed that paying homage to the numerous deities will bring good luck in various aspects of life such as health, longevity, business success, educational accomplishment and family happiness. The streets around the temple are thronged with vendors selling lotus-shaped dumplings, oranges and other foods for the shrines, and paper goods for burning and sending on to the afterlife. The temple becomes very crowded during festival times, with a lively atmosphere, the sound of drumbeats and gongs, and the scent of sandalwood smoke.

The smallest temple is Wat Bumpenchinprot, located in Trok Tao, an alley that runs off from Soi Dr Sun Yat-sen and crosses Yaowarat Road. Occupying the space of only one commercial building, this had originally been a shrine to the goddess Kuan Yin, but was later deserted. The premises were then renovated and used as a Buddhist temple, Rama v bestowing the name. This tiny place of worship is known for the eighteen Buddha images and saints that have been built by the traditional Chinese method known as Tok Sa, using bamboo for the structure, covered with grass-based fabric or leather, and then coated with lacquer and gold.

The Sea of Mud

Bangkok's first paved road, Charoen Krung, was laid out along the swampy bank of the river soon after the Europeans arrived and set up their legations, warehouses, hospitals, homes and churches.
Duration: 2 hours

"March 25—At seven o'clock this morning we weighed anchor, and attempted to cross the bar; but when about half-way over, the ship struck in the soft mud, in which, as the tide fell, she sunk four feet. We had, at the same time, not above four feet water. As the evening tide made, she floated, and we crossed the bar without sustaining any injury. A strong and favourable breeze soon carried us to the mouth of the Menam, a distance of not less than ten miles from the outer edge of the bar, ploughing almost all the way through the thin ooze; and at seven o'clock at night we anchored off the village of Paknam, about two miles and a half from the mouth of the river, upon its left bank."

Diplomat John Crawfurd, on one of the first official British missions to Bangkok, arriving in 1822, was observing the shipping hazard that had always presented difficulties for mariners, and the huge submerged mud bank that stretches out into the sea remains to this day an obstacle to shipping. Continual dredging keeps the navigation channel open, but only for the smaller vessels; the container-carrying

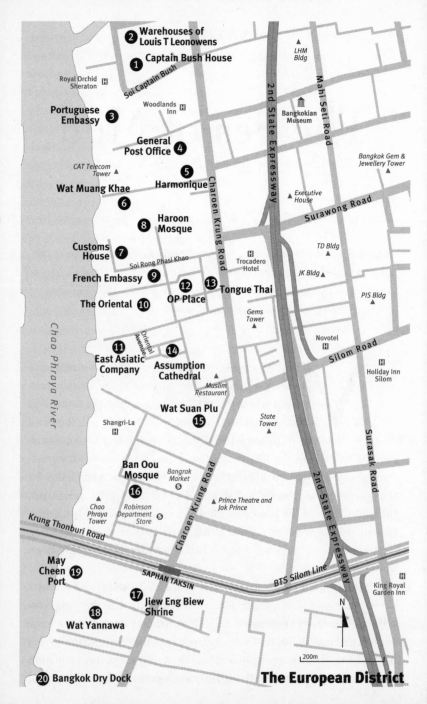

2 **Warehouses of Louis T Leonowens**

1 **Captain Bush House**

Royal Orchid Sheraton H

Soi Captain Bush

Woodlands Inn H

3 **Portuguese Embassy**

4 **General Post Office**

5

CAT Telecom Tower ▲

Harmonique

Wat Muang Khae 6

8 **Haroon Mosque**

Customs House 7

Soi Rong Phasi Khao

French Embassy 9

12 13 **Tongue Thai**

The Oriental 10 **OP Place**

Oriental Avenue

11 14

East Asiatic Company **Assumption Cathedral**

Muslim Restaurant ▲

Wat Suan Plu

Shangri-La H 15

Ban Oou Mosque

Bangrak Market S

16

Chao Phraya Tower ▲

Robinson Department Store S

Krung Thonburi Road

Charoen Krung Road

LHM Bldg ▲

2nd State Expressway

Mahi Seti Road

🏛 *Bangkokian Museum*

Bangkok Gem & Jewellery Tower ▲

▲ *Executive House*

Surawong Road

TD Bldg ▲

JK Bldg ▲

H *Trocadero Hotel*

Gems Tower ▲

PIS Bldg ▲

Novotel H

Silom Road

H *Holiday Inn Silom*

State Tower ▲

▲ *Prince Theatre and Jok Prince*

Surasak Road

Chao Phraya River

May Cheen Port 19

SAPHAN TAKSIN

BTS Silom Line

17 **Jiew Eng Biew Shrine**

18 **Wat Yannawa**

H *King Royal Garden Inn*

N

200m

20 **Bangkok Dry Dock**

The European District

leviathans must use the deepsea port at Laem Chabang, on the Gulf coast near to Pattaya. The bar would be far larger were it not for the fact that the sediment that washes down from the farmlands becomes so liquefied that it washes over the accumulated mud and is swept out to sea, despite the strength of the tide that attempts to push it back again. The Port Authority of Thailand has the responsibility for keeping 66 kilometres (41 miles) of the river dredged for navigation, starting from a point 18 kilometres (11 miles) out to sea, measured from the Phra Chulachomklao Fort at the mouth of the river, which for the charts is marked as Km 0. This stretch is known as the outer bar, and a channel varying between 150 and 250 metres (492 and 820 ft), depending on curvature, is maintained at a depth of 8.5 metres (27 ft) below mean sea level, a formidable and continuous job that requires four types of dredger, namely bucket, shell, backhoe and suction dredgers.

The inner bar channel runs from Km 0 up to the Memorial Bridge, a distance of 48 kilometres (30 miles), and requires considerably less attention, for the flow of the Chao Phraya is strong and the scouring of the water has made the river an exceptionally deep one. Crawfurd sounded the depth of the water and observed that it became deeper the further upstream he progressed from the rivermouth. He measured the depth at the front of the Grand Palace at nine fathoms, which is just over 16 metres (52 ft). Modern charts for the inner bar show a steep-sided U-shape that would be difficult to scramble up if it were on dry land, and with bottom depths that run from 15 metres (49 ft) to more than 20 metres (65 ft). A recent sounding at high tide at the mouth of Klong Bangkok Yai put the depth at 14.5 fathoms, or 26.5 metres (87 ft). In other words, you could drop a seven-storey building into it. Steamship captains of the nineteenth century were, of course, aware of this great river depth between the Bangkok Yai and Noi canals, and they used the stretch of water in front of the Grand Palace to turn their ships round, which must have been irksome for the royal inhabitants.

The Sea of Mud that formed such an effective barrier to the east was typical delta country, and so low-lying that in places the land was below sea level. Ayutthaya had also been built on a low-lying flood plain, and had developed a system of canals for transportation and living, with floating markets at strategic junctions. Bangkok's rulers and inhabitants were therefore perfectly at ease with adopting a similar pattern for the new capital, which is why no roads were built until the coming of the Europeans, who began to settle in the city in large numbers after the Bowring Treaty was signed in 1855. Within a few years they requested Rama IV to build a road along the bank of the river that they could use for walking and riding, and thus was the first road built in the city. The earliest European travellers in the sixteenth century had used the phrase, "Venice of the East" in reference to Ayutthaya, and this was applied with justification to Bangkok until the roads finally began to eclipse the canals. The phrase can still sometimes be found in tourist brochures and guidebooks, presumably written by people who haven't been here since before World War II.

Thailand was of course never colonised, so the phrase "colonial Bangkok" may be a slightly misleading one, but the evocative images it conjures up of colonnaded buildings, rickshaws, and linen-suited Europeans drinking stenghas at the club was real enough. Such a Bangkok did exist, and it revolved around the stretch of Charoen Krung Road that begins at the outer moat, the Padung Krung Kasem canal, where the Royal Orchid Sheraton Hotel stands today, and continued down to the end of the road, at Thanon Tok. On the way, it also occupied parts of the Bangrak, Sathorn and Bang Kolaem districts, each of which has a foot on Charoen Krung. There is a map produced in 1878 by a British sea captain named Alfred Loftus, who was the official topographer and surveyor to the king of Siam, that shows all the embassies, the main businesses and even some of the residencies along Charoen Krung, starting with the German Consulate on the bank of the canal and ending with the offices of the *Siam Weekly Advertiser* perched on the riverside at Thanon Tok. Fifteen years after the road had been completed, it looks a very busy thoroughfare. Today we can stand with our backs to Padung Krung Kasem and see that, in essence, this part of Charoen Krung Road hasn't really changed. The architecture is still shophouses, many of them late nineteenth century originals, and the atmosphere is one of bustling commerce.

Captain Bush Lane is a narrow little thoroughfare running from Charoen Krung down to the river, known nowadays mainly for a collection of arts and antiques shops that are housed in warehouses built by the Japanese in World War II. Captain Bush, however, was one of the best-known Europeans in Bangkok during the second half of the nineteenth century. Born in England in 1819, he had arrived in Bangkok in 1857, shortly after the signing of the Bowring Treaty. Already Western ships were beginning to crowd into the port of Bangkok, and the Krom Ta, or Harbour Department, found itself overwhelmingly busy. The department had divided itself into three divisions: one taking care of European shipping, one of Chinese shipping, and the third taking care of Indian shipping. Rama IV realised that he needed an experienced seadog to act as harbour master, and following discussions with the British consul, Sir John Schomburgk, Captain Bush was appointed to the office, with the title of Luang Wisoot Sakoradit Chao Ta. He immediately reformed the Harbour Department, and 5th August 1859 is recognised today as Harbour Department Founding Day. Bush remained in that position for thirty years, and was a respected and popular local figure. He was amongst the first Westerners to buy plots of land, and built a house here facing the river. Anna Leonowens, who first met Bush when he sailed out to meet her incoming ship on the night of 15th March 1862, finding her with her six-year-old son Louis and the family pet, a large Newfoundland dog, describes him as "a cheery Englishman, with a round, ruddy, rousing face." Anna was distraught that her royal employers had arranged no accommodation, and Bush brought them across the river and provided a room in his house.

Standing at the end of Captain Bush Lane, facing the Sheraton, and in such a sadly ruinous state that it is something of a surprise it stands at all, is a mansion built by a wealthy French wine merchant. In the neighbouring compound are a couple of warehouses that until recent years had a familiar name affixed, for little Louis Leonowens grew into a highly successful man. Louis was a frequent visitor to the Grand Palace, where Anna was teaching the king's son, Chulalongkorn, and other royal and aristocratic children, and he became a favourite of the king himself. Anna left Siam after five years and she sent Louis to a boarding school in Ireland while she went on to America. Louis, now a strong young six-footer, eventually made his way back to Siam. Rama IV was long dead by this time, having contracted malarial fever while on a visit to Prachuap Khiri Khan province to observe the solar eclipse, and Chulalongkorn was now Rama V. Reportedly, the king saw Louis looming above a crowd and called out, "Hello, Louis, do you want a job?" Thus began a career that saw Louis initially as the organiser of a royal cavalry guard, and later as the leader of a security force protecting a surveying team that travelled to Luang Prabang, then part of Siam, and which included Captain Bush's 21-year-old son, George. Louis eventually resigned his royal commissions and became an agent for the Borneo Company, based at Nakhon Sawan, where the Chao Phraya begins, and where he was responsible for corralling the company's timber and floating it down the river in huge rafts to Bangkok. In 1904 he founded the Louis T Leonowens Company, which opened a godown near Captain Bush's house. The company exists to this day, and is part of the American conglomerate the Getz Group, specialising in chemicals, building and architectural materials, agricultural equipment and firearms. The Louis T Leonowens logo is the Giant Swing, which was restored in 1920 using teak from the company's estates.

There is a sharp bend in Captain Bush Lane, at the point where the road turns to the right to follow the riverbank, and here a door is set in a high, blank white wall. This is the entrance to the Portuguese Embassy Residence. The Portuguese had long enjoyed an exceptional relationship with Siam, remaining after most of the other Europeans had been forced to leave in 1688, and in 1820 they were granted permission to build a *feitoria*, a factory, along with a residence to allow a consul to be stationed in Bangkok, rather than the Siamese having to deal with the governor of Macau or Goa. The residence for the first consul, Carlos Manuel da Silveira, was a gracious one, but it was built of bamboo and stucco, and quickly deteriorated in the hot and humid climate. Building began on the new residence in 1860, with stone and glass being shipped in from Goa. Numerous interruptions, including the sinking of an incoming ship carrying building materials, meant that it took fifteen years to complete the building, but the result is the elegant two-storey structure that can be seen today. A 26-metre (85-ft) frontage has three huge arched windows and a veranda flanks the upper floor. Blue and white ceramic tiles from Portugal decorate the entrance, and a lawn leads down to the river's edge.

During those years when Bangkok was opening to Western trade, most of the European nations along with the Americans had their consulates along this stretch of Charoen Krung Road, and the incoming ships would moor alongside their own legations. Next to the Portuguese Consulate had stood the British Consulate. The first British consul, Charles Batten Hillier, had been stationed in Bangkok immediately after the ratification of the Bowring Treaty. The original consulate had been located in rented premises in Bang Kolaem, but permanent premises were clearly necessary and the king, who had developed a high regard for Bowring and the British, took it upon himself to acquire the land. A letter from the king dated 17th July 1856 points out that the chosen piece of land neighbouring the Portuguese Consulate belonged to "many Malayan and Burman people" but that the king was prepared to offer them one *tical* for every one square fathom. The only problem was an area that belonged to a minister in the service of Second King Pinklao. Rama IV pointed out he had no right to compel ministers to sell their land, and suggested that the British wrote to the second king direct. Hillier was felled by dysentery and ended up in the Protestant Cemetery before the year was out, but negotiations were continued by his successor. Once the land was arranged, the king even advanced a loan of 16,000 *ticals* so that building could begin without waiting for the transfer of funds from the Foreign Office in London.

The site was a large one, and along with the residence the British added servants' quarters, two courthouses, a house for the consular assistant, an office building, and a grander residence when the consulate was raised to the status of a legation in 1895. It was all rather splendid, and the size of the legation being far larger than any other of the embassies reflected the scale of British power. Everything began to change, however, when Sir Ralph Paget arrived in 1902 to take charge of the legation. Sir Ralph appears to have been a man of refined sensibilities. Steamships and launches were passing up and down the river day and night, honking and hooting. Two rice mills on the opposite bank had klaxons they continually sounded, and whenever the wind blew from the east the compound was smothered with paddy-ash. Trams rattled along Charoen Krung, enthusiastically clanging their bells. The next-door temple rang its bell daily and loudly to call the faithful. Immediately opposite the legation gates an Italian lady named Madame Staro operated what must have been a very attractive establishment, with loud piano music and female companionship. Sir Ralph was aghast. The place was just so damned noisy, don'tcha know.

He began to cast around for another site, but the bureaucratic wheels in Bangkok and London turned slowly, and it wasn't until 1919 that a suitable plot of land was suggested. Much to the horror of the ambassador of the day, Sir Ralph having long since moved on, the new plot was an area of marsh next to the Saen Saeb canal, a location so remote that even its owner had difficulty travelling there. The new road that ran alongside the land, Ploenchit, petered out a couple of hundred metres east of the site, the land becoming fields and swamp. The legation staff, comfortable in their Bang Kolaem homes, dreaded the idea. The British sea captains, who were required to register their vessels with the legation, complained about the inconvenience. British subjects, who included Indians, Malays and Burmese, faced lengthy journeys out into the wilderness.

But the Siamese government were very happy with the idea: ever since the initial grumblings from Sir Ralph, they had begun to think what a splendid site the legation grounds would make for a General Post Office. The British had established a Consular Post Office in 1858 that handled mail for merchants and missionaries, sending the mailbags by diplomatic pouch to Singapore for forwarding, but this ceased in 1885 when Siam joined the Universal Postal Union and started its own international postal service. The first post office was located in a mansion belonging to Phra Preechakolkarn by the river on the northern side of the second moat, but this wasn't very convenient for foreign customers or for transportation to the mail ships, whereas the British site was. Built in 1927 and clad in dark stone, the

Statue of Rama VII seated next to a 1920s telephone outside the General Post Office.

General Post Office is a rather bulky attempt at Art Deco, a style that had taken root in Bangkok through the building of Hua Lampong Station. Designers of this period had absorbed Egyptian influences following the public interest in the opening of King Tutankhamen's tomb in 1922, and this is apparent in the facade and in the styling of the two giant garudas above the entrance, sculpted by Corrado Feroci. A whimsical statue of Rama VII, seated next to a perfect reproduction of a 1920s telephone, is in the forecourt of the building.

A tiny lane so narrow it is little more than a footpath runs alongside the General Post Office, and along here is a row of ancient shophouses that date back to the earliest days of Charoen Krung. They are actually back-to-back houses, and between them passed a narrow alley. With public access now from the lane only, the houses have become double houses, and this odd effect can be seen by visiting Harmonique, a long-established restaurant in the centre of the row, operated by the family who now own the entire row of houses. Part of the restaurant is set in what was the central alley, roofed over to make an inner courtyard, and made cosy by coloured lamps and curios. Further down this narrow lane, on the river's edge, is a small gem of a temple named Wat Muang Khae, with a marble-clad *ubo-sot* that appears big enough for only a handful of worshippers, and a stumpy but ornate bell tower, presumably holding the bell that so distracted Sir Ralph Paget.

In its prime, starting from the 1880s, this stretch of riverside must have been magnificent, and the great centrepiece would have been the Customs House. Originally the office for collecting duties was on the bank of the Padung Krung Kasem canal but in 1888 Rama v decided that the port itself, as this stretch of the river had become by that time, was the proper place for a customs office and so he commissioned a new building. Joachim Grassi, one of the first of the Italian architects who were to leave such a distinctive identity on Bangkok during Rama v's reign, designed the building, drawing up plans that were similar in style to the Ministry of Defence building that he had designed a few years earlier. There are in fact three buildings: the central building, facing directly onto the river, and a north and south wing at right angles, both of them connecting by elevated corridors to the main building. The style is Neo-Classical, the magnificent façade topped by a giant clock and the apex of the triangular pediment embellished with the emblem of Rama v.

Inside, the central staircase and the floors are made of teak. The ground floor of the three-storey central building was used for ware-housing. The agriculture department occupied the first floor with, facing the river, the inbound tax rice office on the left and the out-bound tax rice office on the right. On the floor above, the liquor duty office was on the left, while on the right was a reception room for foreign officials and traders, which was used for dance parties and which hosted a welcoming party for Rama v when he arrived back in Siam from the first of his European visits. The Customs House can be found down the neighbouring *soi* to Captain Bush Lane, Soi Rong Phasi Khao, the name indicating that it led to the office for collect-ing rice taxes. Wander down this narrow thoroughfare and you will find, directly on the riverfront, on what had once been one of the busiest harbours in the East, the majestic rotting edifice, used now by the Bangrak Fire Brigade, which parks its red trucks in the fore-court and appears to use the building as a dormitory and workshop.

The now sadly dilapidated Customs House once dominated the European riverbank.

The customs office moved further downriver to Klong Toei in 1949, and ten years later the fire brigade moved in, joined in 1968 by the Bangrak Marine Police, and there, it appears, they are determined to stay. The Customs House is maintained by the Treasury Department, and in 2005 a lease was agreed by a hotel development company to turn this beautiful structure into a five-star hotel, which would also give the impetus for the surrounding buildings to be restored as shops and restaurants. We can only wait, and watch, and wonder.

The Customs House was built on land on which stood a small village named Ton Samrong. In the 1830s an Indonesian trader named Musa Bafadel, who plied between Siam, Malaya and Indonesia, decided to settle here. He had a son named Haroon, who prospered and bequeathed his property to his own son, who built a mosque in his name. When the Customs House was built, the Siamese government offered a strip of land to the rear of the building in exchange for the land upon which the timber-built Haroon Mosque stood. The mosque was dismantled and re-erected on the new site, where it stood until 1934, when the son, Yusuf, by now very elderly, decided to replace it with a brick and lime structure. Tucked away in a tiny enclave, with a distinctive green tiled roof and three miniature green onion-shaped domes over the door, it has become a centre, not just for Thai Muslims but for visiting Muslims from India, Pakistan, Malaysia, Burma and Indonesia. Food is prepared and sold by the female residents of the Muslim community who live in the timber houses here. There is a graveyard behind the mosque, the graves marked only by earthen mounds, and in this garden-like setting a number of goats wander, nibbling on the vegetation and providing fresh milk to the community.

The French Embassy Residence is also on Soi Rong Phasi Kao, and like its Portuguese neighbour, it is an unspoiled architectural beauty dating from 1860, and if anything even more ornate. A three-storey timber structure, it has a two-storey front porch with an outdoor staircase on either side. Ornate fretwork runs around the eaves, and there is a veranda on both of the upper floors. A high wall renders this perfectly conserved building invisible, unless you are able to peep from the window of its next-door neighbour, The Oriental.

Ah, The Oriental. Nowhere better symbolises the European presence in Bangkok than The Oriental. And as a modern-day symbol of Bangkok, The Oriental is one of the most famous. Yet the origins of the hotel are obscure and modest. A seaman's hostel was built on the site soon after the Western nations began mooring their ships along the river, but the first record of this venture was a report of its destruction on 11th June 1865, when fire burned down sixty-nine buildings "including the Oriental Hotel", as the *Bangkok Calendar* reported. Nothing else is known until the 1870s, when two Danes, C Salje and F Jarck, emerge as the owners of the rebuilt hotel, with an entry in the *Siam Directory* of 1878 advertising what sounds like commodious accommodation, with "American Bar, Billiard Saloon, Baths, Newspapers kept, Boats for hire, Table d'Hote, Breakfast 9 A.M., Tiffin 1 P.M., Dinner 7 P.M." In 1881 Salje and Jarck sold the hotel to another Dane, Hans Niels Andersen, who realised that Bangkok was becoming more than just a transit point for seamen and traders. He decided to build a new and very grand hotel, and commissioned a local partnership of Italian architects, Cardu & Rossi, to design the place. When the new Oriental opened on 19th May 1887, it was the first luxury hotel in Siam. There were forty rooms, many of them,

much to the alarm of the Thais, who have never been high-rise creatures, located on a second storey. A bar that was big enough to hold
fifty drinkers became immediately popular, one of its earliest patrons
being a young seaman named Jozef Teodor Konrad Korzeniowski,
known to fellow imbibers as Polish Joe, and to posterity as Joseph
Conrad. He had arrived in Bangkok on 24th January 1888 to take command of the barque *Otago*, the previous captain having died at sea,
and although Conrad steered his ship downriver on the 9th February,
never having actually stayed at The Oriental, and never to return to
Bangkok, his name has become indelibly associated with the hotel.

Another regular at the bar was Louis Leonowens, who by the
early 1890s was making a fortune in teak, and when he heard that
Andersen was thinking of selling up and returning to Denmark,
formed a company with Franklin Hurst and bought the hotel for
US$22,000. The Oriental went from strength to strength. In 1903,
with Louis leaving Bangkok and heading back to England to expand
his business (he died there during the flu pandemic of 1919), it was
sold again, but the new proprietor, F S Roberston, left town a few
months later in a flurry of unpaid bills, leading to a temporary closure. A brief succession of owners followed, but in 1917 Siam was
drawn into the war against Germany, and suddenly business was
not so good. Some of the gloss came off the hotel. A sniffy article in
1920 by a French writer named Henri Cucherousse ("a small place
with forty bad, comfortless rooms in an old building on the bank of
the river...it must be ten years since the place had a coat of paint")
hurt not just the pride of the owners but the pride of the foreign (or,
at least, the non-French) community. An indignant response in the
Bangkok Times pointed out the splendours of the hotel and ended
with the dignified flourish: "We think M Cucherousse owes us an
apology for his harsh remarks."

An even greater public relations disaster almost happened in
1923. William Somerset Maugham, then at the height of his pop-
ularity, was travelling through Burma and Siam and then on to
Haiphong, in Vietnam. He arrived in Bangkok by train from Chiang
Mai, and took a room in The Oriental. Soon he began to feel very ill.
He took his temperature. "I was startled to see that it was a hundred

and five. I could not believe it, so I took it again; it was still a hundred and five... I went to bed and sent for a doctor." The doctor diagnosed malaria, and Maugham queasily recalled a night on his way down through Siam when he had incautiously slept without a mosquito net. Quinine had no effect, and his condition worsened. His temperature climbed higher and he lay close to death. During his delirium he heard Madame Maria Maire, the manager, talking to the doctor. "I can't have him die here, you know. You must take him to the hospital." The doctor agreed, but suggested waiting a day or two. "Well, don't leave it too long," she replied. Maugham recovered to find himself extraordinarily clear-headed, and sat in his room writing a distinctly bilious child's fairy story about a fictitious king of Siam and his nine daughters.

During World War II the Japanese Army requisitioned the hotel and used it as an officers club, under the management of the Imperial Hotel in Tokyo. After the Japanese defeat, the American forces moved in and the hotel was used as a transit camp for prisoners of war. In 1947 the hotel came back to life when a consortium led by a French photojournalist, Germaine Krull, and including Jim Thompson, the future Thai Silk King, bought the property. Once again The Oriental was back in business, and in 1967 the hotel moved into the modern era when it was purchased by ItalThai, a construction and mercantile company owned by Giorgio Berlingieri, an Italian engineer, and Dr Chaijudh Karnasuta, a Thai. Their aim was to turn it into a world-class hotel, and they appointed a 30-year-old German named Kurt Wachtveitl as general manager. Wachtveitl, who retired in 2009, proved to be a genius amongst hoteliers, and the remainder of the story would fill a book.

The Oriental today is something of a very clever illusion. Fame and tradition help create the impression for the visitor that he is entering the lobby of the fabled old hotel, whereas the lobby is part of the River Wing, an outwardly conventional multi-storey block that was built in 1976 when the land upon which the Chartered Bank had stood for almost eighty years was acquired. The Oriental management decided that, in the absence of any known founding date for the hotel, the opening of the River Wing should mark the centenary, and so 1876 has been the official founding year ever since. The ten-storey Garden Wing, atop of which is perched the famed Le Normandie French restaurant, dates back to 1958. Yet Hans Niels Andersen's hotel, which opened in such a blaze of glory in 1887, is still here, known today as the Authors' Wing, and it casts an almost mystical spell over the curious jumble of structures. One is hardly aware, walking along the corridor from the lobby to take afternoon tea in the Authors' Lounge, of transiting a century of architectural styles. Stepping out onto the lawn to admire the white frontage with its embossed pediment and wooden shutters, one hardly notices the adjacent tall buildings. Much of this magic is woven in the warren of windowless back offices hidden in the River Wing, where the arcane art of hotel management has reached its apogee, but it is more than this, for somehow the spirit and the history of the old hotel has permeated everything and everyone. The visitor is in The Oriental, one of the greatest hotels in the world. Or, at least, he would be if the Mandarin Oriental Hotel Group of Hong Kong, operator and part owner of the hotel for forty years, had not a few years ago, in an extraordinary rush of blood to the head, renamed the graceful old legend as Mandarin Oriental, Bangkok.

Temple of the Chinese Junk

Our second route through the European district takes us to an offshoot of Chinatown and one of Bangkok's oddest temples, and on to the final resting place of so many of those early expatriates.
Duration: 2 hours

D irectly next to The Oriental, separated from it only by the narrow thoroughfare known as Oriental Avenue, and occasionally floated as a "wouldn't it make a wonderful extension" idea, is the old headquarters of the East Asiatic Company, which grew out of Andersen & Co, founded by Hans Niels Andersen around the time he was purchasing The Oriental. Along with the hotel, Andersen had also purchased The Oriental's retail store, ship chandlery, ice factory, bakery, and aerated water factory. Some of this land was used for his own company, which encompassed shipping, logging and sawmills, and when the East Asiatic Company was founded in 1897 this prominent riverfront site was chosen for the offices. The building was completed early in 1901 and is designed in a neo-Palladian style, with a balustraded staircase leading to the first-floor entrance, arched fanlights over the shuttered windows, and the company logo of an anchor embellishing the pediment. The building has stood empty for many years, although it is in a reasonable state of preservation. East Asiatic's warehouses, huge arched structures built with concrete frames and brick infill (the bricks were

Headquarters of the East Asiatic Company, whose founder also built The Oriental.

imported from Middlesborough, in England), located further along Charoen Krung Road, have recently been brought back to life as part of the Asiatique leisure and shopping complex, a commendable venture that combines conservation with modern needs, and opens up the riverfront to the public.

Asiatique is operated by the same people who operate OP Place, a lovely old building dating from 1905 that stands on the remnants of Chartered Bank Lane, and which houses antique shops, art galleries and boutiques. Elsewhere in this little parcel of land there is a graceful villa from the reign of Rama VI, which houses The Oriental's China House restaurant, and some original shophouses, one of which is home to Tongue Thai, a restaurant noted for its Thai food and Old Bangkok ambience. The area is, however, disfigured by the expanse of tottering corrugated fencing that encloses the land behind Thai Home Industries, a series of handicraft shops housed in former monks' quarters. This has been here for countless years. Why it cannot at least be tidied up, I really do not know.

The East Asiatic Company building is divided into two blocks, connected by an enclosed bridge, and passing through the passageway one is in a tiny and completely enclosed township, that of the Catholic community that has grown up around Assumption Cathedral. Here is a beautifully proportioned square such as might exist in any French cathedral city, as Assumption owes its origins to French missionaries. The Roman Catholic Archdiocese of Bangkok can be traced back to 1662, when the Vicariate Apostolic of Siam was created. The first French missionary active in Siam had been a Franciscan, Bonferre, who had sailed up to Ayutthaya from Goa on board a Portuguese ship in 1550. A small Catholic community grew and after the granting of the Vicariate Apostolic by Alexander VII, Siam, which by this time was a great power in the East, gave shelter to Vietnamese, Japanese and other Christians fleeing their own countries. In 1673 a bishop, Father Louis Laneau, was appointed, and the church entered the spiritual care of the Society of Foreign Missions. Father Laneau was head of the Roman Catholic mission for Indochina, and was based at Ayutthaya, where King Narai was sympathetic to the Catholic Church. Despite the uprising against the Europeans in the wake of the 1688 Siege of Bangkok, and the destruction of Ayutthaya by the Burmese almost a century later, the Catholic Church maintained a status in the country, the community being an integrated part of Siamese society.

In 1809, in the year that Rama II ascended the throne, and with Bangkok taking shape as a great and prosperous city, a missionary named Father Pasquale Gallo obtained permission from the king to build a cathedral. Designed by a French architect and built with materials imported from France and Italy, the cathedral was completed in 1821 and named Assumption to commemorate the passing of the Virgin Mary to heaven. As Christian missionaries began arriving in Bangkok in considerable numbers from the middle of the nineteenth century, the community around Assumption grew. Early in the twentieth century the cathedral was rebuilt, being largely funded by a Catholic Chinese philanthropist named Low Khiok Chiang, a Teochew immigrant who founded a trading company named Kiam Hua Heng, on Charoen Krung Road. One of his early ventures was the import of Singer sewing machines, which had been invented by an American named Isaac Merritt Singer in 1851 and which a few years later appeared in Siam, when Anna Leonowens

Assumption Cathedral, centre of a large Catholic community on the bank of the river.

arranged for a machine to be brought in from Singapore and presented to Rama IV. So successful did Singer become after Kiam Hua Heng took on the distributorship in 1889 that it was spun off into a separate company and remains on Charoen Krung Road today as a publicly listed company and a leading retailer of electrical appliances. Groundwork for the new cathedral started at the beginning of 1910 and work was completed in 1918. Extensive repairs had to be undertaken when Allied bombs fell in the area during World War II.

Tall and rectangular, the cathedral is constructed of red brick, a striking contrast to the stucco-clad eighteenth century churches in Bangkok. The architectural style is Romanesque, with a symmetrical structure that has two 32-metre (104-ft) towers flanking the entrance, the pitched roof of the nave between them reaching a height of 25.6 metres (83 ft). The corners of the building are reinforced with limestone bricks, the white stone forming a contrast with the glowing red of the bricks, and the semi-circular arches over the doorways and windows are supported by non-structural Romanised pillars. The main doorway is multiple layered, the door itself deep inside the vestibule. Inside, the rich décor blends neoclassical and

French colonial themes and is lit by stained glass windows set behind domed arches supported by Romanised pillars. Fresco paintings and bas reliefs adorn the walls, statues of saints line the altar, and the barrel-vault ceiling is set with golden stars in blue panels.

Outside in the square, the Annunciation Convent and the Catholic Centre face the cathedral. To the right is Assumption College, a boys' school founded in 1885 and the third oldest school in Thailand, and to the left is the building of Assumption Printing Press, looking completely unlike a printing works, with its magnificent classical portico and its colonial colonnades, but which has played a very significant role in the affairs of the diocese since the nineteenth century and inside which can be found an intriguing collection of antique printing machinery. The Roman Catholic Archdiocese of Bangkok today ministers more than 80,000 souls. Pope John Paul II visited the cathedral in May 1984, a visit that is commemorated by a statue in the grounds.

Tucked in behind Assumption, on a lane that is opposite the foot of Silom Road and which runs down to a public river pier, is a Buddhist temple that is off the tourist trail, oddly enough given its location, but which has some remarkable old timber architecture. Wat Suan Plu can be reached via an alley off Charoen Krung or through the imposing white gate almost opposite the Shangri-La Hotel. The *ubosot* is traditional, although more richly embossed than many temples and with exquisite panel paintings and large and finely detailed *naga* and angel figures on the gable ends of the three-leaved roof, but it is the monks' quarters and the other buildings in the compound that really capture the interest because they are all made from wood with a clapboard effect, and have been stained cream and red. Follow the lane that runs alongside the Shangri-La, and you come out opposite the Ban Oou Mosque, founded by Muslims from Java who came to Bangkok in the time of Rama IV. Within this small area of land on the riverbank, therefore, within one minute's walking distance of each other, we find three religions living peacefully together.

Dr Dan Beach Bradley, writing in 1835, at a time when Western influence was minimal in the affairs of Siam, commented that there was not one square-rigged ship in the Chao Phraya River. The entire trade of Siam was carried out by Chinese junks, of all sizes from fifty to five hundred tons. The larger vessels plied between Bangkok and Singapore, Batavia and Canton, while the smaller ones traded along the eastern and western coasts of the Gulf. They were carrying rice, timber and gemstones on the outward-bound journey, and bringing back tea, silk, paper and fancy goods from China, or fabrics, glassware and European products from Singapore and Batavia. Junks running the China trade would make only one voyage a year, taking advantage of the southwest monsoon in June to sail from Bangkok, and of the northwest monsoon to return late in January. Bradley writes of a flotilla of sixty to eighty junks moored in the river from February to June, forming two lines in a huge floating bazaar. Each of the ships was freighted with the goods of several merchants, who would display their products on the deck until everything was sold.

The Portuguese had been in treaty relations with Siam since 1820, but very little came in direct: most of the trade was with Portuguese territories such as Goa, Macau and East Timor. A community of Muslim merchants was shipping between Bombay and Bangkok under the British flag, but only at the rate of three or four ships a year. Twenty years after Bradley's observations, the situation and the riverscape were to change dramatically. Foreign trade now flourished, as did foreign fashions. Now the junks rode at anchor beside tall-masted sailing ships and the early steamers. Godowns and sawmills were built at the river's edge, their memories enshrined in names such as Soi Rong Luey Misglug (Klugg's Sawmill Lane) and Soi Rong Luey Asiatic (East Asiatic Sawmill Lane), which survive today.

Rama III, who reigned from 1824 to 1851, foresaw that the supremacy of the Chinese junk was not going to last for ever. The king had in his youth been given responsibility for foreign trade and relations, and when he became king he devoted much of his time to both the politics and the mechanics of international trade. He is known to Thai history as the Father of Trade. Steamships were faster and more efficient than sailing vessels. China under the Qing Dynasty was weakening, and the strength of the Western countries was growing. The king felt that a reminder of how Siam's prosperity was achieved was needed for the generations to come. On the bank of the river, shortly before ships reached Bangkok, was a village named Ban Thawai, or Tavoy Village. Populated by people originally from Tavoy, in Burma, the settlement had a market for trading water buffalo. There was a temple here of unknown age named Wat Khok Kwai, which translates as "Temple of the Buffalo Pen". During the reign of Rama I the temple was accorded royal status and renamed Wat Khok Krabue, *krabue* being a more formal word for buffalo. In the temple grounds, directly on the riverbank and visible to all passing ships, Rama III built a chapel that is a stone replica of a Chinese junk. *Yan* in Thai means "craft" or "conveyance", and *nawa* is a vessel or boat, and so the temple was renamed yet again, this time as Wat Yannawa.

The building of Charoen Krung Road had the odd effect of turning Wat Yannawa around by 180 degrees. Whereas the temple had originally faced the river, now a large gate was built on the new road and this became the main entrance. The *ubosot*, dating back to the renovations of Rama I, was originally the front of the temple with the later junk *wiharn* looming behind it: now, the huge Chinese junk obscures the view of the bell tower and *ubosot* to the rear. Built of concrete, the junk chapel measures 43 metres (141 ft) from end to end and is 5 metres (16 ft) high in the centre. Two *chedis* stand on the deck, representing the masts. These structures have given the temple its local name, *sampao chedi*, which means "junk with *chedis*" (the word "junk" entered the English language in the sixteenth century via the Portuguese word *junco*). Narrow stone steps inside the hull lead up to the deck, and the wheelhouse at the rear is the altar.

On the northern side of Wat Yannawa, right up against the red-painted iron fence of the temple, is an area of riverbank that has played a significant role in Bangkok's history, and in particular that of the Chinese community. Labelled prosaically as "Soi 52", it is known to the locals as Soi Wang Lee. When the southern half of Charoen Krung was built, this stretch of the road between the legation district and the Western residential district at Bang Kolaem became an extension of Chinatown. Consequently, many Chinese immigrants landed at the pier next to the temple, and were absorbed into the community. The landing was not without its hazards. A ship sank here and many were drowned. The wreckage remained a danger to navigation for several years, Captain Loftus noting the position on his map and commenting that "several anchors have been lost here". Near to this spot the Jiew Eng Biew shrine was built by Chinese immigrants for a group of Hainanese who had set sail from their homeland bound for Bangkok, only to be mistaken for pirates off the coast of Vietnam and slaughtered.

In 1908 a group of Chinese merchants formed the Chino-Siam Steam Navigation Company in an attempt to break the Western monopoly on passenger and cargo shipping between Bangkok, Singapore, Hong Kong, Shantou and Haikou, and they made their port at the land around the Chinese jetty. It became known as May Cheen Port, after the Thai name of the company. Three rice mills were founded in the immediate vicinity, adding their smoke and clamour to the din from the sawmills and the general hubbub of commerce, and this became one of the most congested parts of Bangkok. It also became an area noted for its revelry, particularly after the Wang Lee family, successful Chinese immigrants who made a fortune from rice mills, acquired the land and, in 1927, erected two rows of elegant shophouses at right angles to the river, flanking the port. The development included the Prasitiphon, a bar with Thai and Western hostesses, a band playing dance music, and the raucous atmosphere of a portside saloon. After World War II it faded, and became a noodle shop. Sadly, in a controversial piece of vandalism, this area has recently been cleared, but right up to the end it was still possible to see the faded lettering above the interior doorway, saying: PLEASE ENTERTAIN HERE.

On the southern side of Wat Yannawa is a row of shophouses, one prominent establishment making and selling vendors' carts, and several others dealing in marine engines, paint and tarpaulins. At a gap in the row, through a modest gateway, and unexpected in this urban setting, is a large dockyard. British entrepreneurs founded the Bangkok Dry Dock in 1865, Captain Bush being one of the shareholders. Built to service sea-going cargo vessels, the dock was conveniently sited for all the foreign ships coming into Bangkok, and it

The end of the line for this tram at the former terminus of Thanon Tok.

became one of the most prominent businesses along the riverbank. The dock was requisitioned by the Thai Royal Navy during World War II, and subsequently badly damaged when bombed by Allied forces. After the war the dock was handed back to its British owners, but the 45.7-metre (150-ft) timber-built No 1 dock had been almost completely destroyed. A ferro-concrete replacement more than twice the length was built and there are now two docks, handling vessels up to 4,000 dwt. The company shares were gradually bought up during the 1950s by Thai interests, which explains the name: The Bangkok Dock Company (1957) Limited.

And so you trudge on down Charoen Krung Road, beginning to realise what a long road it is, and no doubt a spiffing place to drive one's horse and carriage. Over Klong Bang Kolaem you go, where until the early 1940s, until it was washed away in serious flooding, there was a thriving floating market. We are now in the old Western residential district of Bang Kolaem, an area that grew up even before Charoen Krung Road was laid because (a) everyone travelled by boat, and (b) there was nowhere else. But there is nothing left of this now, except for a blank iron door set in a high wall.

The Protestant Cemetery, the final destination for so many members of the Western community, owes its beginnings to Colonel William Butterworth, formerly of the Madras Army, who became Governor of the Straits Settlements in 1843. Butterworth had become friends with Rama IV before the king had ascended the throne, and in those days before the Bowring Treaty and the appointment of a British consul, much of the dealings between Siam and Britain were done through Singapore. In 1851, Butterworth wrote to the king, pointing out that there was no burial ground for Christians of the Protestant faith who died in Bangkok. The king himself had been aware of this, and he readily acceded to Butterworth's request that land be provided. A man named Nai Muang had owned a site by the river, and had absconded when he got into debt. The land had passed into the hands of one of his creditors who, although the record isn't clear, appears to have been related to the Scottish merchant Robert Hunter. The Western community felt the site would serve their needs perfectly. Measured out by the traditional Siamese units, it was 5 *sen* and 8 *wah* long, and with a width of 1 *sen* 1 *wah* and 2 *sok*. A *wah*, which is still used today, is the fingertip-to-fingertip measurement of a man's outstretched arms. A *sen* is equal to 20 *wah*, while a *sok* is an elbow length. Converted into metric, the land is 216 x 43 metres (708 x 141 ft). The price was 10 *chang*, or 800 baht, and the king paid for the land out of the royal coffers. The burial ground was presented to the foreign community on 30th July 1853.

Passing through the iron door, the traffic noise dimmed by the high wall, the visitor is in a peaceful spot that could easily pass for an English churchyard. Administered by the Protestant Cemetery Committee, with the burial register kept at Christ Church on Convent Road, the cemetery is maintained entirely by voluntary contributions. A stroll amongst the graves here will reveal the resting place of many of the earliest foreign settlers. The grave of Dr Daniel Beach Bradley, with its tall obelisk and forbidding black lettering, evokes an image of the man himself, who died in 1873 at the age of 69. Next to him lie his two wives, Emelie and Sarah. This part of the cemetery is in fact given over to the American missionaries: the Reverend Samuel Jones Smith, John Taylor Jones, John Carrington,

William Greenstock, the Reverend Cyrus Chilcott, Alanson Reed; names familiar to us from Bradley's own writings. George Bradley McFarland, compiler of the Thai-English dictionary that is still a standard work today. Jennie Neilson Hays, whose grieving husband built the Neilson Hays Library on Surawong Road in her memory. Hamilton King, American ambassador, who died in 1912 and has an old-established restaurant in the Dusit Thani Hotel named after him. There is an impressive tomb for Admiral Sir John Bush, who died in 1905 at the age of 86, the monument erected by Rama v himself. Nearby lies Bush's son George, buried beneath a large monument with a skull and crossbones relief, also erected by the king. His Majesty was particularly benevolent in commemorating those of his foreign servants he felt had given a long and devoted service. Henry Alabaster, who died in 1884, a diplomat who had helped in the surveying and construction of Charoen Krung Road and who had become a trusted advisor to the king, has the largest and most imposing memorial of them all.

On one of my recent visits as I stood contemplating the monument erected "In Memory of the Deceased Members of Club Concordia", a woman emerged from the small chapel on the riverbank. Reassuring me that her dog wouldn't bite me, she apologised for the length of the grass. She was in charge of routine maintenance, and having watched me taking notes had probably assumed I was an official. *Nam tuam tuk wan*, she explained. The ground was flooded every day now because we were in the rainy season, and the grass could not be cut. I assured her I was just looking round, and she retreated behind her chapel to await the dry season. The ground was indeed waterlogged. Anyone venturing off the path would in all possibility sink down to prematurely join the sleepers under the long grass. Doubtless, however, those laid to rest under these white stones have long since dissolved into the marshy water, their remains sucked into the river and born downstream, over the bar and into the ocean.

Not far below the cemetery, Charoen Krung ends at Thanon Tok; the point where, as the Thais, totally unused to the concept of roads, pointed out that had the road continued, it would have fallen into the water. Although this was largely a residential district, there was still plenty of commerce here. Thai Tobacco, its factory backing directly on to the cemetery but now empty and its fate uncertain, was originally built to process tobacco leaf sent down by river from the plantations around Chiang Mai and Chiang Rai. There used to be sawmills and woodyards down here, and there is an old-established fireworks factory still in existence. A Chinese undertaker has his business on a corner site, the opulent walnut-wood coffins with their distinctive lotus-bloom shapes stacked up at the frontage (I wouldn't be seen dead in one of those) and the surrounding buildings decorated with feng shui mirrors to reflect the bad luck back at him. There are several small Muslim communities, marked by the green domes of their mosques, and there is a large hospital.

The trams had rattled down this road all the way from the City Pillar to Thanon Tok, the oldest and longest of all the Bangkok tram routes. The line had started out as a venture by the indefatigable Captain Loftus, who in 1887, along with Danish naval officer Andreas du Plessis de Richelieu, gained a royal concession to run horse-drawn trams along this route. The concession was later transferred to a Danish company that electrified the line in 1894, the first electric tramway in Asia and predating Copenhagen's own electric trams by about ten years. The line was closed in 1963. A lone yellow tram now sits in front of the offices of the Metropolitan Electricity Authority's Yannawa branch, close to where the trams performed a U-turn. A restaurant named The View now occupies the site where the offices of the *Siam Weekly Advertiser* stood and next to this are the two floating docks of Wangchao Shipyard. At the point where the river bends sharply there is the Krung Thep Bridge, a steel truss structure that opened in 1959 and is modelled after the Memorial Bridge. This too is a bascule bridge, still in working order, the leaves operated by electric motors.

The Village of Love

Walking the length of Silom Road will take us from the European district through an Indian neighbourhood and up to an area of Christian churches, convents, hospitals and schools, before ending at the city's most famous red-light district.

Duration: 3 hours

As with the name of Bangkok itself, no one seems to know quite how the name of Bangrak originated. The general opinion is that it derives from a huge rak tree that grew in the muddy ground of a canal, Klong Tonsoong. All the locals and visitors knew this landmark, for the flowers of the tree are woven into garlands, and for a small village set in flat swampland it would have been prominent. Others say the name dates from the early part of the nineteenth century, when Catholic missionaries set up a medical care centre here: the word *raksa* meaning "to cure sickness". But *rak*, written in a different way, can also mean "love". And so Bangrak is now known as the Village of Love, illustrated by the procession of young couples who pass through the district registry office on St Valentine's Day to exchange their wedding vows.

The footprint of Bangrak runs along the river from the southern side of the Padung Krung Kasem canal to Sathorn Road, thereby spanning the old European legation district. There are three roads laid out in parallel at right angles to the river, each of them running up to the far border of the district at Rama IV Road, while one side of a fourth

The mansion of Luang Sathorn, who developed Sathorn Road.

road, Sathorn Road, forms the eastern border. The oldest of these is Silom Road. Western merchants had petitioned the king directly after the signing of the Bowring Treaty for a canal to link Padung Krung Kasem with shipping at Klong Toei, and the Hua Lampong canal had been dug in 1857, arrow-straight across the fields and marshland to the big bend in the river, halving the journey time. The earth dug out to form the canal was heaped alongside and was the first instance in Bangkok where a walkway was built alongside a canal. When the Silom canal was cut between the new waterway and the river in 1858, it followed the same pattern. With the building of Charoen Krung, and the southeastward spread of the city, the demand for roads and development land grew. These two thoroughfares were upgraded, earth being dug from the sides of the road to raise the surface, which was then covered with a layer of rocks and brick. The road alongside Hua Lampong became Rama IV Road. Luang Sathorn Racha Yuk was the first person to privately fund the construction of a canal and road across his property when he built Sathorn Road in about 1890. He made a profit by selling off plots of land on either side of the canal to private owners, and built himself an ornate mansion that is one of the

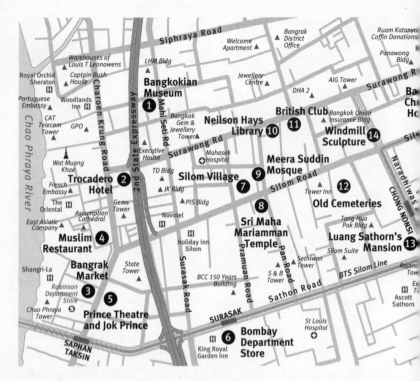

few on this sadly despoiled road that remain. Luang Sathorn did not live to enjoy his success, dying of influenza in 1895 at the young age of 38. The mansion became the Hotel Royal in 1927, and then from 1948 to 1999 housed the embassy of the USSR, and later, Russia. It is now a boutique hotel and part of the Sathorn Square development. Luang Sathorn's success in selling land to wealthy investors encouraged Chao Phraya Surawong Wattanasak to construct Surawong Road a few years later, and four noblemen of the rank of *phraya* to build Siphraya Road in 1905. (*Si* means "four". There was a fifth nobleman in the venture but he held the lesser title of *luang*. He was later elevated to *phraya*, but not before the road was completed: otherwise it would be called Haphraya!). There was no canal built along Siphraya, because by this time canal building in Bangkok had come to an end. The noblemen regarded the road as a commercial venture, running from the customs area and emerging banking district through land that was ripe for development.

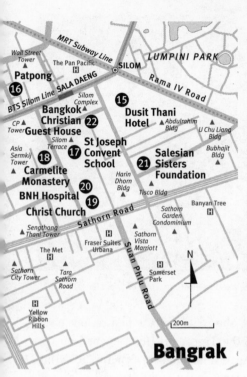

In addition to being the home of the embassies and the port, this stretch of Charoen Krung started to become a desirable residential neighbourhood for Europeans, especially with the advent of the trams (there being a first-class section in the tram, in which ladies were required to wear hats). Siphraya Cross evolved into a fashionable European shopping centre. The banks were in this area, all three of them (Hongkong & Shanghai, Chartered, and Siam Commercial), and there was a hospital, founded by the French. J Antonio, the photographer whose work is an important record of Bangkok in Rama v's time, and who wrote the classic *1904 Traveller's Guide to Bangkok and Siam*, had his studio here. The offices of the *Bangkok Times*, founded in 1887, were here. Kiam Hua Heng, astounding everyone by importing the recently invented Singer sewing machines, became the leading dry goods store. In the 1920s the Chirathivat family, Chinese immigrants from Hainan, opened a small shop on the corner of Captain Bush Lane, selling international newspapers and magazines. Named Central Trading Store, it grew into Thailand's largest retail conglomerate, responsible today for all those Central and Robinson's department stores, all those Centara hotels, and much else besides. Indian and Burmese gemstone traders moved in and this became the city's gemstone centre, a position it retains to this day, with gems and jewellery being one of the country's prime industries. The Indian presence here remains a strong one, with Indian trading companies, spice shops and restaurants, and Indian

A modern windmill sculpture signifying the origins of the name of Silom Road.

ownership of the Holiday Inn. The 1920s saw the first serious challenge to The Oriental, when the Trocadero Hotel opened on the corner of Surawong Road in 1929, a magnificent structure towering four storeys, with European management and a Parisian chef, and charging the same rates as its august neighbour. Today the hotel is in a sad state externally, with cheapo shops all along its ground floor level and its graceful façade encrusted with air-conditioning units, and it describes itself as an economy hotel. At the far end of the shopping centre, the foot of Sathorn Road, the Bombay Department Store opened in 1903, a great attraction for the well-heeled residents who were moving into their newly-built mansions. The Thai-Chinese Chamber of Commerce (TCC), which had been founded in 1910, later bought the building at a bargain price, and at the beginning of 1930 moved in and used it as their headquarters. When the Imperial Japanese Army occupied Siam during World War II, they took over and used the building as their command centre. The TCC moved back in after the war was over, and later built a new tower block to the rear of the premises. Today, the building, an exceptional example of its type, houses the Blue Elephant Cooking School and Restaurant.

Silom Road takes its name from windmills built to draw water from the canal to irrigate the market gardens and orchards, *si lom* being the word for "windmill" (it's a different *si* to the word for "four"). This is why you see windmill names and signs attached to restaurants and shops, and why the big modern steel sculpture was placed at the junction when Naradhiwas Road was cut in the mid 1990s. Bangrak Market grew up at the foot of Silom and thrives to this day, inhabiting the little streets around Robinson's department store and behind State Tower, which looms above the ancient pawnshop on the corner. A little further on stands a row of crumbling shophouses, and midway along them is the tiny decaying skeleton of a cinema awning, placed over a narrow alley that leads to the Prince Theatre. Originally known as the Bangrak Cinema, it is believed to date from 1908, which would make it one of Asia's oldest picture houses. Jok Prince, near the theatre entrance, has been serving the best rice *congee* in this area ever since anyone can remember, and there are other eating-places that are part of the neighbourhood fabric, such as the Muslim Restaurant, on the corner of Charoeng Krung and Silom, which has been here for at least seventy years. Having been founded by Hajee Maidin Pakayawong, a goat butcher at the market, fresh goat meat is the speciality, with goat biryani and goat liver masala high on the list of favourites.

During the first half of the twentieth century, this was a pleasant part of Bangkok in which to live. Silom Road still had its canal and was lined with rosewood trees. From 1925 a tram ran alongside the canal to Rama IV Road, itself still with a canal, and then past the green expanse of Lumpini Park and up to Pratunam, for those who wanted to visit the market there, or they could disembark at the top of Silom and catch a tram to Hua Lampong, where there were two railway termini. Although the tram was discontinued in 1962, and the Silom canal filled in not long after, there is still the opportunity to see what life must have been like by visiting the home that has been turned into a private museum, the Bangkokian Museum.

Charoen Krung Soi 43 still retains faint traces of the classy residential neighbourhood it was before World War II, when a small canal used to flow along here, and houses occupied large compounds. One of these belonged to the family of Waraporn Suravadi,

who still lives on the compound but has turned three of the buildings into a museum displaying everyday objects used in the first half
of the last century. Waraporn, who was born in 1939, says her family
has owned the compound since her great-grandfather's time.

To one side of the compound is a single-storey shophouse. Many
families built shophouses on their land, which is why you so often find
splendid old houses buried behind commercial property. Waraporn
has converted this into a gallery that holds mainly kitchen utensils
and domestic equipment, such as a sewing machine and a charcoal-
heated iron. There is a kitchen range powered by charcoal, and a rice
miller that is so large and heavy it is mounted in a frame and worked
by a pulley. Some items have simply disappeared from society, such
as the snuff inhaler with a mouthpiece you use to blow the snuff up
your nose. By the door is a crumbling stack of once-smart leather
suitcases, formerly the possession of Waraporn's mother's first husband, Dr Francis Christian. Dr Christian was an Indian by birth,
who had gone to Dublin to study medicine. The couple had met in
Penang. They returned to Bangkok, and Dr Christian decided to set
up a practice. A traditional wooden house was built to the rear of the
compound in 1929, intended as a clinic, but the doctor died before
seeing his first patient. He was only forty years old. The house now
forms a second gallery, with many of the good doctor's possessions
still intact, including his large framed surgeon's certificates.

The third gallery is inside the main house, which was built in
1937. Although it is constructed of teak, the house was carefully
painted to look as if it is concrete, at that time an expensive but
fashionable material. Waraporn's mother had by this time married
Bunphum Suravadi, and the house is that of a prosperous family, a
comfortable home for the three little daughters who grew up here. It
is handsomely and tastefully furnished, equipped with Qing Dynasty
blue porcelain and crockery from Johnson Brothers of England, with
an English piano and an expandable dining table standing on sturdy
lion's paw legs. Upstairs, the bedrooms have four-poster beds draped
in mosquito netting. Waraporn, who has been a teacher all her life,
charges no entrance fee and regards the museum as a service to keep
alive the memories of how Bangkok once was. There is also a small

museum on the premises, operated by the Bangkok Metropolitan Administration and displaying old photographs of Bangrak.

From the Bangkokian Museum it takes only a few minutes to walk through the back roads to what was another graceful old family home. Fronting onto Silom is a cluster of teak houses, standing on a two-acre compound, and built in the Southern Thai style known as *panya*, which uses square elements for the upper storey. They were erected about 1908 and there were ten of them, owned by the Thai-Chinese Aksornramat family. In 1978, some of the buildings having become dilapidated, the family demolished what could not be saved and built a connecting bridge between the remaining structures. Inside the compound they opened a restaurant and small shops and boutiques. Known as Silom Village, it is one of the most attractive and prominent features of Silom Road, the restaurant popular with tourists and locals alike and the buildings in an excellent state of preservation.

Almost opposite Silom Village is the unmistakable landmark of the Sri Maha Mariamman Temple, a typical Southern Indian temple with its riot of carved and brightly coloured Hindu gods and goddesses. Immigrants from Tamil Nadu built the temple in the late 1860s, and today it is the primary Hindu temple in Thailand, as well as being the oldest. Within the compound are three shrines, and the procedure is to pray first at the shrine of Ganesh, then at the shrine of Karthik and finally at the shrine of Sri Maha Mariamman. There are also shrines for the worship of Lord Siva, Brahma and Vishnu, and inside the main temple hall at figures of Mahalakshmi, Saraswathi, Kali and Hanuman. Known generally as Wat Khaek, *khaek* being the generic Thai word for "Indian", the temple stands on the corner of Pan Road, a narrow lane whose opposite corner is a blaze of saffron-coloured garlands for worshippers and which would brighten up anyone's living room, regardless of their religious beliefs. Every year, in September or October, the Dussehra festival, the remover of bad fate, is staged here, a ten-day event that on the final day sees this part of Silom closed to traffic and the streets decked with yellow garlands and candles, while the image of Sri Maha Mariamman is carried in a procession along the road.

Directly opposite Wat Khaek is a lane named Soi Pradit, and here can be found a community of Muslims originally from Indonesia. They have been in Thailand a long time, having originally settled in Ayutthaya. The Meera Suddin Mosque rises up amidst the small wet market that makes this a crowded thoroughfare, and has its origins in a timber house that was converted into a mosque in 1912. In 1983 a Muslim businessman named Manit Hadji Muhamud Maidin built the present structure on the land, using his own funds, and it remains today a privately maintained mosque, independent from the Religious Affairs Department.

Continue on Soi Pradit and you will emerge onto Surawong, with the graceful rotunda of the Neilson Hays Library on the corner, half buried behind green foliage. There can be few more tranquil places anywhere in the city for book lovers to sit and read, and along with the lending library there is a reference section that includes a selection of books on Bangkok and Thailand, tucked inside an ancient cabinet. In 1869, a year into the reign of Rama V, the Ladies Bazaar Association in Bangkok, a charitable organisation founded three years previously, founded the Bangkok Ladies Library Association to meet the reading needs of the increasing English-speaking community. The books were initially stored in a private residence on the Baptist compound, and later they were removed to the vestry of the Protestant Union Chapel in Charoen Krung Road, where they were stored rent-free until 1900. Jennie Neilson was a Danish Protestant missionary who arrived in Siam in 1881. She married Dr Thomas Heyward Hays, an American who was head of the Royal Thai Navy Hospital, in 1887, and they made their home at Silom Road. Jennie became actively involved in the Bangkok Ladies Library Association, which became more costly and difficult to administer after 1900, when the Protestant Chapel moved and temporary accommodation had to be found. First of all, the books were stored in the house of a lawyer on Charoen Krung, and then in 1909 they were moved to a large room on the upper level of the premises of Falck & Beidek, in Chartered Bank Lane. In 1914, Jennie became president of what by now was named the Bangkok Library Association, and the decision was made to buy a plot of land on Surawong Road, where a modest building was erected to act as a permanent library. In 1920, Jennie died suddenly of cholera. Dr Hays felt that her devotion to the library should be commemorated, and he commissioned Italian architect Mario Tamagno to design a building that he then gifted to the Association. The new building was opened on 26th June 1922. Tamagno, already renowned for other works in Bangkok, including Hua Lampong Railway Station, designed a rotunda for the main entrance and a single-storey building with classical Romanesque interior columns, teak window frames and beautiful wood flooring. King Rama VI presented a large writing desk, bearing the royal insignia, which is still used today.

Nowadays the rotunda entrance is closed because of its proximity to the busy street, and the entrance is to the side of the building, via a tree-shaded courtyard. The dome is used as an art gallery, but everything else remains the same as the day the library opened, there having been only a brief period of closure when the Japanese Army used it as a barracks. The library is staffed entirely by women volunteers, following the wishes of Dr Hays, who wanted the tradition of the original Association to continue, and it is run by a committee of twelve women. Dr Hays himself died two years after the library opened, at the age of 70, and is buried in the Protestant Cemetery with Jennie.

Next to the Neilson Hays Library stands the British Club, set well back from the road, its 1910 clubhouse being visible only to members and their guests, who pass through a gateway emblazoned with the BC plaque and find themselves contemplating a large lawn, a number of tennis courts and a pleasant swimming pool. Inside, with the sombre wood panelling and the ceiling fans, it is almost as if the past century never happened. The club was founded on St George's Day, 23rd April 1903, by a small group of British businessmen and diplomats, and occupied a small wooden building standing on the same plot of land as it does today, Surawong Road having only recently been completed. It was, of course, solely a male preserve. To the eastern side of the club stood the Danish-owned Siam Electricity Company's Bangkok Lawn Tennis Club, and a small canal ran along the west side to join the Silom canal. Membership grew, and in 1910 the present clubhouse was built, the old house being demolished to create space for what is now the front lawn. In 1919 the tennis club was acquired and gave the club the seven tennis courts it has today, and increasing the land area to three-and-a-half acres. As with the Neilson Hays Library, activities were cut short in December 1941 when the Japanese invaded Siam, using the club as an officers' mess. The club was reclaimed after the war, and was back in business by 1946.

The British Club and the Neilson Hays Library share a back gate onto a lane that leads to Silom, and opposite here, on both sides of a thoroughfare that the taxi drivers know as *soi prachaa farang*, or "foreigners' cemetery lane", are the remains of several old grave-yards. The most prominent is a now defunct Catholic cemetery, distinctive because of its two-storey gatehouse on Silom Road, but with the graves now removed and the plot overgrown, waiting for a destiny at present unknown. At the rear of the cemetery, where a wall divides it from a modern office block, there is a gap between the old graveyard wall and the newer wall. When the building was first erected, some wag plugged this gap with a coffin lid, which remained there for years until it rotted away.

On the other side of the lane is a Chinese burial ground, the graves packed in close together, the land flooded with goo and patrolled by pi-dogs with a distinctly chippy attitude to anyone attempting a short-cut. A few families live in shacks on the edge of the ground, and are only marginally friendlier towards strangers than the dogs. A Buddhist graveyard lies next to this, and is now largely pressed into service as a carpark. Beyond this there used to be yet another Chinese burial ground, but it was cleared a few years ago to make way for a development that includes a hotel, shops and office space. So much for the Thais' fear of ghosts.

There are very few buildings still standing from the early days of Silom Road, those that are being generally private residences hidden behind high walls in the back *sois*, or pressed into service as charming restaurants. Some masterpieces have sadly been lost, such as Baan Surasana, which stood on the site of the Bangkok Bank. The bank had been formed in 1944, when the Japanese occupation of

Siam resulted in the closure of the British, European and American banks. A group of Thai courtiers and businessmen founded the bank, which was initially operated out of two adjacent shophouses in Chinatown. It is now Thailand's largest bank. When the head offices were completed on Silom in 1980, the building was, at twenty-five storeys, for some years the tallest tower in Thailand. It just topped the twenty-three-storey, 82-metre-high Dusit Thani Hotel, completed in 1970 and itself only slightly smaller than the Chokchai Building on Sukhumvit Road, which had opened the year before as Bangkok's first high-rise office building.

The Dusit Thani, which took its name from the fanciful miniature city created by Rama VI, was a landmark in more ways than one. Thanpuying Chanut Piyaoui had opened her first hotel, the Princess, on Oriental Avenue at Charoen Krung Road directly after World War II. By the 1960s it was becoming apparent that tourism represented a significant future industry for Thailand, and Thanpuying Chanut, who by now had seen first-hand how top hotels overseas operated, decided to build a first-class international standard hotel in the centre of Bangkok. It thereby became one of the first new-generation five-star hotels to open in the city, along with the Siam Intercontinental on Siam Square, now demolished, the President on Ploenchit, which is now the Holiday Inn, and the Hilton on Silom, now also a Holiday Inn. The Dusit Thani was built on the site of a mansion, and despite its height was constructed without the use of a tower crane, there being none in existence in Bangkok at that time. Ropes, pulleys, ramps, and baskets of building materials were the methods used, with the workforce being housed in the basement as the building grew above them. The hotel remains essentially unchanged to this day, a pleasantly rambling and unhurried setting that is not unlike a small town in itself.

Convent Road is a leafy lane at the top end of Silom, with some old eating-houses on the corner, a decent Irish pub, a very attractive conversion of an old timber house into a French restaurant named Indigo, and several other outstanding restaurants and nightspots. Wander further along this road, however, away from the lights of Silom, and we are into a hushed Christian world.

On 3rd June 1861, a meeting of non-Roman Catholic Christians, most of them British, had been held at the British Consulate to consider the possibility of building a church. The Catholic Church already had several places of worship in Bangkok, and indeed a resident bishop. The Protestants had nowhere to gather except in one of the houses of the American missionaries. The meeting resolved to ask Rama IV for a suitable piece of land, and the king rapidly responded with the offer of a parcel of riverbank just to the south of Wat Yannawa, part of which was owned by the Siamese government and part being leased by the Borneo Company. Funded by a combination of local subscriptions and a grant from the Treasury in London, the Protestant Union Chapel was opened on 1st May 1864.

The years passed, and by the end of the century the congregation, which by now had its own full-time chaplain, had outgrown the modest premises. Further, the chapel's neighbour, the Bangkok Dock Company, which had come into existence a year after the church, was an extremely noisy one, and the ships on the river were a continual disturbance to the solemnity of the services. The new roads were opening up what had been rural areas and creating suburbs, and no one now relied on the river and canals for transport. In 1903 the Church Committee approached Rama V, asking for permission to sell the land that had been gifted by the king's father, and use the funds to purchase a new site and erect another church. Again, the king's reply was prompt and kind, not only giving his permission but also presenting another site, nearly three times as large, on Sathorn Road. The letter from the king said that the site measured 2 *sens* and 10 *wahs* on the north and south sides, and 2 *sens* on the east and west sides, giving an area of about 2,000 square *wah*, "free from disturbing influences, and eminently suitable for establishing a place of worship". The letter gave permission for a church to be established on the land, with the provision that the rights granted did not include the right to use the premises for the internment of the dead. As the Protestant community already had its own burial ground on Charoen Krung Road, the burial rights did not arise. The king's letter was dated 7th April 1904. On 19th July, Mr J S Smyth, "Long Jimmy", a local architect, submitted plans and a model of a new church that

Christ Church, built on Convent Road by the Anglican community.

he said could be built for the 57,000 *ticals* offered, and said that he would supervise the construction free of charge. The Borneo Company bought the land on which the riverside church stood, and Captain Bush then bought the land from the Borneo Company to extend the Bangkok Dock. The hymns of praise were replaced by the clangour of the dockyard, and everyone was happy.

Building of the church began in August and was completed early in 1905. Christ Church was chosen as the name, suggestions of saints' names being dismissed as conscious rejections of popery, and the dedication service was held on the evening of Sunday, 30th April. Today, the church stands as an island of tranquillity on the maelstrom of Sathorn Road. Built in a simple Gothic style with plaster-covered brickwork in the walls and pillars, the church stands on a foundation of teak logs and has a tiled roof supported by teak timbers. The sanctuary is tiled in marble. There are two aisles, north and south, with an organ at the east end of the north aisle and the vestry in a corresponding position on the south aisle. The roof rises to 13.7 metres (45 ft) and the square tower to 15.8 metres (52 ft). Five handsomely carved teak ceiling fans were installed on each side of the nave in 1919, but these days air-conditioning is included. A bell, tuned to the note of F, hangs in the tower. Services are held in English and in Thai, and up to 450 worshippers can be accommodated. Christ Church is part of the Anglican Church in Thailand and comes under the Diocese of Singapore.

Convent Road takes its name from St Joseph Convent School, founded in 1904 by the Sisters of Saint Paul de Chartres, initially to meet the needs of Europeans living in Siam. Today the school is one of the leading private schools in Bangkok, noted especially for its English Programme. The Sisters of Saint Paul de Chartres had first arrived in Bangkok a few years earlier, in 1898, to take care of St Louis Hospital, which had been founded by Archbishop Louis Vey, who was the Apostolic Vicar of the Roman Catholic Mission in Siam. St Louis Hospital is today a thriving non-profit private hospital that occupies 32 hectares of land on the other side of Sathorn Road. Directly opposite the high wall of St Joseph Convent is another high wall, topped with high railings, behind which is a small community of nuns of the Order of Discalced Carmelites, who live under their vows of silence and prayer.

If you cut through to Sala Daeng Road you will find the Salesian Sisters Foundation, which provides Mass and other services in Italian and Spanish. On Sala Daeng Soi 2 stands the Bangkok Christian Guest House, owned by the Foundation of the Church of Christ in Thailand. Protestant missionaries had first arrived in Bangkok in 1826 through the American Board of Commissioners for Foreign Missions, who had initially sent Karl Gutzlaff, followed by a group led by the Reverend Jesse Casswell and then, arriving in 1834 as a missionary physician, Dr Dan Beach Bradley. American Baptists arrived in 1833. In 1840 the American Presbyterian Mission sent two missionaries, the Reverend William P Buell and Mrs Seignoria Buell, and out of this had grown the Presbytery of Siam Mission, which was very active in establishing schools, hospitals and churches in Bangkok and other parts of the country. The Church of Christ in Thailand was founded in 1934 by the merger of several Protestant groups, mainly Presbyterian congregations along with the Lutherans from the German Marburger Mission, and is today considered to be the largest Protestant church in Thailand. After World War II, the Church of Christ had purchased land between Silom and Surawong roads, renovated some wooden buildings that stood there, and inaugurated the Bangkok Christian Hospital in 1949. The hospital today stands on the same site and is one of the largest general hospitals in Bangkok. One of its buildings is named the Moh Bradley Building, after Dr Bradley. The Bangkok Christian Guest House provides accommodation for a steady stream of missionaries, social workers, aid providers, medical personnel and NGO personnel passing through Bangkok.

The BNH Hospital, formerly known as the Bangkok Nursing Home and which stands beside Christ Church, has no religious affiliation but evolved out of the British community at the time the church was being planned. In 1897 there had been a meeting between community members and the British Resident Minister George Grenville, held at the British Legation, to discuss the founding of a hospital modelled on contemporary British practice. A proposal was put to Rama V, who endorsed it and instructed officials to supervise the founding of the hospital as a non-profit organisation: the monarch also provided an annual grant of 960 baht. The Bangkok Nursing Home was a modest affair, located in rented accommodation near its present site and staffed by two nurses sent out from the Colonial Nursing Association in London in 1898. In 1901 the Bangkok Nursing Home Association raised a loan of 50,000 baht and purchased the plot of land on Convent Road on which the hospital now stands. A charitable non-profit institution, and one that has undergone several financial crises in its history up until relatively modern times, the BNH has fund-raising in its DNA and is well known for its high-profile annual bed push.

There are those cynics amongst us (and shame upon them!) who declare that Bangrak, the Village of Love, is so named because the red-light district of Patpong lies at its heart. Whatever reputation Patpong has for debauchery, it is nonetheless a village, and it grew in the same unplanned way that characterises so much of Bangkok.

Poon Pat was a Chinese immigrant from Hainan Island who in the early twentieth century was working as a rice buyer for a company in Bangkok. Part of Poon Pat's territory included the Ban Moh district in Saraburi Province, to the north of Bangkok, and looking into the rice yields there, he realised there was something odd about the soil. During the monsoon rains, erosion would often reveal what the farmers called white earth, laying a metre or so below the topsoil. Nothing would grow on or near the white earth, and new topsoil had to be shovelled back over it before rice seeds could be planted. Poon Pat took a sample back to Bangkok, where it was found to be almost pure calcium carbonate, a mineral that is necessary for the production of Portland cement. At that time cement for Siam's roads and buildings had to be imported, and so the discovery was of great value. In recognition of his service to the nation, Rama vi bestowed upon Poon Pat the title Luang Patpongse Panit, the "luang" roughly equivalent to viscount and with the "panit" signifying the title had been conferred for services to commerce. Poon Pat adopted Patpongse (the "se" is silent) as his new Thai family name and quickly adapted to the life of nobility.

Directly after the end of World War II, Poon Patpongse purchased an undeveloped plot of land that lay between Silom and Surawong roads. The only building of any significance on the plot was a teak building that had been occupied by the Hongkong & Shanghai Bank, and which had been taken over by the occupying Japanese in 1941 for use as their military police headquarters. Poon Patpongse had been looking for a large plot to use as the family compound, and he paid 59,000 baht for the land, which had been used for fruit growing. Deciding to cut a six-metre wide driveway from Surawong into the property, Poon Patpongse handed the job over to his son Udom, and took the family away on holiday to Hua Hin. Udom had studied at the London School of Economics directly before the war, and later at the University of Minnesota, and he sensed a business opportunity. He doubled the size of the road and drove it through to Silom, envisaging a district where offices could be built to accommodate the Western companies that were coming into Siam during the restructuring that was taking place following the war. By this time Siam was Thailand, a constitutional monarchy, and was eager to take its place in the new world order. When his father had calmed down

A sign on a go-go bar in the red-light district of Patpong.

he saw Udom's logic. Finance was raised to build shophouses at the Surawong end of the road, and then Udom put the next part of his plan into action. Familiar with the Western way of doing business, and knowing they distrusted time-honoured Asian practices such as key money, a large upfront deposit that the landlord puts in the bank to earn interest, he sought out potential tenants and offered them straight Western-style rental deals. Companies began moving in, notably airlines, as Bangkok began to emerge as a destination and as a staging post for other Asian cities. News bureaux, shipping lines and the US Information Service all opened offices here, and a Japanese man named Mizutoni opened the first restaurant, Mizu.

The Vietnam War changed everything. Udom saw that the American GIs who were stationed in Bangkok, or passing through, were going to be looking for somewhere to spend their R&R dollars. He started offering leases to Western businessmen to open bars and nightclubs. New Petchburi Road became the centre for bordellos and massage parlours, while Patpong quickly became a lively area for bars catering both for the local businessmen and the military. Only in the late 1960s with the opening of the Grand Prix Cocktail Lounge & Bar did Patpong start to emerge as Bangkok's premier red-light district. Taking over the premises from a barbershop, this was the first bar in Bangkok to feature girls dancing go-go, clad only in bikinis, if that. Like all great ideas in Bangkok, it wasn't lonely for long.

Patpong's glory days were the 1970s and 1980s, for after the GIs had left the reputation of the place kept on spreading and the tourists and tired businessmen took their place. When the street market was opened in the early 1990s (being a private thoroughfare the road can close whenever it wants to) the area lost much of its raunchy quality and a lot of that business moved to Nana Plaza and to Soi Cowboy. Today, open-fronted bars and music outlets cater for bemused tourists and shoppers, while many of the go-go bars with their semi-nude girls remain half-empty (or so I am reliably informed). But if you wander along Patpong in the daytime, admittedly not the best time to look at the place, you will see Udom's shophouses still standing. Seldom can a property investment anywhere have paid off quite so handsomely. Oh, and Mizu is still there, unchanged since the day it opened, and, I sometimes have my suspicions, still with the original staff.

The Hidden Island

*There are two sections to this walk and it is necessary to take a taxi
from Rama III Road to Phra Pradaeng and on to Bang Krachao,
where it is also advisable to travel by car or by bicycle in order to
cover the entire island.*

Duration: 1 day

L ooping around Bangkok is an inner ring road made up of
sections of urban road that were already in existence and
which over the course of several years were upgraded to
arterial road status. The stretch that runs alongside the river from the Rama III Bridge to the port district of Klong Toei, where
it changes its name and heads out through the northern suburbs, is
Rama III Road.

Despite its riverside route, there is little that is scenic about
Rama III Road. It had earlier become a semi-industrialised zone,
with industries such as cement and sheet metal spreading down
from the port and taking up large plots of land on the bank of the
river. In the late 1980s, the Bangkok Metropolitan Administration
decided to designate this as a second business district, and cut a
road directly through to Sathorn and Silom roads, alongside the old
Chong Nonsi canal. Bangkok Bank established part of its head office
here, the Krung Sri Bank set up its head office, the SV City mixed-
use complex was built, and Montien opened their five-star Riverside
Hotel. The Asian financial crash of 1997 put paid to most of the

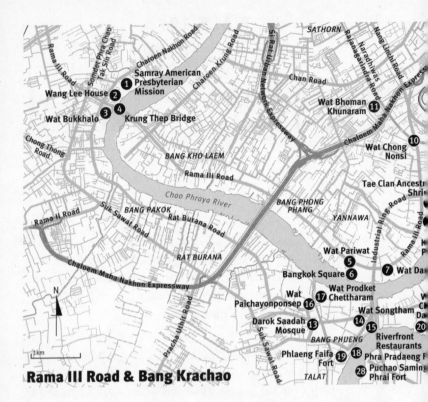

Rama III Road & Bang Krachao

other grand schemes, scarring the district for years with half-built projects. Recent years have seen some life emerging in this area, greatly encouraged by the feeder bus that serves the Skytrain station at Sathorn Road, but dreams of a thriving riverside business district still seem rather remote.

Although the riverfront is hogged in most places by industry and commercial developments, rendering the river itself invisible, there are a series of beautiful riverside temples that continue on in their timeless way. To begin an exploration of these, it is necessary to start on the other side of the river, at the foot of the Rama III Bridge, not at a Buddhist temple but at one of the first footholds of Christianity in Bangkok, where the Americans founded the Presbyterian Mission in 1849.

The Catholics have always been in Bangkok, before even the city was founded, represented principally by the descendants of the

Portuguese of Ayutthaya, who over time had been absorbed into Siamese society and regarded as just another community with different religious beliefs, alongside the Cham Muslims, the Indian Hindus, the Chinese Taoists and others. The Protestants, however, didn't arrive in Bangkok until 1828, when the London Missionary Society sent the Reverend Jacob Tomlin and the Reverend Carl Gutzlaff. More missionaries arrived in 1833, these being sent by the American Board of Commissioners for Foreign Missions. Intending to direct their efforts towards the Chinese population, they settled in a house near to Wat Samphanthawong in Chinatown. This is the group that Dr Dan Beach Bradley joined when he arrived in 1835, and in that year the mission moved across the water to the Kudi Cheen community. Missionaries from the American Presbyterian Mission began arriving in 1840 and stayed initially with the other Protestants in Kudi Cheen, where the influence of the community was growing, due in no small part to Bradley's energetic work as a medical doctor, teacher and importer of Siam's first printing press.

The Presbyterians founded their own church, initially holding services and meetings in their living quarters, and by 1857 they were able to buy a plot of land at Samray, a village on the Thonburi side that took its name from the samray trees that grew there on the riverfront. Here they decided to build a church, and although it took five years to raise the funds and construct the building, Samray Church opened in 1862. Although Samray may have seemed an odd destination, this part of the riverbank was quickly being transformed from a wilderness into an industrial area, and the population was growing. There was also the large population of Westerners directly across the river, at the lower end of Charoen Krung Road. Samray became the centre of the Presbyterian community, and along with the church there was a boys' school, a printing press, and housing for the missionaries and the local people who became involved with running the community. The school was later to move across the river, where it became the Bangkok Christian College.

Samray Church is reached via the quiet lane of Charoen Nakhorn Soi 59, a thoroughfare that is little more than a footpath, and the church sits directly on the riverbank, fronted by a green lawn. A small jetty is there for anyone travelling by boat. The original church fell into disrepair half a century after it was built, and this present structure was erected in 1910, taking the same design. A belfry was added as a separate structure in 1912. The lines of the church are clean and simple, with three arches on the plain flat frontage, which is adorned only by a cloverleaf pattern and the year of construction. In recent years the church has been painted a dark yellow, which no doubt had some of the more conservative members of the congregation shaking their heads, but, contrasting with the red-tiled roof, the effect is rather pleasing. The river originally came almost to the church steps, but reclamation during the latter half of the twentieth century has added enough land for a congregation to gather. A church office and community hall was added in 1963. Some of the church land was sold off to members of the congregation in 1916, and as a result the lane has several very pleasant old wooden houses dating from this time. The cemetery is at the entrance to the lane, separated from Charoen Nakhorn by a high wall, and is immaculately kept.

Immediately next to Samray Church are the remains of one of those industries that brought so many people into the locality during the second half of the nineteenth century. The origins of the Wang Lee family business have been described earlier on in the section on the old Thonburi harbour. There were five rice mills owned by the family, three of them being located here. One was on the site of the present Anantara Hotel: it burned down in 1976. Another was on land that has recently been cleared, except for the magnificent

One of a pair of ancient Chinese shrines flanking the Krung Thep Bridge.

teak house built for the owners, which although dilapidated still stands on the riverfront next to the church and is apparently due to be restored. The third can be found on the other side of the Krung Thep Bridge, renovated and converted into a restaurant. The mill came under the name of Long Heng Lee, and an original signboard hangs proudly inside the restaurant. On this site, too, is a house built for the owners, which has been restored and acts still as a residence. The mill dates from the 1880s or 90s, the timber construction being very typical of the time. Wang Lee was not the only operator of rice mills in this area: by 1903 there were eleven mills in this immediate area, out of a total of almost fifty in Bangkok.

On the far side of the restaurant is a temple that, to the best of my knowledge, is the only one in Thailand that is set on top of a three-storey building. Wat Bukkhalo was founded in 1767, and while the original *ubosot* is still here on the riverbank, a chapel and a number of *salas* have been built on the roof of the community centre; the temple is a striking sight for anyone passing across the Krung Thep Bridge or the Rama III Bridge in a southerly direction, particularly early in the morning when the sun catches the red and gold structures perched on top of their white platform.

It was probably the Chinese millers or sailors who built the two Chinese shrines on either side of the Krung Thep Bridge, and they predate the bridge itself. Again, for anyone passing over the bridge, in either direction, they present an intriguing flourish of red and white gables and rampant dragons, but as with most Chinese shrines there is no known history: they are simply modest places of worship. The Krung Thep Bridge was opened in the middle of 1959, and at the time was only the second road bridge across the river. Although lacking the splendour of the Memorial Bridge, it is still a fine example of steel truss design, and it too has a bascule span for allowing the passage of large ships. Unlike the older structure upriver, the bridge can still open. Fuji Car Manufacturing Co Ltd built the bridge, which has a total length of 626.25 metres (2,053 ft). The neighbouring Rama III Bridge was opened in 1999 and was built as part of the inner ring road, taking the strain off the older structure.

Rama III Road does not readily give up its temple treasures, certainly not to the casual passer-by. Wat Chan Nok is directly on the riverbank, a small and pretty temple that is reached only by entering Soi 6 and proceeding to the end of the lane; unless viewed from the river, it is otherwise invisible. Wat Bang Khlo is similarly hidden, reached by travelling along Soi 20, or admired from the Montien Riverside Hotel next door. Wat Pariwat is the first visible temple, occupying a huge area of land between the river and the road, next to the clothes shops and restaurants of Bangkok Square, and visible from some distance because of the striking deep-blue colouring of the *ubosot* roof tiles. Much of this temple structure is very modern, and contemporary images are to be found in the compound, including Captain Hook and his pirate companions helping to hold up the eaves on one of the roof structures, and the footballer David Beckham, who appears as a golden embossed image on the base of the principal Buddha figure. Although only 30 centimetres (11.8 in) high, and standing at the end of a frieze of *garudas* supporting the altar, this image has become so well-known amongst locals that the temple is increasingly known as David Beckham Temple. Placed there in 1998, with the enthusiastic permission of the abbot, the figure is wearing a football shirt bearing the name of team sponsor

Sharp. The Thais are football crazy, and Beckham's name is revered, so perhaps it is not surprising to see him turn up as a deity in a Bangkok temple. "Same-same but different", as the Thais might say.

Wat Dan, nearby, is another substantial temple and serves as a particularly extensive monastery, its cluster of accommodation around the thoroughfare that passes through the compound being home to a large community of novice monks, many of them pre-teen youngsters who spend time there during the annual Rains Retreat, and who appear to be easily diverted when a foreigner walks past their windows, peering out with friendly if distinctly un-monk like grins.

Continuing along this side of the road, there is a modest temple archway across a narrow lane, and walking down here will lead us past a school and into the compound of Wat Klong Phum, built beside a tiny canal and enjoying a pastoral setting on the bank of the river. The school is part of the temple, and within one of its buildings the Bangkok Metropolitan Administration maintains a small district museum. A wrought-iron fence further along Rama III Road reveals what at first appears to be a small Chinese temple with a low roof and blue ceramic tiling on the wall, but which is actually the frontage of the Tae Clan Ancestral Shrine, and behind this is a large and beautifully proportioned courtyard with a river frontage.

Further up Rama III Road the Chong Nonsi canal runs beneath the road to empty into the river, where there is a sluice gate and pumping station. On the corner where Naratiwat Road was cut to link Rama III with Sathorn and Silom stands Wat Chong Nonsi, one of Bangkok's oldest temples, dating from at least the latter half of the seventeenth century. The grounds of the temple contain more than thirty *chedis*, and there is an ornate bell tower with a balcony. Although the *wiharn* is relatively new the *ubosot* is original, displaying the characteristic boat shape of its time, and rather austere, being painted white and with its roof aged into a light brown colour. Measuring only 20 metres (65.5 ft) long by 10 metres (32.8 ft) wide, this building could be overlooked as being simply an interesting survival in an urban landscape, except that on its inner walls are some of Bangkok's most remarkable murals, painted between 1657 and 1707, and famous for depicting the everyday and sometimes bawdy lives of ordinary people within its scenes from the Jataka. This is the earliest surviving temple mural in Bangkok, and the only Ayutthaya-era temple in which both the murals and the architecture are of the same period, with no renovations. Because of its historical purity and value the *ubosot* is usually kept locked and viewed only on request.

Behind Wat Chong Nonsi, its canal-side setting lost when the road was laid, is a Mahayana Buddhist temple that is regarded as being one of the finest examples of Chinese temple architecture in Thailand. Wat Bhoman Khunaram is a fairly recent structure, built in 1959 by a Chinese spiritual master who later became the temple's first abbot. The buildings and artworks in this five-acre compound are a mixture of Thai, Chinese and Tibetan styles, and the enormous black and gold alms bowl that towers over the roof is a familiar local landmark. King Bhumibol in 1970 came to perform the raising of a tiered umbrella above the main building, and to commemorate the visit his initials have been placed above the temple entrance. Wat Bhoman is the centre of the Chinese Order of Buddhist Monks in Thailand.

Rama III Road, for most of its length, is double-decked. As the confined surroundings made it impossible for the highway engineers to add slip-road ramps, the elevated section subsides to ground level for major junctions. Viewed from sideways on, the road would look like a massive switchback. Taxi drivers appreciate this. The way is usually uncongested and the driver can really put on a turn of speed, sailing along the elevated sections, lurching down the ramps that are corrugated with expansion and drainage joints, and landing with a satisfyingly springy bounce on the flat pad of the ground deck before flooring the pedal for the up ramp. For the taxi driver who spends most of his day in a semi-mobile carpark, it must be exhilarating. For the passenger who, to take a random example, has just drunk a large cappuccino at his local Starbucks, it can, however, be alarming. At such a time the passenger may turn his eyes to the horizon, like a seasick sailor, and if he looks towards the river he will see a remarkable sight: a long wall of almost unbroken green jungle. This only begins at the upper end of Rama III, roughly from the SV City complex, and with almost no riverside temples from here on, as the river flows into the industrialised port district at Klong Toei, there are few ground-level vantage points. Perhaps the best place to view the river is from the mouth of the Chong Nonsi canal, where the curious observer will be rewarded with a Conradesque view of coastal freighters chugging past against a jungle backdrop, heading to and from one of the small jetties, or further up to the shipyard at the Krung Thep Bridge; and he may wonder just where the city has gone.

A map will soon provide the answer. The river here describes an enormous loop that doubles back upon itself and almost touches at the district named Phra Pradaeng. The effect is to create what is effectively an island in the middle of the city. A small canal, Klong Lat Pho, was cut in 1628 to allow light craft to bypass the loop, but the angle of the cutting was such that the river flow could not inundate it, as happened further upstream at Thonburi. Klong Toei, which occupies most of the loop on the Bangkok side, had long been a port town, going back centuries to when the ocean came a lot further inland, and so this part of the river was important to shipping. The cutting of the Hua Lampong canal during the time of Rama IV gave the port even more importance, connecting it both with the city centre and the waterway that led through to the rich rice-growing province of Chachoengsao. It is from the lower end of this canal that Klong Toei takes its name: the southern end of the canal became known for the pandan plants, *toei*, that grew along the waterside. Klong Toei was developed as a modern port starting from 1938, but its limited capacity for heavy shipping and the traffic chaos caused by trailer trucks on land resulted in the founding of Laem Chabang deep-sea port in Chonburi province early in the 1980s. Amongst all this volume of trade and encroachment of human habitation on both the Bangkok and the Samut Prakan sides of the river, the land within the loop has remained almost totally undeveloped. Referred to either as the Phra Pradaeng peninsula, or more often Bang Krachao (although the Thais refer to it as Krapow Moo, which means "pig's stomach"), this is a huge area of green countryside in which quiet villages snooze down peaceful lanes, where many people travel by bicycle, and where small temples are buried away amongst the greenery. The visitor could easily imagine that he is upcountry was it not for the occasional startling

Gateway to Phlaeng Faifa, one of the forts built to protect the Chao Phraya estuary.

sight of a familiar Bangkok tower poking up from beyond the trees.

A few years ago, two magnificent new bridges opened across the Chao Phraya at the neck of the peninsula, taking the highway across the water next to SV City, with a necessarily tightly woven cloverleaf junction between the two. At the same time the Lat Pho shortcut canal, which had measured no more than 15 metres (49 ft) wide and 2 metres (6.5 ft) deep, and which ran for just 600 metres (656 yds) across the narrowest part of the isthmus, was widened to 65 metres (213 ft) as part of a flood alleviation scheme. The bridges have rendered Bang Krachao more easily accessible, although as there is no reason for anyone to go there, the peninsula remains as quiet as it was before the bridges—which are called Bhumibol I and Bhumibol II, and which complete the inner and outer ring roads—were built. (The bridges are cable-stayed spans with gigantic A-frames at either end. The frames are an abstract rendering of the traditional Thai form of greeting, the *wai*, a charming notion for anyone entering the city via the river, although sadly these days this is generally confined to the crews of container ships.) There are three ferry crossings: those from Wat Klong Toei Nok and Wat Bang Na Nok are for foot passengers and cyclists, with landings directly on the island, and the third being a car ferry whose captain sits in a tiny cabin atop a square tower at the stern, and which plies from Puchao Saming Phrai Road in Samut Prakan to Phra Pradaeng. Near to Phra Pradaeng ferry pier and perched on the river's edge is a row of restaurants known only to local Thais, and which afford memorable views of giant container ships travelling to and from Klong Toei.

Phra Pradaeng sits on the west side of the thin strip of land where the Chao Phraya almost meets itself, and is a crowded little town that seems to be not quite of Greater Bangkok, a feeling enhanced by the cycle-rickshaws that still ply the streets. But there is more than this: the temples are different, some of the older people dress in a different way, and sometimes even the festivals are a little different, Songkran for example being held a week later than in central Bangkok. This is Mon territory, settled after the fall of Ayutthaya, when it became prominent in helping to guard the entrance to the Chao Phraya. Rama I ordered a fort to be built here in 1809, and in 1815 Rama II commanded another eight forts to be built. The Mon immigrants having proved such fierce enemies of the Burmese, several hundred Mon men and their families were settled along the river to man the forts and to populate the town that the king was building here, Nakorn Keunkan. The community has grown from that original migration. Phlaeng Faifa, the only remaining fort, is to be found near the ferry pier, although there is little left except for a solid archway and the earthworks topped with stone ramparts and ancient cannon. The site is now a small public park. Most of the other forts have been completely lost and forgotten, their stones long ago taken away for other building works, but the ruins of one, Puchao Saming Phrai, can be found on the Samut Prakan side of the river, almost directly opposite, completely neglected except for a row of rusting cannon along the riverbank.

So thoroughly did the Mon settle Phra Pradaeng that there is only one Thai Buddhist temple amongst the thirty-eight temples within the administrative district of Amphoe Phra Pradaeng: all the others are of the Mon Buddhist sect. Wat Prodket Chettharam was built in the time of Rama II and stands on the bank of the Lat Ruang canal, which was cut at that time by Mon immigrants under the direction of the king; the depth of the Lat Pho canal was reduced because of the saline water that was travelling upstream and seeping into the irrigation system that fed the orchards established there. Klong Lat Ruang passes in a diagonal fashion across Phra Pradaeng to avoid inundation by the river, and was too narrow for larger shipping. In 1907 the Maenam Motorboat Company, a subsidiary of Siam Electricity, which owned Bangkok's electric trams system, set up a steam tram that ran parallel to the Lat Ruang canal because the waterway was not large enough to handle their boats. The trams were later converted to petrol but the system was abandoned in 1940 because of wartime fuel shortages. Wat Prodket's position next to this quiet and clean waterway has enabled the creation of a small moat around the central *chedi*, an attractive area set with stone benches. Although designed for devotees of the Thai style of Buddhism, Wat Prodket shows strong elements of Mon design in its architecture. The roofs of the *ubosot* and *wiharn* are both covered with Mon ceramic shingles and there are no rooftop decorations, giving a slightly cropped look to the outline, while the gables are flat and with a vine pattern made from ceramic fragments placed on stucco. A Chinese gate leads over the moat, and there are Chinese pavilions. The temple has both a sitting Buddha, in the Subduing Mara position, and a Reclining Buddha. Inside the *wiharn* are Dharma illustrations performed in Western art style, which is extremely rare, and inside the *mondop* is a representation of the Buddha's footprint, inlaid with pearl.

Facing Wat Prodket on the other side of the Lat Ruang canal is Wat Paichayonponsep, distinctively Mon in design, its entrance arch painted in red ochre and its flat eaves embossed with ceramic patterns. A leafy pathway leads alongside the canal, and with a large screen of trees and a small waterside village, this spot has a rural atmosphere.

Following the canal road from Wat Prodket leads through a Muslim community, with the green domes and tall minaret of Darok Saadah Mosque towering over the houses, and picking up the main road here will take us over the canal to Songtham Road, and to one of the most prominent local landmarks, Wat Songtham, set near the ferry pier and resplendent behind a magnificent red-and-gold fence. The enormous Mon-style *chedi* dominates the southern corner of the compound, its gleaming white base formed into three tiers, with rows of golden Buddha images encircling the *chedi* on each tier. The red-and-gold theme is carried through to the bells that hang outside the *ubosot*, and each of the monk images placed in a line in a nearby *sala* is heavily encrusted in gold leaf. Wat Songtham dates from the time of Rama III, and is a royal temple, second class. Alongside the temple runs Phetchahung Road, and following this leads over the Lat Pho canal and across the entire length of the Phra Pradaeng peninsula.

The scenery begins to change immediately: the narrow streets have gone, to be replaced by green countryside and small villages, and an unhurried way of life. Away from the two-lane road there are orchards, jungle, mangrove swamps, and hidden temples. This is still Mon country, settled at the same time as Phra Pradaeng and in the years after, the Mon language can still be heard and Mon script seen on older buildings. Turning under the archway for Wat Chak Daeng will lead us along a narrow country lane to an old wall decorated with green Dharma wheels and into the temple compound, which enjoys a garden setting on the bank of the river. A traditional stupa has been built here next to the water, a mound-like construction made from red clay bricks, reminding us that the Mon were outstanding makers of unglazed clay pottery. Next to the stupa is a

Small private ferry service plying between Rama III Road and Bang Krachao.

golden *chedi* atop the cream-coloured *wiharn*, surrounded by small golden Buddha images: the *chedi* is floodlit at night, a striking sight from the far side of the river at Phra Pradaeng. A small notice next to the temple relates that it was built by a Mon community who had fled from Ayutthaya and settled here during the Thonburi era.

Follow Phetchahung Road a little further, and there is a turning for Wat Bang Nam Phueng. This lane leads through fields and woodland, across a bridge that spans a narrow waterway, and here we are at one of the peninsula's few conscious attempts at a tourist attraction: a floating market. A number of vendor boats line the canal side, covered by netting to reduce the sun's rays, and visitors walk along concrete walkways to the stalls and the food outlets, so this is not really a floating market at all: although, admittedly, "concrete walkway market" doesn't quite have the same cachet. Bang Nam Phueng Floating Market is a recent innovation by the villagers themselves and designed primarily for Thais, and consequently is a lot less pushy than other floating markets that cater to foreign visitors. There are some quality handicrafts and food products from the OTOP project available, some reasonably priced clothing, and of course, good food. The market is open only at the weekends but is well worth a visit. An added attraction are the sampan rides that are available along the canal, which unlike most of Bangkok's *klongs* is clean and fragrant. Along the lane that runs past the market is one of the community's two temples, Wat Bang Nam Phueng Nai, a small temple that has a tiered stupa topped with a golden image, and beyond this are green fields and orchards.

Taking the lane that leads to the ferry pier for Bang Na brings us to the second temple, Wat Bang Nam Phueng Nok (*nai* and *nok* mean, respectively, "inner" and "outer"), which is far larger than its sibling and sits on the river's edge. A large golden Buddha is seated facing the ferry pier, and a fat Buddha is placed in the cemetery, its tummy button used for offerings. Behind the temple buildings on the pierside are the original chapel and ordination hall, dating back to the early days of the Mon settlement, but long neglected and crumbling away. They are hidden now behind overgrown trees, with small homesteads up against the walls, their exterior décor gone, their interiors bare, the remains of ancient murals still to be seen on the walls. The Buddha images are still here and are regularly visited.

At least two other temples on the peninsula have allowed their former buildings to fall into disuse, although not to the extent of Wat Bang Nam Phueng Nok. Wat Pa Kedi has a disused chapel crammed in behind a newer structure, and although stripped of its grandeur is sound enough. The small original chapel at Wat Bang Krasop, although mainly plain brick and stucco on the outside, is in a good state of repair and has beautiful mouldings over its windows and the doorway arch. What appears to be a new chapel in the compound was having its interior images painted during a recent visit, enormous swirling designs of purple and gold, and was the work of just one artist, working alone on a scaffold.

Phetchahung Road ends at the ferry pier looking out across at the yellow gantry cranes of Klong Toei, and Bang Krachao will almost certainly remain as unspoiled jungle island. The late 1970s had seen protection orders placed on the peninsula, the original intention having been for controlled leisure development. The developments never happened, and the Thais have become conservation minded in more recent times. About a tenth of the total area of almost a thousand acres is protected, acquired and maintained as Sri Nakhon Khuean Khan Park by the Royal Forest Department. With its nature trails, cycle paths and large lake where boats can be hired, the park attracts a modest number of local tourists. There is a refinery near to the bridge, and some warehousing, but otherwise there is no industry. Recent years have seen some residents offering homestay accommodation, there are companies that operate cycling tours, there is a place displaying Siamese fighting fish, and a handful of residents who have been peacefully making incense sticks for several generations have now, to their bemusement, become a tourist attraction. Life is quiet here. There is no police station. You will look hard to find an ATM. The restaurants are all very local, most of them roadside stalls. The modern city is only a ferryboat ride away, but there is no hurry to travel back across the water.

The Jim Thompson Legend

*From Bangkok's mainline railway terminus, this walk takes us to a
temple with a coffin shop and then on to the home of the man who
is responsible for one of the most enduring mysteries of the East.*
Duration: 2 hours

On one of my first visits to Bangkok, more than thirty
years ago, I stayed at the old Sheraton on Surawong,
which is now the Tawana, and on Sunday morning I
took myself for a quiet walk. I had no guidebook, and
no idea where I was going. I walked to the top of the road and turned
left, heading for the temple whose red roofs I could now see, when
I chanced upon a most curious shop. Its window contained nothing
except photographs of corpses, many of them in poor condition. I
later learned that this was the office of Ruam Katanyu, one of the
two main charitable operations in Bangkok that collects dead bodies from the streets, rivers, canals, burned buildings, and anywhere
else life may have expired, and brings them here either for collection by relatives or for cremation at the temple, Wat Hua Lampong.
Any dead body not identified has its photograph pasted in the office
window in case someone might later recognise it. Ruam Katanyu
also performs a rudimentary ambulance service, delivering the sick
and injured to hospital. The vehicles of the body snatchers are mainly converted pickup trucks, and the only thing to distinguish them

The design of Hua Lampong terminus combines classical and industrial elements.

usually as they speed through the traffic is a flashing amber light on the cab roof. At a small chapel next to Wat Hua Lampong Thais donate money for coffins for the unclaimed bodies. Anyone can do this, and it is very much an act of compassion. Donators receive two slips of paper, one to attach to an empty coffin, the other to burn at an altar. Donations are usually 500 baht. Wat Hua Lampong itself is an imposing structure, occupying a large area on the corner of Siphraya Road, and unusual in that the *ubosot* and *wiharn* are both raised on a one-storey high platform. A lifesize figure of Rama V is seated in a shrine at the platform. It is a royal temple, third class, and in 1996 to celebrate the fiftieth anniversary of the ascension to the throne of King Bhumibol Adulyadej, Wat Hua Lampong underwent extensive renovations. The Golden Jubilee seal, depicting two elephants flanking a multi-tiered umbrella, is featured extensively in the remodelling.

The word *lampong* means "loudspeaker" but is also used for a type of flower whose bloom forms a loudspeaker shape, while *hua* means "head" or "bulb". This area must have been used for growing these flowers in the past, and in addition to the temple taking its name from the locality, as did the canal that was later buried under

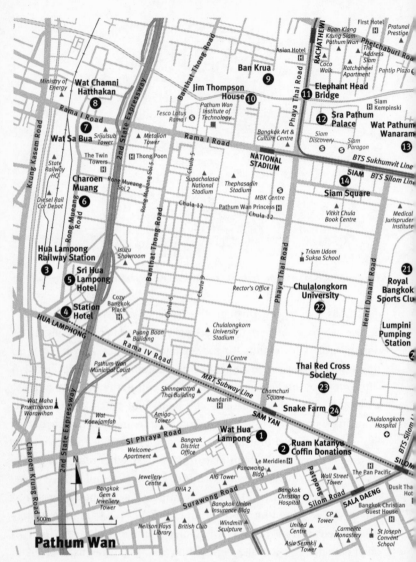

Rama IV Road, on the other side of the street and a few minutes walk to the northwest stands the mainline railway terminus that has also taken the name. And whereas Wat Hua Lampong stands on the border of Bangrak district, Hua Lampong Railway Station stands in Pathum Wan, the name meaning "lotus forest". Clearly, the muddy, swampy land here had once been very fertile indeed.

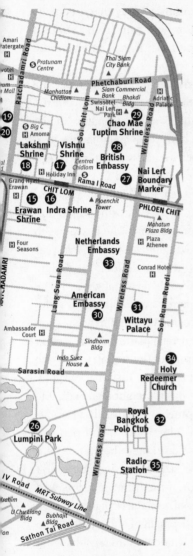

Siam's first railway was the Paknam line that ran from Bangkok to what is now Samut Prakharn, at the mouth of the river, a distance of 21 kilometres (13 miles). Opened in April 1893 by Rama V, it was a Belgian-Danish joint venture, with the steam locomotives built by Kraus of Munich. The Bangkok terminus was built on the edge of the Padung Krung Kasem canal, for easy access to the wholesalers and markets in Chinatown, just across the bridge, for the main purpose of the line was to bring in goods from ships at deep anchor at the river mouth along with fish and other produce. The one-metre gauge line had ten stops and proved very quickly to also be a popular commuter line, providing a rollicking ride for passengers alongside the Hua Lampong canal, and then turning to run directly alongside the river, crossing the small canals along its route via timber bridges before puffing to a halt at Paknam Market. The line closed down in 1960, but the route can still be followed today by road, becoming a distinct thoroughfare of its own after Rama IV Road ends, and after the tail end of the old Hua Lampong canal

emerges briefly into daylight to disgorge into the river, for there is a long thoroughfare here named Thanon Thang Rot Fai Sai Kao, "the road that skirts the railway line". There is almost nothing to see now, as the rails were torn up, except for a spur that heads into the port area at Klong Toei, which for some reason has survived. One of the original Kraus locomotives has recently been installed near the Paknam terminus, although enthusiasts say that it actually ran on the Mahachai-Mae Klong line that was built from Thonburi to Samut Songkhram at about the same time, Kraus supplying the engines for both ventures.

Laying of the northern and northeastern railway lines, under the newly formed Royal State Railways of Siam, began in 1891, and the terminus for both was built near to the Bangkok terminus of the Paknam line. The Royal State Railways built their maintenance yard nearby, but the railways proved to be such a success that a much larger station was soon required. The maintenance yard was moved to Makkasan in 1910, where it can still be seen, much of it in a state of picturesque industrial ruin, and the building of Hua Lampong station began. Mario Tamagno, one of the Italian architects who has left such a distinctive mark on the city, and who was under a twenty-five-year contract to Siam's Public Works Department, undertook the design. Before coming to Bangkok Tamagno had studied and taught in Turin, one of Italy's great industrial centres, where new architectural styles were emerging for the factories and the company buildings.

Built by Dutch engineers, and with fourteen platforms, the station opened on 25th June 1916. Standing in front of the station today, one can see how Tamagno drew inspiration from his Turin background. That vaulted iron roof with its girder design, combined with the blue, green and clear-glass skylights, somehow sits easily in architectural terms above the Greco-Roman columns of the portico and the Renaissance-style wings on either side. Enter the station and the dimensions are a delight: despite its size, Hua Lampong is still to a human scale. The iron girder design of the frontage is followed throughout the building to support the roof, and the skylights, orange and clear glass at the far end, give the interior a light and airy feel. The offices on the upper level still have their window shutters, enhancing the European style of the era. Tamagno's design initiated a style that later came to be known as Thai Art Deco, used in grand buildings such as the General Post Office and Chalermkrung Royal Theatre, as well as in smaller premises such as shophouses in Chinatown. Take a short walk from the station along Rama IV Road and over the canal bridge to the Maitri Chit Junction, and you will see how, with a clear

A riverbus plying the Saen Saeb canal passes the Jim Thompson House.

view of Hua Lampong in front of him, the designer of a handsome block of shophouses has erected a pediment that is a miniature duplicate of the station frontage.

There is an old photograph in one of the books I have about Bangkok that always amuses me. It was taken at the beginning of the city's railway era, the photographer standing on the bank of the Padung Krung Kasem canal, and in the foreground is a hotel proudly bearing the name HOTEL HOVEL. I can only assume that it was supposed to be Hotel Novel, and that the Thai usage of the English language was as whimsical then as it is now. But other than this the picture is interesting because it shows that in this area, to the front of the old Paknam Railway Station, the kind of inexpensive hotel accommodation that grows up around a railway terminus had already started to appear.

Exit the station today, and towards the left there is a big sign looming above the rooftops of a very elegant row of shophouses and bearing the words STATION HOTEL. The entry to the hotel is not exactly salubrious, being tucked down an alley lined by food shops that appear distinctly uninviting to even a usually happy enough consumer of street food. The lobby, though, is spacious and very

Chinese in style, and the rooms, at about 250 baht, are not expensive by any standards. The Station Hotel is, however, not an ancient structure, the manager estimating about fifty years, so unless this is a reworking of an earlier building there is no great antiquity here. Pity. It all sounded rather romantic. By contrast, in Rong Muang, the lane that runs directly alongside the station, is something of a gem. The Sri Hua Lampong Hotel is housed inside a building that must have been here since the station itself. This is a very traditional old Thai-Chinese establishment. The reception desk is a small table in the far corner of the Chinese-style lobby, and there is a seating area made from tables and benches that once graced a railway carriage.

Opposite are the very attractive buildings that house the station offices, and further on along Rong Muang, past the big overhead conveyor that connects the Bangkok Mail Centre with the station, is the little village of Charoen Muang, once famous as an umbrella-making district. These are the big sun umbrellas found shielding the tables in garden cafes and the grounds of hotels. There are only a handful of these workshops still open, the main business of the district now being in wrought ironwork and steel products, and there are numerous shops that between them could probably offer anything needed in this line, ranging from an imposing set of gates, through to engine bolts and flanges. Rong Muang leads all the way alongside the station marshalling yards and emerges onto Rama 1 Road, Wat Sa Bua tucked into the corner where the ramp leads up onto the main road, its monks' quarters sporting unless I am very much mistaken the art of Rong Muang in their fence and gateway, and a boldly embossed lotus pond over the main gate to illustrate the temple name. Directly opposite is Wat Chamni Hatthakan, its graceful Chinese-style floral gables rising in pastel blues and creams above the courtyard, porcelain forming the vases and flowers. Vividly coloured paintings adorn other gables, and on one, overlooking the front wall, is a small, embossed image of a Reclining Buddha that acts as an advertisement for the golden figure reclining inside.

Continue along Rama 1 Road, and directly under the National Stadium terminus of the BTS Skytrain is Soi Kasem San 2, which leads through to one of the strangest stories in the East.

The Jim Thompson House is a classic example of how a good story can make a tourist attraction. Had Thompson not disappeared in such mysterious circumstances in 1967 I doubt if the house would be so popular: in fact it would probably have been pulled down by now to make way for an apartment block. Before entering that intriguing gateway at the end of the lane, however, step out onto the canal pathway and gaze across the lumpy grey waters at the village opposite.

Ban Krua is where Jim Thompson's interest in the fragments of glowing silk that he found from time to time in stores throughout Bangkok and in traditional homes eventually came into focus. The story of how he built up the silk industry from its almost extinct folk-art level to become world-famous is well known, but the reality of the small community of Ban Krua is a little more obscure. By the time Jim Thompson came on the scene, directly after World War II, silk weaving in Bangkok had almost died out. There was little demand for the material, which was mostly used by that time for ceremonial occasions. Most of the looms in the city had closed, and only at Ban Krua was silk weaving done on an appreciable scale. The residents of Ban Krua are Muslims, ethnic Cham people who migrated from Cambodia to Siam during the reign of Rama I. They had fought alongside the king's troops during engagements against the Burmese, and as a reward had been allocated the land on which they live to this day. The community had brought with them the art of silk weaving, and Thompson had traced the origins of the silk that he so much admired to this village. Ban Krua had been transformed after he discovered them, in the late 1940s, for the community became his main silk production site, supplying silk thread and pigments, and creating patterns and designs. The canal water was still clear in those days, and was used for the washing and dyeing of the thread.

Thirty years ago there was a tiny ferry that plied from the watergate of Jim Thompson's house across the canal, a toothpick-thin canoe that could hold only two people and the oarsman: the clumsy foreign visitor would grip the sides of the boat in terror lest he be pitched into the water. These days the longtail boats that blare their way along the canal, their sawn-off truck engines causing a backwash that slaps furiously against the walkway, have made this small service an unviable one and a small footbridge crosses the water just a few metres from the house. In essence, the village has changed little since Thompson's time. Old timber houses face out across the water, little shops sell sweets and drinks, and washing hangs everywhere. Along the walkway the houses are so tightly packed it is not easy to see how to enter the village. The alleys are so narrow that often only one person can pass at a time, and some are cul-de-sacs, leaving the visitor with the embarrassing possibility of blundering into someone's living room. One of the easiest routes is the alley directly opposite the Thompson House watergate, for it leads to the green-painted mosque in the centre of the village. Anyone searching for gracious old teak houses is, however, going to be disappointed: the village had originally been built with whatever could be found, and even in the wider back-alley that forms the outer boundary of the village, where there are some bigger and more substantial homes than those by the canal, the design is, at best, prosaic.

Along the waterfront I found a small open-fronted shop with several colourful bolts of silk in a glass case, and when I asked where the silk came from I was told there are weaving sheds in Soi 9 and Soi 11. The *sois* aren't marked, but I was directed to a narrow opening between the houses. I almost had to squeeze my way in, but I soon heard the familiar clickety-thud-clickety-thud of a loom. Through a doorway I spied an elderly gent hanging hanks of newly dyed black-and-scarlet silk over a pole to dry, and stepping past him (no one seems to mind you invading their privacy) I saw a mediaeval sight, a lone worker in a courtyard toiling over a steaming cauldron of dye, dipping the raw hanks into the liquid. Taking great care not to slip on the stone floor of the courtyard, and thus possibly emerging from the village a startlingly different colour to when I entered, I progressed into a low room where a solitary girl sat at an ancient wooden loom, weaving the most beautiful shimmering silk. The girl smiled pleasantly at me as she worked the treadle with her feet, and operated the warp with a piece of cloth dangling from the overhead part of the frame. There were, she said, a couple of other weavers nearby, and at the top of Soi 9 I found a house with two looms, and close by a shed with another five looms packed in together. These

are the workshops of Lung Aood Ban Krua Thai Silk, an independent business owned by Manassanan Benjarongjinda, more usually
known as Lung Aood, who is in his seventies and kept on working
after the disappearance of Thompson in 1967, and the transfer of the
silk weaving to Korat, which is where the company's silk farms are
located. Lung Aood has a thriving family business, supplying mostly regular customers, along with some walk-in trade. His wooden
house is production centre, warehouse and shop, and from here the
visitor can buy something that really is a part of Thai culture and
history, and for a reasonable price.

Initially, Thompson had been living at The Oriental, where he was
a shareholder. Needing more room, he moved into a rented house on
Sathorn Road, and then built a small frame-house opposite Lumpini
Park. When that became too small, Thompson began searching
around for another plot of land, and eventually purchased the plot
on the side of the canal. It had once been part of a large estate where
an aristocratic family kept a summer palace, but the land had long
been parcelled off and sold. Thompson built, or possibly to be more
correct, assembled his house here, using six separate buildings from
a variety of places and owners. The most important section, which
became his drawing room, was an early nineteenth-century house
from the weavers' village. Thompson had been admiring the house,
with its teak walling and delicate carving for several years, and when
he moved it onto the site he reversed the walls so that the carvings
faced the inside. The kitchen building also came from the weaving
village, and had had an earlier existence as part of an old palace.
Most of the remaining elements he found in Ayutthaya, dismantling
the houses, stacking them on barges, and floating them down the
river and thence by the canal directly to the site. He also found in
Ayutthaya the large bricks that he used for the terrace, and the green
Chinese tiling, which had been used as ballast on rice boats returning from China, and which he set in the parapet. Thompson completed his house in 1959.

This compound has changed considerably since I first came here,
many years ago. A teak house has been erected as a large shop and
museum, and opposite is another house with a restaurant and a

very pleasant little café. But the house itself is unchanged since Jim Thompson last walked through the door, and I personally never tire of visiting it.

The story of Thompson's disappearance is well-worn in the telling. In March 1967, Thompson was on holiday in the Cameron Highlands in Malaysia, staying with friends in a bungalow named Moonlight Cottage. Thompson's friends, who were taking an afternoon nap, heard him taking a chair out onto the patio. Then they heard his footsteps briefly on the gravel path. After that, runs the story, he was neither seen nor heard in this world. It is all very appealing; a perfect mystery story. A man ascends a mountain and vanishes into thin air. Thompson's background as a wartime spy and subsequent emergence as the Thai Silk King add the glamour, and time has done the rest.

I don't know what happened any better than anyone else. But some while back I travelled to the Cameron Highlands on an unrelated assignment, and took some time out to do a little hunting around. I asked a taxi driver if he could find Moonlight Cottage, and as the Cameron Highlands is little more than a collection of English-style villages, he got me there easily enough. The cottage is slightly above the level of the road, hidden by trees. There is a short driveway, and we arrived quite suddenly on the front lawn. There were windows open, but no one seemed to be around. Feeling rather furtive, I took a few pictures and then got back in the car. I was there for less than five minutes. During that time I had the distinct impression that not even I could have got lost in the surrounding jungle. The house stands alone, but it is not remote. Thompson had actually got lost while walking with his host a day or so previously, but they had emerged soon enough onto the nearby golf course.

By a stroke of luck I found the journalist who had been on the spot at the time, and who had broken the story of the disappearance. A local man, he later gave up writing and when I met him he was manager of the Smokehouse Hotel, a Tudor-style building straight out of the Sussex Downs. He told me that while the search was underway they watched the skies over the jungle for circling birds, a sure sign that something (or someone) was dead amongst the trees. There were no birds. A psychic arrived on the scene and said he was receiving images of the missing man, giving a very plausible name as being instrumental in Thompson's sudden disappearance. The psychic was not taken very seriously, but before he left he had performed an impromptu reading on the young reporter that had been so accurate that the middle-aged man now standing in the lobby of the Smokehouse was still in awe. Somebody, somewhere, knows something. But nobody has ever gone public. Maybe it is just as well—the truth might spoil a thundering good story.

Many years ago, I went with a photographer to write a feature story on the Thompson House. We went in the evening so we could get some mood shots. The custodian in those days was a man named Bill Riley, who had been one of Thompson's friends. With the day's visitors gone, Riley went across the compound to fetch a couple of gins. The photographer was out in the garden. I sat alone in the house, on the big couch in the living room. Everything was very quiet. I felt the skin on the back of my neck tingling. This is not a good house to be in. I don't think it was the ghost of Jim that was bothering me: it didn't feel like that. The house itself seemed to have a malevolent quality. It sighs and groans in the breeze. Floorboards creak overhead. The images grin blindly from their niches. It was reassuring to hear the familiar tones of the photographer swearing in the garden, and I was greatly relieved when I heard Riley, who had a gammy leg, come stamping back with the drinks. I might have put it down to my imagination, but then some years later I was talking to a director of the Jim Thompson company, an American who had recently arrived in Thailand. He told me he had slept in the house for a couple of nights, and he vowed that he would never, never do it again. He shuddered at the memory.

The Lotus Forest

*Walking through what was once rich agricultural land, our
route takes us past a royal palace and through Bangkok's prime
shopping district to a neighbourhood of small Hindu shrines,
ending at the city's first public park.*
Duration: 4 hours

The Elephant Head Bridge, adorned on all four corners
with elephant head pilasters, carries Phayathai Road over
the Saen Saeb canal. At the foot of the bridge, and running almost to Siam Square, is a high wall pierced by a
single gate. The enormous trees that shade the wall indicate a sylvan
land away from the mad rush of traffic, but there is no sign at the
gate as to what lies beyond.

The official name of the bridge is Saphan Chalerm Lar 56, and it
was built in 1908, the name commemorating the fifty-sixth birthday
of Rama v, who had built a bridge every year since 1894, out of his
own funds, to mark his birthday. It is the fifteenth of the seventeen
"Chalerm" bridges built during the king's reign, the series ceasing
with his death, although Rama vi followed the policy for a number of years with the Charoen series, until he ran out of places to
build them. Thereafter the king donated birthday funds to hospital
building. The Elephant Head Bridge has been widened in recent
years and is no longer quite the whimsical structure it was, but it
is nonetheless one of only three remaining Chalerm bridges: one

crossing the Saen Saeb canal a little further down at Ratchadamri Road, an original but plainer structure, and the third, 53, an even more modest bridge directly under the Saphan Taksin Skytrain station at Charoen Krung Road.

Saen Saeb canal was dug by order of Rama III during a conflict between Siam and Vietnam, who were fighting over Cambodian territory. The canal, which took three years to build, starting from 1837, was cut from a point near the Mahakan Fort in Bangkok through to the Bang Pa Kong River, in Chachoengsao Province, allowing large numbers of troops and equipment to be transported by water to Cambodia. By the time Rama IV came to the throne the canal was a more tranquil waterway, with an abundance of lotus flowers growing in the waters and the mud in this area, and so the king named the new palace he directed to be built here, on the canal bank, Sra Pathum Palace, or Lotus Pond Palace. Alongside it he built a temple, Wat Pathum Wanaram. It is from the palace and temple that Pathum Wan district takes its name.

Sra Pathum Palace was built for royal recreation in what was then open fields, and today the royal estate here covers forty-three acres, although the palace and its grounds covers only seventeen of them, the remainder of the land being leased to commercial buildings, including Siam Paragon and CentralWorld. Before the recent developments the Siam InterContinental Hotel and its gardens stood on this land. The hotel had opened in 1964, being one of the first of Thailand's new international hotels, and its gardens were vast. No one realised quite how vast until the hotel was demolished about a decade ago, and only then because the grounds could be seen from the Skytrain, itself completed only a few years previously. The Skytrain also revealed Sra Pathum Palace, until the high buildings were later erected, and until that time few people had actually seen it. Sra Pathum, however, holds a very important place in Thai history. Here lived Queen Savang Vadhana, twenty-seventh daughter of Rama IV, consort to Rama V, mother of Prince Mahidol Adulyadej, and grandmother of both King Ananda Mahidol, Rama VIII, who died at a young age in 1946, and King Bhumibol Adulyadej, Rama IX. The wedding of Prince Mahidol and Princess Srinagarindra, the Princess Mother, took place here, and this is also where they made their home. Here, too, took place the wedding of their son King Bhumibol to Queen Sirikit in 1950. Prince Mahidol had died here in 1929, after which the Princess Mother lived here as a widow until her own death in 1995. Queen Savang died here in 1955 at the age of 93. Today, Sra Pathum Palace is the residence of Princess Maha Chakri Sirindhorn.

Despite the solid wall of shopping malls along one half of Siam Square's northern side, and the concrete beams of the Skytrain overhead, there is still a significant remnant of the early days here, with the pink pastel wall of Wat Pathum Wanaram, lotus blooms in panels along its length, and on top of the pillars. The temple was founded in 1857 by Rama IV, when the only way to get here was by boat along the canal, and it is designated a royal temple third class. The ashes of Prince Mahidol are buried here, along with those of the Princess Mother, and amongst the buildings is a *sala* constructed from the crematorium of the Princess Mother. The principal Buddha image in the *ubosot* was brought from Vientiane, in Laos, during the reign of Rama III. Somehow the compound, with its bodhi tree, its white *chedi* and its shrine fragrant with incense smoke, manages to be peaceful and serene, and if the visitor wanders down the gravel path and past the monks' quarters he will find himself in a miniature forest, a place for anyone who wishes to meditate, and for those studying at the Dharma centre in the grounds. The temple underwent grim publicity in 2010 when several civilians were shot and killed here during the government clashes with the Red Shirts, who had barricaded the nearby Ratchaprasong junction.

Diagonally across the Ratchaprasong junction is the Erawan Shrine, another site where violent tragedy has struck in recent years. On the morning of 21st March 2006, a Muslim man had smashed the Hindu image at the shrine, and for his trouble had been beaten to death on the spot by two street sweepers. The dead man, his father later explained, had been mentally ill, rather than driven by any hatred of the Hindu religion or the deity Than Tao Mahaprom, who is represented at the shrine. The image in place today was installed two months after the incident, and is a far more valuable (and stronger) image, being made from an alloy of nine metals, including gold and silver, unlike the previous image, which was made of plaster covered with gold leaf.

The Erawan Shrine is one of Bangkok's most famous attractions, a courtyard of intense colour, music, the clanging of bells and swirling incense smoke, made even more colourful by the bright blooms of the flower vendors outside on the pavement. Devotees offering prayers and hoping for wishes to be granted, or giving thanks for earlier good fortune, can hire the shrine dancers to accompany their prayers. A small sum of money is paid to the woman seated at a small wooden desk, the amount varying according to how many dancers are requested, a scale being posted on a signboard on the wall. Two xylophones and a double-headed drum provide the music. A dance usually lasts for three minutes. Spare a thought for the dancers, for they work long hours: usually every other day, with a shift that can last from 8 a.m. to 4 p.m., or 4 p.m. to 10 p.m.

The Erawan Shrine is not old, having been founded in 1956 to reverse a series of misfortunes and mishaps that had occurred since work began three years previously on building the Erawan Hotel next door. The Erawan was a government venture, the first of the international hotels built after World War II, and the aura of bad luck that surrounded the hotel prompted the consultation of one of Thailand's leading astrologers, Luang Suwichanphaet. He explained that the time of the laying of the foundation stone had been inauspicious, and that to correct it a shrine to appease the spirit of the land would have to be built within the grounds of the hotel. An image of Than Tao Mahaprom, the four-faced deity also known as Brahma, was decided upon. A sculptor named Chit Phimkowit, who worked for the Fine Arts Department, undertook the design of the image that was unveiled on 9th November 1956. The replacement image that was installed according to very precise directions between 11 a.m. and 11.59 a.m. on 21st May 2006 is an exact replica. The original Erawan Hotel, named after Brahma's thirty-three-headed elephant, thrived for more than thirty years before being demolished and replaced by the present Grand Hyatt Erawan.

A revered Hindu shrine in a Buddhist country is not so surprising given the relationship between the two religions, and Brahma

Incense sticks are lit at the Erawan Shrine as an offering to the Brahma image.

ceremonies are very much part of significant occasions in Thailand. Hinduism travelled out of India via merchants, sailors and artisans from the Coromandel Coast and settled in parts of Southeast Asia more than a thousand years ago, rooting deeply into the Khmer empire at Angkor and on the island of Bali. Of the Hindu gods who became entrenched in Siamese culture, Vishnu became favoured by royalty, Brahma by the priestly class, and Shiva by women wishing for children. Over the centuries, Hinduism in Siam evolved in a different way to the Indian beliefs. Scholars say that the Thai beliefs are based on a more ancient form of the religion, unmodified by the bhakti doctrine that effected such changes in India, and being far more ritualistic.

For reasons that no one seems to know, the junction at which the Erawan Shrine stands, nowadays increasingly referred to as Ratchaprasong Square, has evolved as a concentration of Hindu shrines. There are six of them, including the Erawan Shrine, each devoted to a different deity. Brahma is the god of kindness, mercy, sympathy and impartiality, each virtue represented in the four faces of the image. Visitors to the Erawan Shrine purchase an "offering set" from one of the stalls, which will cost about fifty baht and includes twelve incense sticks, four candles, four jasmine and marigold garlands and four pieces of gold leaf. They then walk around the shrine in a clockwise direction and offer three incense sticks, one candle, one garland and a piece of gold leaf to each face of the Brahma image. Indra, the god who takes care of humankind, the supreme ruler with his lightning bolt and thousand eyes, is represented in the jade coloured image at the front of Amarin Plaza, next door to the Erawan Shrine. Small elephant figurines and fresh marigold garlands are the offerings here. On the opposite side of the road, Vishnu, the god of mercy, is mounted on his celestial vehicle Garuda in front of the InterContinental. He was erected in 1997, in the wake of a fire that badly damaged the hotel shortly before it opened, and is there to protect local businesses and the wellbeing of all worshippers with a mighty power that deflects evil spirits from the vicinity. Offerings here are yellow items, such as marigold garlands, pieces of yellow fabric, and even Thai desserts such as *tong yip* and *tong yod*.

Next to the InterContinental stands Gaysorn Plaza, and here on a plinth outside the fourth floor stands an image of Lakshmi, the goddess of luck, wealth and fertility. She is the consort of Lord Vishnu, and her presence is believed to enhance his power. Offerings are dark pink lotus blossoms, coins and sugar cane. Ganesh, the elephant god, sits in a shrine in front of the Isetan department square at CentralWorld, on the other side of the junction. He is the son of Shiva, the lord of the gods, accidentally beheaded by his father who was then directed to decapitate the first creature he saw, to provide a replacement head. The creature happened to be an elephant. Ganesh has a mouse as his celestial vehicle, and is known for his creativity, love of the fine arts and encouragement of success. Offerings here are marigold garlands, milk, traditional desserts, sugar cane and fruit such as bananas and apples. Close to the Ganesh Shrine is the shrine of Trimurti, a combination of the qualities of three gods: Brahma the Creator, Vishnu the Preserver, and Shiva the Destroyer. Hence this is a very powerful shrine. Thais regard Trimurti also as being the god of love, and the belief is that he descends from heaven to this shrine at 9.30 p.m. every Tuesday and Thursday, which is why you will find young Thais praying here fervently at these times and offering the traditional nine red incense sticks, red candles and red roses.

Many years before Siam Square was laid out, the adjacent area had briefly been part of Thailand's first airport. Aeroplanes came surprisingly quickly to Siam. The Wright brothers flew the world's first powered aircraft in December 1903, and only seven years later, at the beginning of 1911, a Belgian pilot named Charles van den Born sailed into the port of Bangkok to give a series of flying demonstrations, part of a Far East tour that had started in Saigon and after Siam went on to Hong Kong and Canton. One of the few pieces of land suitable for an aircraft was that of the Royal Bangkok Sports Club, and here M van den Born set up his machine, a Farman Mk IV biplane named Wanda, built by the Anglo-French pilot and aircraft designer Henry Farman. Between 31st January and 6th February, with an extra day added on 9th February due to demand, Thai and foreign dignitaries were carried aloft for a glorious few minutes at a payment of fifty baht each, circling over Sala Daeng before landing back at the racecourse. The newly enthroned Rama VI, king for only four months, watched the demonstrations avidly. Bangkok Aviation Week had been organised by the Societe d'Aviation d'Extreme Orient, formed by a man named Karl Offer in response to the growing interest in aviation from the Far East.

Siam began making arrangements to send three young Thais to France for pilot training, and they left for Paris at the beginning of the following year. The training was extensive and intensive, for the three pilots were to return and form the nucleus of the Royal Thai Army flying unit. At the same time, the Ministry of War ordered seven aircraft: three Breguet biplanes and four Nieuport II monoplanes. A fourth Breguet was purchased by Chao Phraya Aphai Pubet, who donated the machine to the Ministry, the first of a steady stream of donations from other wealthy Thais that was to play a significant part in building the nation's fleet of planes.

The eight aircraft and the three pilots arrived in Bangkok together with a French mechanic towards the end of 1913. Once again, the Royal Bangkok Sports Club grounds were used as the runway for the fledgling air force, being not only flat but also surrounded by open fields in case of accidents. Hangars for the aircraft were built in the grounds of the Police School, which, as it does today, occupied the large area of land at the top of the racecourse. Here the new aircraft were assembled and on 29th December the first demonstration flights took place. The Sports Club's land was however unsuitable as an increasingly busy aerodrome, being too small and too swampy, and the decision was made to move the new Aviation Section to higher ground at Don Muang. Although there was no road out to the remote airfield, the railway line passed the site, and this enabled the Army Supply Department to quickly prepare the landing strip, hangars and housing. The three pilots touched their aircraft down on the airfield for the first time on 8th March 1915, and Don Muang remains the base for the Royal Thai Air Force to this day.

Until the Skytrain was built and rather spoiled the view, clever photographers were able to stand on the golf course in the centre of the Royal Bangkok Sports Club and photograph what is now the Four Seasons so that the splendidly designed hotel appeared to be a mansion in the centre of a vast green estate, with manicured lawns and tranquil ponds. The Club remains essentially unchanged to how it was at the dawn of aviation, a green sward in the centre of the city that has grown around it. Franklin Hurst, the English businessman who was, along with Louis Leonowens, later to buy The Oriental, had in 1890 submitted a request to establish a racetrack and sports field. A fifteen-year lease was signed between the Ministry of Interior and Mr Hurst in 1892 for an area of land at Sra Prathum, the present site, measuring 457 metres (500 yds) wide and 822 metres (900 yds) in length, at a rent of 200 baht per year. A club was formed, appearing at various times as the Gymkhana Club, Bangkok Gymkhana Club, and the Race Course Society. In 1901 Rama v granted a royal charter that established the Royal Bangkok Sports Club. The Club now holds twenty-six race meetings per year, while the only other race-track in Bangkok, the Royal Turf Club, established at Dusit in 1961, holds another twenty-six race meetings. The Royal Bangkok Polo Club evolved out of the Sports Club in 1919, and in 1924, when it was known as the Bangkok Riding Club, leased land from the Crown Property Bureau just off Wireless Road, where it remains to this day, occupying a huge area of land tucked amongst country lanes unknown to most people, and accessed via Soi Polo.

The entrance to the Royal Bangkok Sports Club is on Henri Dunant Road and consequently much of the length of the road is lined on its east side by a long, low wall with overhanging trees. Much of the opposite side of the road also has a pleasant green appearance with an assortment of low-key buildings, and it is only when you slip into one of the little *sois* that will take you into Chulalongkorn University do you realise just how huge and diverse this campus really is: an enormous learning institute, right in the heart of Bangkok, yet almost invisible were it not for the throngs of students entering and leaving.

Chulalongkorn University, Thailand's first institution of higher learning, was officially founded in 1917. Its history dates back a little further, however. During the second half of the nineteenth century, Siam was struggling to remain independent of the designs of the colonial powers, primarily Britain and France. King Chulalongkorn, Rama V, maintained a policy of strengthening the nation's institutions and thus its sovereignty, and this hinged upon improving the educational system so as to produce capable personnel for running the public and private sectors. In 1871 he founded a school at the Royal Pages Barracks within the Grand Palace, which was later greatly enlarged and given the name Suan Kularb. Other schools followed. In 1899 Prince Damrong, a younger brother of the king, submitted a proposal to found a civil service training school, and this produced a steady stream of graduates for the government each year. Because the curriculum was founded upon court service, Siam still being an absolute monarchy meant that the students had to spend time as royal pages; so the institute took its name from the origins of the educational system and became known as the Royal Pages School.

King Chulalongkorn passed away in 1910, the threat of colonisation largely a thing of the past. But his son, Rama VI, understood that the original intention had been to establish a multi-discipline institute of higher learning, open to all, and designed to meet the developing needs of Siam. He therefore expanded the Royal Pages School and named it the Civil Service College of King Chulalongkorn, on 1st January 1911. The college received its original funding from the remaining sum of money contributed by members of the royal family, government officials and ordinary citizens to erect a statue of King Chulalongkorn. The money was not inconsiderable: with interest, it amounted to 982,672 baht and 47 satang. Rama vi also donated a palace in Pathum Wan district that had been the home of his late brother, Crown Prince Vajirunhis, for the college, together with an adjacent plot of land measuring about 523 acres in area, for its use and future expansion. First to be erected was the Administration Building, designed by a British architect, Edward Healey, in the traditional Thai architectural style. Within a few years, in 1917, the king felt the college was ready to become Chulalongkorn University. Initially there were just 380 students taking classes in four faculties, which were located in the two campuses. The Faculty of Medicine was located in an annex at Siriraj Hospital, while the Faculties of Public Administration and of Engineering were at the Administration Building and the Faculty of Arts and Science was located at Prince Vajirunhis's palace. The palace of Crown Prince Vajirunhis, who had died from typhoid age 16, is a lost architectural treasure. It had been built in 1881 to a design by an unknown British architect, who had clearly drawn his inspiration from Windsor Castle. A three-storey riot of Gothic, with a four-storey central tower surmounted by battlements, it quickly gained the nickname "Windsor Palace" amongst the expatriate community. The Thai name was Wang Klang Thung, "palace in the centre of a field", or more usually just Wang Mai, "new palace", which was adopted as the name of the sub-district that today covers the site. When it became part of the Chulalongkorn campus, Windsor Palace was modified to hold classes and laboratories, and Prince Mahidol himself instructed medical students here in pre-clinical courses.

Following the Siamese revolution in 1932 that abolished absolute monarchy, the property came under the Ministry of Education's Department of Physical Education. In 1935 the palace was demolished to make way for the Suphachalasai Stadium, part of the National Stadium complex. Elements made from imported marble have been excavated in recent years and stand now outside the Chulalongkorn University School of Sports Science.

Walking through the Chulalongkorn University campus today, the grace of the older buildings in their parkland setting provides an appropriate framework for higher education, while even the later, more prosaic structures have been softened by the greenery. Before the land was built upon it was overgrown with vegetation and rain trees, and these trees have become a symbol of the university. Generations of students have read and reviewed their lessons under the shade of the rain trees. With the old trees dying off in the middle of the last century, King Bhumibol visited the campus and planted five saplings in 1962, three on the right side and two on the left side of the football pitch in front of the auditorium. Most recently, at the time of the university's eightieth anniversary celebrations, a programme was undertaken to plant eighty rain trees throughout the campus.

Although most of the extensive land holdings of the university are related to the campus itself, an interesting diversion was made in the mid 1960s when Siam Square was laid out on university land immediately to the north of the campus. The aim was to lease out the land to shop owners and use the funds for benefitting the university. Siam Square, however, quickly took on a life of its own as Bangkok's first shopping mall district, a trendy place around which the city's equivalent of the Swinging Sixties revolved. Nowadays, Siam Square is Bangkok's prime shopping and leisure district, the building of the Skytrain interchange having been decisive in adding accessibility for a destination that is also serviced by some twenty-five bus routes and even by boat, via the Saen Saeb canal. Consequently, this is the place where youngsters continue to meet, and the thirteen steps in front of Siam Centre have been one of Bangkok's prime people-watching locations for two generations.

Siam Square was laid out in 1965, and a couple of years later, at the beginning of 1967, the Siam Theatre opened, specialising in the showing of foreign movies. The Lido Theatre was built the following year, and the Scala appeared in 1970. The Bangkok Bank building, British Council building, and the Siam Bowl were all built during this period. In the late 1970s, with the economy flourishing, a host of fast food joints, boutiques and tutoring services opened. A small police station with four officers, plus a fire station, was set up on Siam Square Soi 7, opposite Siam Theatre, in 1980. MBK Centre, also known as Mahboonkrong (after the parents of developer Sirichai Bulakul, Mah and Boonkrong) was opened in 1985 on the western boundary of the university's land. Rama I Road marks the northern boundary of the square, and the commercial developments on the other side of the road, although they are assimilated into the notion of Siam Square, actually stand on royal land that was originally the grounds of Sra Pathum Palace. In terms of sheer size and glamour, they outdo the humbler premises within the square. The first beer garden, now a familiar sight in front of shopping malls throughout the city at the end of the rainy season, was a Kloster event held at Siam Discovery Centre in the mid-1980s. The large courtyard area between Siam Discovery and Siam Centre is today used for the same purpose, and for other events. The opening a few years ago of Siam Paragon, the Kempinski Hotel, Centara Grand and the Bangkok Convention Centre and CentralWorld have all added to the allure of Siam Square, and indeed, to the traffic congestion. The Skytrain and its associated elevated walkway is the best way to travel here.

Henri Dunant, in case you were wondering, had nothing to do with Chulalongkorn University. He was the Swiss founder of the Red Cross. The Thai Red Cross lies on the other, southern side of the university campus, between the university and Rama IV Road. In 1893, a territorial dispute between France and Siam over land along the Mekong River flared into a brief war that resulted in many casualties on both sides. There was no charitable organisation available to offer medical aid to the soldiers and civilians, and a lady of the Siamese Royal Court, Thanpuying Plien Pasakornravongs, gathered together a group of female volunteers and proposed to Queen Savang Vadhana that the king's permission be sought to set up "The Red Unalong Society of Siam" for this purpose. King Chulalongkorn's response to the proposal was favourable, for he understood how the society's creation could further help the progress of Siam. Funds totalling 443,716 baht were collected, and Queen Savang Vadhana was appointed as patron, Queen Saowapha Bhongsri as society president, and Tanpuying Plien as society secretary. The names Red Unalom Society and Red Cross Society were used alternately until 1910, when the former disappeared and the name Siamese Red Cross Society was adopted. Later this was changed to the Thai Red Cross Society, and the organisation was officially recognised by the International Committee of the Red Cross in 1920.

The Snake Farm within the Red Cross compound, formerly the Pasteur Institute, is now known as the Queen Saowapha Memorial Institute, and was set up to produce anti-venom serum for snakebite victims nationwide. The Pasteur Institute of Paris helped to develop this facility, which was opened in 1923 by Queen Savang. It was only the world's second snake farm, the first being in Brazil. Venomous snakes are milked daily to make snakebite antidote, one of Bangkok's oldest and most popular tourist attractions. The Chulalongkorn Faculty of Medicine at Siriraj Hospital evolved to encompass several disciplines, including dentistry, pharmacy and veterinary science, and eventually many of these were carved away to form what is now the Faculty of Medicine Siriraj Hospital, part of Mahidol University. Chulalongkorn's Faculty of Medicine and Chulalongkorn University Hospital today stand on a large area of land immediately to the south of the Royal Bangkok Sports Club, the hospital having been opened in 1914.

Sandwiched into a piece of land between the Club and the Faculty is the Lumpini Pumping Station, drawing its water supplies from the Bangkhen Water Treatment Plant, in the north of the city, and using four massive pumps to deliver water supplies to the surrounding area. Lumpini is one of twenty distribution stations that operate in conjunction with three main transmission stations to supply the city, and it was built in 1979. Despite its enormous pumping capacity, Lumpini's output can be controlled from a single desktop computer. The distinctive water towers that supply the pressure have in recent years had offices built into the previously empty space between the support struts, forming a practical and economic use of land to house the Thai Red Cross AIDS Research Centre, the Red Cross symbol woven in a striking fashion into the wall of the compound.

Ratchadamri Road, leading north from Silom, had been completed in 1903, largely to provide access to the Royal Bangkok Sports
Club. The land on the opposite side of the road to Chulalongkorn
Hospital was an open field that had recently become popularly
known as Sala Daeng, after the red-coloured pavilion of the same
name that formed a stop on the Paknam Railway. Rama VI began in
the early 1920s to plan what was designed to be the greatest exhibition ever to take place in Siam. The first had been the National
Exhibition, held at Sanam Luang in 1882 to celebrate Bangkok's centenary, and other fairs had been held over the years since at Dusit,
and a series of large agricultural fairs had been held adjacent to Sra
Pathum Palace. Now the king planned a magnificent showcase for
the nation, to be held in its own exhibition grounds. He granted
the Sala Daeng field for this purpose, a huge area of 142 acres, and
the grounds were landscaped to accommodate the various pavilions to their best effect. Two lakes were dug in the northeastern
and southwestern parts of the park: the large lake and its islands
near Ratchadamri Road was to display the works of the Treasury,
while the smaller one near Wireless Road was to be surrounded by
foreign commercial pavilions, Chinatown enterprises, and produce
from what was then known as Monthon Ratchaburi, the Ratchaburi
Circle, five provinces close to Bangkok. Each ministry was to have
its own pavilion, while three exhibition halls for major industries
would be placed near Rama IV Road. Canals such as the Silom, Hua
Lampong, Ratchadamri and Saen Saeb canals would provide access,
along with the roads, and the government granted the concession
for a new tramway, the Silom Line, that would run from Charoen
Krung Road to Pratunam. The Samsen tramway was extended from
its Hua Lampong terminus to Sathorn Road via Sala Daeng. The
opening date for the exhibition was set for 23rd January 1926. Then,
on 25th November 1925, the king died, at the age of 44. The exhibition was officially cancelled on 1st January, and Lumpini Park, named
after the birthplace of the Buddha, became a public park in the man-
ner of the great parks of Europe. Corrado Feroci sculpted the statue
of the king erected in 1941 at the entrance to the park, and the open
area around the statue is today used for public ceremonies.

Mr Sukhumvit

Our walk takes us from what was a century ago swampland on the bank of the Saen Saeb canal, down through the embassy district to the site of Bangkok's first radio station, and then back up to the beginning of modern Bangkok.
Duration: 2 hours

On the corner of Ploenchit and Wireless roads stands a curious object. About three metres (10 ft) high and cylindrical in shape, it is made of concrete and is entirely blank. No door, no window, nothing. From time to time it has provoked lively comment in the letters page of the English-language newspapers, where it has generally been referred to as The Thing. Is it a wartime pillbox, part of the pumping apparatus for the nearby Saen Saeb canal, a toilet, or something to do with the sewers? For the answer we have to go back many years, to a remarkable man.

Lert Sreshthaputra was born in 1872 to a well-respected Bangkok family that lived near the southern end of the second moat. Young Lert showed early signs of being a very enterprising person, having his birthdate changed by a venerated monk to give himself a more auspicious astrological sign. When his schooling was finished he worked as a clerk for the soda water and soft drinks section of the Singapore Straits Company, which later became known as Fraser & Neave. By the age of 22 he had risen to be a partner in the business, but his ambitions went far beyond this: he had saved enough money to set up on his own, and he opened a store on Charoen Krung Road, near to where it crosses the Padung Krung Kasem Canal. By now he was called Nai Lert, or Master Lert, and this is the name that appears above the shopfront in old photographs. Nai Lert's store began by selling sewing machines, canned foods, carbonated lemonade, and other imported goods, and it prospered. Nai Lert gained more fame when in about 1910 he imported the new ice-making equipment, being the first person in Siam to be able to solidify water, an art that drew astonished crowds to such an extent that an exhibition was staged in the Sala Sahathai building, next to the Temple of the Emerald Buddha.

Around the time Nai Lert opened his store, the tram service along Charoen Krung Road had been electrified, and the street was evolving as the most fashionable shopping district in town. And then something else happened. Around 1900 the first motorcar appeared in Siam. Owned by Chao Phraya Surasak Montri, the vehicle was of an unknown make and was described by an envious noble as looking like a steamroller set on solid rubber tyres and topped off by a flat roof. Possessing a feeble engine sufficient to propel the vehicle along level ground but without the power to climb humped bridges, it nonetheless required fuel. When in 1904 a son of Rama v, travelling in Europe, ordered a Daimler-Benz to be delivered to Siam, which he then presented to his father, a motorcar was something every wealthy Siamese wanted to own. This proved a decisive time for Nai Lert, who took on the concession for Shell motor spirit. His store became one of Bangkok's few filling stations, and he expanded the premises. Motorcars did not remain a novelty for long. Nai Lert had started a horse-drawn carriage service for hire to the affluent to tour the city's new roads, and in 1910 this evolved into a bus service using engine-driven vehicles, importing the motors from England and appointing a team of local carpenters to build the bus bodies, following a design that Nai Lert himself sketched out with chalk on the cement floor of his shop. A distinctive white colour, the first White Bus route ran from Pratunam to Siphraya Road, and this was followed by the White Boat service that ran along the Saen Saeb canal, bringing people in from as far afield as Nongchock and

Minburi, where they disembarked at Pratunam. He imported Fiat motorcars and rented them out with drivers by the hour, starting Bangkok's first taxi service. He built pleasure boats and sea-going vessels that fished the Gulf of Siam and transported goods to and from provincial towns along the coast. He built the Hotel de la Paix, in the Saphan Lek Bridge area, which offered English beer, Scotch whisky, and tasty sausages made by his wife. King Rama VI came to lunch shortly after it opened.

In 1915 Nai Lert did something that really made people shake their heads in disbelief. He purchased, from the royal family, twenty-five acres of swampy land alongside the Saen Saeb canal. Bounded by what are now the top part of Wireless Road, Ploenchit Road, and Soi Chit Lom, the investment seemed a whimsical one. The city was spreading outwards in the southeast, the Bangkok Sports Club was not that far away, and there were several big houses a little further to the south of Nai Lert's land. But in the area of the canal the ground was soggy, and best used for growing rice. In fact rather than attempt to cross the rough and marshy ground by vehicle, Nai Lert himself travelled by canal to inspect his new acquisition. To ensure there was no mistake as to the ownership of the land in this wilderness, Nai Lert set up a series of massive stone boundary markers in the shape of up-ended cannon barrels and various forms of ordnance. There were six of them, and only The Thing remains. Another Thing, in the form of a bullet, existed outside the Swissotel Nai Lert Park until 2003, when it was hit by a car and destroyed.

In 1922 the British finally made up their minds to leave the riverside compound on Charoen Krung Road, having been offered almost half of Nai Lert's plot of land, some twelve acres, at an advantageous price that allowed them to both buy the land and erect the new embassy buildings from the proceeds of the sale of their original site. The misgivings of the British minister, Sir Robert Hyde Greg, who was something of a traditionalist, were mollified by the designs for the new Residence. The first structure to be erected was the war memorial, paid for by British subjects in Siam and unveiled in 1923. The statue of Queen Victoria was transported to the site (the statue was boarded up by the Japanese in World War II, but they thoughtfully provided a peephole so that Her Majesty would not be left in complete darkness), and Sir Robert took up residence in the completed compound in 1926. The embassy has in recent years sold off the section of land facing onto Ploenchit Road, which is being developed by Central Group as a hotel and other commercial property. Not a bad move, all in all, as this has always been a rather glum corner, with its high, grey wall. But I do worry about the future of The Thing, which is looking rather decrepit these days and could well fall victim to any official who decided it was an unsafe structure. Losing this humble but significant landmark would be a great pity.

Soon after he had bought the land, Nai Lert had built a teak house next to the canal where he would take his family from time to time to escape the turmoil of Charoen Krung, where they had their main residence and where the company offices were located. Towards the latter part of the 1920s he decided to move his family full-time to the peace and quiet of his canal-side property, and a second house was built there, a small canal and a pond dug, and spacious gardens laid out. Today the property is known as Nai Lert Park and lies directly behind the Swissotel, which is owned by his descendants. Standing on eight-a-half acres it had opened as the Hilton International in 1983, and occupies the land on which Nai Lert built a depot for his White Bus Company. A bronze statue of Nai Lert is seated near the entrance, although the beautiful white automobile that had belonged to him and was parked alongside the statue was moved to the house after the destruction of the boundary marker, on the perfectly reasonable assumption that if a Bangkok driver can destroy a ten-foot high stone bullet with a single blow, a vintage motorcar would not stand a chance.

Descend the flight of steps that leads down from the hotel main entrance, follow the pathway to the bank of the canal, and you will find one of the city's most curious shrines. Chao Mae Tuptim is a female spirit, *tuptim* being the Thai word for both ruby and pomegranate. No one knows quite how long this shrine has been here, or why. Very possibly it dates back to the early days of the canal, with scattered villages along the banks and passing boats stopping to make offerings. A large fichus tree stands here, and these trees, with their twisting aerial roots, are traditionally regarded as an abode for spirits. Why it was decided the tree was the home of the goddess Tuptim is a mystery, as is the goddess herself, and her reputation for fertility. It only takes a few wishes to come true, and a shrine can achieve a reputation. Whatever the history is, the tree and its spirit house has drawn generations of supplicants bearing the offerings of phalluses, and hundreds of them have been left here. Some are tiny and placed in the branches, some are baked like cakes and left to dissolve into the elements, and some are real whoppers, elaborately carved from wood and painted in varying shades of red and pink.

Although Ploenchit Road may have looked remote to the British legation staff gloomily contemplating a long trudge from their comfortable homes in Bangrak or Bang Kolaem, to the British sea captains who had previously only to step off the deck of their ship and into the embassy garden to get their paperwork sorted, and to the servants who quite possibly had fears of crocodiles and tigers, the new British Embassy by 1926 was not really that remote. The tram rattled up Silom Road as far as Pratunam, the roads were good enough for the motorcars that were becoming commonplace, and there was always a boat ride along the canal that was eventually to become Wireless Road. Civilisation ended in fields and pathways where Sukhumvit now runs, true enough, but on the immediate south side of Ploenchit Road, or the trail that passed for Ploenchit Road, were some very desirable residences.

Take, for example, the house of an Englishman named Henry Victor Bailey, a wealthy adventurer who settled in Siam and ran an architectural practice, along with importing motorcars and blue-and-white porcelain from China. Bailey designed and built a house for himself here in 1914. A large timber residence, large enough to house himself and his three Siamese wives, it stood on stilts and had a broad veranda and a billiards room. Bailey died in 1920, and the house was sold to the Siamese Treasury. In 1947, after the conclusion of World War II, Thailand, in a gesture of appreciation to the United States, handed over the property and ten acres of manicured gardens for use as the official residence of the American ambassador, which it remains to this day. Then there was Wittayu

Palace, built for Prince Rangsit in 1925. The prince had studied in Germany, and he was also an avid collector of Asian and European antiques. When his collection became too large for his palace at Pomprabsatrupai, the prince had bought land here and commissioned Swiss architect Charles Berger Lang to design a new palace in a Swiss-German style. The prince designed the interiors himself, and asked the architect to specify a thick wall so that he could maintain a constant temperature for his fragile collection. Prince Rangsit died of a heart attack in this house in 1951, and it passed to his descendants, who maintain the house and its collection in its original form. Then there was the residence of Dr Alphonse Poix, a French doctor who was a physician to Rama V. A white-painted two-storey structure with a three-storey tower and beautifully carved gables, the house was built in the last years of the nineteenth century and in 1948 was purchased by the Dutch government to be used as a residence for their ambassador.

The coming of the British Embassy to this part of the city had a profound influence on what was to become known as Wireless Road, because most of the embassies of the world's leading nations had moved here within twenty or so years. Those that couldn't find premises in Wireless Road moved into the nearest places they could find, such as Soi Thonson, Soi Ruam Rudee, and the upper part of Sathorn Road. This in turn led to a large population of expatriates in this area, and this led to the establishment of Western schools and kindergartens, of which Ruam Rudee, a quiet thoroughfare whose name translates roughly as "love lane", became the epicentre. It also led to the founding of one of the world's oddest Catholic churches, the Holy Redeemer Church on Soi Ruam Rudee, which at first glance and even at subsequent close examination looks like a Thai Buddhist temple. In 1948 the Bishop of Bangkok had asked the Redemptorists to establish a foundation and parish in Bangkok to serve the growing English-speaking population. Four American Redemptorists duly arrived and began searching for a suitable plot of land to build a church. They rented accommodation not far from the site of the subsequent church, and they established a temporary chapel: the chapel appears to have been distinctly makeshift, because with admirable brio they dubbed it Our Lady of the Garage. They eventually found a suitable piece of land, tucked into the L-shape of the lane, and a suggestion by Bishop Fulton J Sheen that the traditional style of architecture be used, was followed. It was an inspired decision. The church, completed in 1954, holds services in Thai and English, and plays, as they say, to packed houses. Holy Redeemer also founded two schools, a local parish school for Thai students and an international school, the latter now located outside the city and one of the most successful and prestigious of Thailand's international schools.

So, why is this leafy thoroughfare called Wireless Road? Travel on down to the end of the road and you will find, opposite Lumpini Park, a scene of most awful desolation, at least, at the time of writing. One doesn't need to be an old-timer to remember when this huge area, fifty-one acres of royal land, was the Armed Forces Preparatory School. Founded here in 1958, it was a parade ground and playing field where cadets drilled and worked out, attended classes in the buildings facing Rama IV Road, and lived in the warren of barracks behind the buildings. In 2000 the school moved out to Nakhon Nayok, and the Suan Lum Night Market moved in. The market always seemed a dodgy venture, with very little security of tenure for the vendors and investors, and a rather strange location for a market that didn't open until 9 p.m. and had little walk-past trade. It closed in 2011 and the developers bought a large piece of land on Ratchadaphisek Road. Some of the vendors moved there, and some went to Asiatique, on Charoen Krung Road. Suan Lum was bulldozed, and remains to the present as a flat area of rubble and weeds. Except, that is, for a very high radio mast that has a small building at the base, and appears to be a functioning island in a sea of desolation.

Radio, as with so many other technological developments, came early to Siam. Two experimental transmitters were installed in the early years of the twentieth century, one at Golden Mount, high above the city, and the other at Si Chang Island, off the coast of Chonburi. Both were used by the Royal Thai Navy for ship-to-shore communications. In 1919 Rama VI used both these transmitters to proclaim the birth of radio broadcasting in Siam, but the technology

Nai Lert's cannon-shaped boundary marker outside the British Embassy.

was primitive and local resistance to something so unnatural was strong. In the early 1920s Prince Purachatra Jayagara, the Prince of Kamphaengphet, was appointed Minister of Commerce and Communications. He had a natural interest in technology, and installed a small transmitter in his palace at Luang Road, near to the second moat. The test broadcasts proved encouraging, and on 31st May 1928, Station 4PJ, carrying the prince's initials and broadcast from the Post and Telegraph Office at Wat Liab, went on air. In 1930 the Telegraph Act was amended to allow the public to own radio receivers. To cater for the new demand, a radio station was established at Phayathai Palace.

Following the coup in 1932, the national radio station was moved to Sala Daeng, next to the Paknam Railway station. Renamed Radio Bangkok, it had a new call sign, 7PJ, and a 2.5kW transmitter. Tests were also carried out here on a shortwave transmitter, 8PJ, to reach overseas. After World War II the government, which retained a monopoly on radio broadcasting for many years, built larger and more powerful transmitters elsewhere. But that radio mast poking up from the rubble on the corner of Wireless Road marks one of the starting points.

Visitors staying in the Sukhumvit Road area, or travelling on main roads in other parts of the eastern side of Bangkok, are bewildered by the fact that a railway line runs at ground level through the city. The already clogged traffic comes to a complete standstill at the clanging of a warning bell, the barrier is lowered, and a couple of minutes later a train of seemingly several miles in length clanks its way between the waiting lines of traffic. The railway line is for freight, and links the marshalling yards of Bang Sue, in the north of the city, with the port and oil refinery at Klong Toei. It also marks very clearly, and as effectively as a moat, where the old city ends and the new one begins: for Sukhumvit Road, visible beyond the railway barrier, is an exuberant arterial highway that forms the main hotel, shopping and tourism district, and which beyond the suburbs runs along the eastern seaboard to eventually end 400 kilometres (248 miles) away in the province of Trat, on the Cambodian border.

The Saen Saeb and Bang Kapi canals were dug to the east of the city in the time of Rama III, with the former being the main waterway for agricultural produce and military use, while the latter flowed along what are now Ploenchit and Sukhumvit roads and connected a network of small canals, creeks and drainage ditches that stretched all the way to Klong Toei. In the time of Rama IV, at the request of the newly-arrived Western traders, the Hua Lampong canal was cut eastwards along what is now Rama IV Road to connect the third moat to the river. The land through which these waterways passed represented a rural idyll, with fields, orchards, rice paddies and villages threaded by the waterways.

With the building by Rama IV of Sra Pathum Palace, the eastern part of the city became a popular residential area for nobility and high-ranking officials, with plots of land being used to build country estates. When the Westerners arrived they pushed the city further to the east by opening their embassies in the Wireless Road district, and setting up home there. Nai Lert and an enterprising Indian Muslim named Lek Nana bought large plots of land between the Saen Saeb and Bang Kapi canals, and began to develop them. The trail that ran alongside the Bang Kapi canal was paved as a two-lane road in 1940, as far down as Soi 19. Beyond that, the way remained little more than a track. A large number of Indians began arriving in Bangkok in the 1940s, and they bought up plots of land along the paved road and beyond, where they were able to erect inexpensive housing for themselves. With Klong Toei now a modern port, road traffic increased.

Businesses began to move into the area, and the road that was known as the Paknam Trail, as it led towards Paknam, at the mouth of the river, needed to be developed systematically. Canals were filled in, and new roads made. The patchwork of roads and trails grew, evolving into an arterial highway that needed a name. Prasop Sukhum had been the first Thai to study at the Massachusetts Institute of Technology, travelling to the United States in the early 1930s, and had been greatly influenced by the American style of highway building. Returning to Bangkok, he started as an assistant engineer with the Department of Sanitation and progressed to the position of chief engineer of the Highways Department. He was responsible for much of the new infrastructure that underpinned Bangkok, as the city developed and grew with astonishing rapidity after World War II, becoming a megacity whose continuing expansion seems to have no end. So successful was Prasop Sukhum's career that the king bestowed upon him the formal title of Phra Pisan Sukhumvit. There was an initial suggestion that the highway be named after Lek Nana, who modestly declined, and so Mr Sukhumvit, in 1950, by a casual flip of history's coin, became world famous for the road that leads eastwards out of the Sea of Mud, absorbing the little farming and fishing villages and leaving the historic districts far behind to create a different kind of Bangkok.

INDEX

The Tuttle Story: "Books to Span the East and West"

Many people are surprised to learn that the world's largest publisher of books on Asia had its humble beginnings in the tiny American state of Vermont. The company's founder, Charles Tuttle, came from a New England family steeped in publishing.

Tuttle's father was a noted antiquarian dealer in Rutland, Vermont. Young Charles honed his knowledge of the trade working in the family bookstore, and later in the rare books section of Columbia University Library. His passion for beautiful books—old and new—never wavered throughout his long career as a bookseller and publisher.

After graduating from Harvard, Tuttle enlisted in the military and in 1945 was sent to Tokyo to work on General Douglas MacArthur's staff. He was tasked with helping to revive the Japanese publishing industry, which had been utterly devastated by the war. When his tour of duty was completed, he left the military, married a talented and beautiful singer, Reiko Chiba, and in 1948 began several successful business ventures.

To his astonishment, Tuttle discovered that postwar Tokyo was actually a book-lover's paradise. He befriended dealers in the Kanda district and began supplying rare Japanese editions to American libraries. He also imported American books to sell to the thousands of GIs stationed in Japan. By 1949, Tuttle's business was thriving, and he opened Tokyo's very first English-language bookstore in the Takashimaya Department Store in Ginza, to great success. Two years later, he began publishing books to fulfill the growing interest of foreigners in all things Asian.

Though a westerner, Tuttle was hugely instrumental in bringing a knowledge of Japan and Asia to a world hungry for information about the East. By the time of his death in 1993, he had published over 6,000 books on Asian culture, history and art—a legacy honored by Emperor Hirohito in 1983 with the "Order of the Sacred Treasure," the highest honor Japan bestows upon a non-Japanese.

The Tuttle company today maintains an active backlist of some 1,500 titles, many of which have been continuously in print since the 1950s and 1960s—a great testament to Charles Tuttle's skill as a publisher. More than 60 years after its founding, Tuttle Publishing is more active today than at any time in its history, still inspired by Charles Tuttle's core mission—to publish fine books to span the East and West and provide a greater understanding of each.